Urban America: The Policy Alternatives

Urban America:
The Policy Alternatives

David A. Caputo

Purdue University

 *W. H. Freeman and Company*
San Francisco

Cover photo: U.S. Geological Survey.

Library of Congress Cataloging in Publication Data

Caputo, David A   1943–
   Urban America.

   Includes bibliographical references and index.
   1.   Cities and towns—United States.   I.   Title.
HT123.C36   301.36′3′0973   76-7351
ISBN 0-7167-0556-7
ISBN 0-7167-0565-6 pbk.

Printed in the United States of America

10 9 8 7 6 5 4 3 2 1

For Alice, Christopher, Elizabeth, and Jeffrey

Contents

Preface

As the United States celebrates its two-hundredth birthday, it is difficult to imagine the living conditions and political institutions that existed in the late 1700s. One must wonder what was unique about that period of American history that helped forge the political institutions and compromises that provided the basis for the survival and growth of the United States to the present time. The nation has endured major social, economic, and political difficulties in the past 200 years and has experienced substantial change.

The contention is frequently heard these days that American institutions have failed to adapt themselves to the political, economic, and social changes affecting society, with the result that the United States is now faced with the problem of surviving amidst technological changes and social forces that may ultimately render these institutions hopelessly obsolete. Perhaps this situation is most evident in the cities and suburbs of the nation.

The Founding Fathers apparently had no preconception of the importance and size that cities would obtain in the next 200 years. Indeed, it can be logically argued that the nation's cities, rather than the states, could be expected to be partners of the national government because of the cities' inevitable growth and emerging dominant role in America's economic, social, and political life. Regardless of one's view in this argument, the contemporary American city has indeed become a key determinant of America's social, economic, and political destiny, and any understanding of the future of American politics and of the nation as a whole requires consideration of the role of the cities and the changes that have resulted from their growth.

This book does just that. Its central theme is quite clear. Urban politics in the United States both directly affects and is directly affected by national political institutions and policy decisions made at the national level. Therefore, the political leaders and citizens of America's urban centers, as well as the leaders of the three branches of the national government, have a variety of possible policy alternatives available to them. If the correct choices are made among these competing alternatives, and if they are vigorously pursued and implemented, dramatic changes could result that would affect the present and future structure and fabric of life in the United States. Thus the policy alternatives must be clearly stated and understood both by individual citizens and by political leaders in order that they may consider the possible implications of these alternatives for American society. In this book an attempt is made to discuss the alternatives, their implications, and the likelihood of their selection, as well as to describe the present and possible future aspects of urban life.

In the final analysis, the central issue facing policy-makers at all levels of American society is the impact their decisions will have on the quality of life in the future. This issue is extremely important at the urban level, because policy decisions made by urban leaders inevitably will have a direct and measurable influence on the life styles and individual alternatives and destinies of the citizens residing in their particular urban area.

In this book a basic assumption is that individuals and groups have considerable control over their own destinies and the destiny of society. The policy-makers deciding the fate of urban America have a variety of resources at their disposal as well as a set of parameters that limit the choices open to them. Consideration of policy alternatives in a rational and positive manner is an important and vital step toward bettering the quality of life of those residing in urban America, in both the immediate future and the long run. An appreciation of the forces limiting the choices and alternatives and hence the participants is as important as understanding the policy alternatives and their implications. Thus, the historical, institutional, and behavioral material usually utilized in the study of urban politics is combined in this book with the relevant policy analysis material to provide a comprehensive overview of urban America and its possible future course.

The book has no explicit ideological theme other than "pragmatism." At times, the statement of policy alternatives and their subsequent analysis will seem inconsistent with both liberal and conservative political ideologies and may seem at variance with current and popular positions. At times, the policy recommendations may reflect the acknowledgment that conflict or other unpopular forms of action may at times be necessary in order to better the quality of life in America's urban centers and in the nation as a whole. Contemporary ideologies, with their emphasis on consistency and personal interpretation, often fail to take into account the realities of modern America and the complexities of America's urban problems. A two-hundred-year historical precedent has set the stage for and perhaps will even limit future change, but it has not provided panaceas for or rapid solutions to the difficult and complex problems facing the United States. In this volume I consider a variety of policy alternatives in order to present an overview of contemporary urban America that should enable the readers to develop and assess meaningful policy alternatives of their own as well as to evaluate those put forth by others. The interested reader will find suggestions for further reading and exploration scattered throughout the book. My hope is that the reader will be a more enlightened and sophisticated observer of urban politics and its complexities as well as a more perceptive policy analyst as a result of having read it. To the extent that I succeed in these goals, my work will be a success.

I would like to thank the many who have contributed to my increased knowledge and understanding of urban politics and urban policy-making. This includes the many policy-makers who have taken time to talk with me, my colleagues within the discipline who have been helpful, and the citizens and public officials of urban American who have taken time to participate in my research.

I would also like to thank those who have given me the personal encouragement necessary for my research and writing—especially my wife, Alice, who has had to spend a lot of time without me. Her patience, encouragement, and, above all, understanding, are appreciated. My parents and children understood my preoccupation and absences and encouraged me to continue the work. Diane Amos, Viki Doty, Dotty Eberle, Rita Lynch, Betsey McCormick, Ruth Messenger, and Carol Roberts all assisted at various stages in typing the manuscript. Richard Lamb's encouragement was instrumental in my completing the project and Richard L. Cole, Jesse McCorry, Jeffrey L. Pressman, and Alan Saltzstein read an earlier draft and made numerous helpful comments and suggestions.

What follows is a highly personal view of the urban policy choices facing this nation, but a view based on supporting empirical and theoretical evidence. I assume full responsibility for it and ask only that the reader give it serious consideration and thought.

Lafayette, Indiana
October 1975

David A. Caputo

Urban America: The Policy Alternatives

Chapter 1

Urban America and the Cities

Introduction

Urban America can be viewed in a variety of ways, but perhaps the two most useful are the "snapshot" and "motion picture" perspectives. The snapshot perspective provides a frozen image of a very dynamic process at a particular point in time, whereas the motion picture perspective attempts to record the events occurring in a rapidly changing society over a longer period. The 1970 census data supply the information needed for a snapshot or "still" view of America's urban centers because they capture and freeze the changes occurring in American society in 1970.

Consider for a moment the information in Table 1-1, which indicates the population totals for the nation's 200 largest Standard Metropolitan Statistical Areas. A *Standard Metropolitan Statistical Area* (SMSA) is a metropolitan area including one city of 50,000 or more people, or two or more adjacent cities with combined populations of more than 50,000. Even a quick look at the table reveals the importance of these 200 SMSAs for the life and vitality of the nation. Traditionally, an *urban area* has been defined as any area with a population of more than 2500. It should be readily apparent that this low population figure has accounted for estimates that

Table 1-1 SMSA Rank and Population of America's 200 Largest SMSAs,
1970

RANK	SMSA	1970 POPULATION
1	New York, N.Y.	11,575,749
2	Los Angeles–Long Beach, Calif.	7,404,697
3	Chicago, Ill.	6,977,611
4	Philadelphia, Pa./N.J.	4,822,245
5	Detroit, Mich.	4,203,548
6	San Francisco–Oakland, Calif.	3,108,026
7	Washington, D.C./Md./Va.	2,861,638
8	Boston, Mass.	2,753,700
9	Pittsburgh, Pa.	2,401,362
10	St. Louis, Mo./Ill.	2,363,346
11	Baltimore, Md.	2,071,016
12	Cleveland, Ohio	2,063,279
13	Houston, Texas	1,985,031
14	Newark, N.J.	1,859,096
15	Minneapolis–St. Paul, Minn.	1,813,587
16	Dallas, Texas	1,556,324
17	Seattle–Everett, Wash.	1,434,611
18	Anaheim–Santa Ana–Garden Grove, Calif.	1,420,676
19	Milwaukee, Wisc.	1,403,887
20	Atlanta, Ga.	1,390,247
21	Cincinnati/Ohio/Ky./Ind.	1,384,983
22	Paterson–Clifton–Passaic, N.J.	1,357,930
23	San Diego, Calif.	1,357,854
24	Buffalo, N.Y.	1,349,211
25	Miami, Fla.	1,267,792
26	Kansas City, Mo./Kans.	1,256,327
27	Denver, Colo.	1,229,798
28	San Bernardino–Riverside–Ontario, Calif.	1,214,307
29	Indianapolis, Ind.	1,111,352
30	San José, Calif.	1,066,932
31	New Orleans, La.	1,046,470
32	Tampa–St. Petersburg, Fla.	1,012,594
33	Portland, Oreg.	1,007,130
34	Phoenix, Ariz.	968,487
35	Columbus, Ohio	916,228
36	Providence–Pawtucket–Warwick, R.I./Mass.	914,110
37	Rochester, N.Y.	882,667
38	San Antonio, Texas	864,014
39	Dayton, Ohio	852,531
40	Louisville, Ky./Ind.	826,553
41	Sacramento, Calif.	803,610
42	Memphis, Tenn./Ark.	770,217
43	Fort Worth, Texas	726,086
44	Birmingham, Ala.	739,274
45	Albany–Schenectady–Troy, N.Y.	722,094
46	Toledo, Ohio/Mich.	692,488
47	Norfolk–Portsmouth, Va.	680,600
48	Akron, Ohio	679,239
49	Hartford, Conn.	663,891

Table 1-1 (Cont.)

RANK	SMSA	1970 POPULATION
50	Oklahoma City, Okla.	641,801
51	Syracuse, N.Y.	636,596
52	Gary–Hammond–East Chicago, Ind.	633,367
53	Honolulu, Hawaii	630,528
54	Fort Lauderdale–Hollywood, Fla.	620,100
55	Jersey City, N.J.	607,839
56	Greensboro–Winston-Salem–High Point, N.C.	604,720
57	Salt Lake City, Utah	557,635
58	Allentown–Bethlehem–Easton, Pa./N.J.	543,809
59	Omaha, Nebr./Iowa	542,646
60	Nashville–Davidson, Tenn.	541,142
61	Grand Rapids, Mich.	539,225
62	Youngstown–Warren, Ohio	537,124
63	Springfield–Chicopee–Holyoke, Mass./Conn.	529,922
64	Jacksonville, Fla.	528,865
65	Richmond, Va.	518,319
66	Wilmington, Del./N.J./Md.	499,493
67	Flint, Mich.	497,950
68	Tulsa, Okla.	475,264
69	Orlando, Fla.	428,003
70	Fresno, Calif.	413,329
71	Tacoma, Wash.	411,027
72	Harrisburg, Pa.	410,505
73	Charlotte, N.C.	409,370
74	Knoxville, Tenn.	400,337
75	Wichita, Kans.	389,352
76	Bridgeport, Conn.	389,153
77	Oxnard–Ventura, Calif.	378,497
78	Lansing, Mich.	378,423
79	Mobile, Ala.	376,690
80	Canton, Ohio	372,210
81	Davenport–Rock Island–Moline, Iowa/Ill.	362,368
82	El Paso, Texas	359,291
83	New Haven, Conn.	355,538
84	Tucson, Ariz.	351,667
85	West Palm Beach, Fla.	348,993
86	Worcester, Mass.	344,320
87	Wilkes-Barre–Hazelton, Pa.	342,329
88	Peoria, Ill.	341,979
89	Utica–Rome, N.Y.	340,670
90	York, Pa.	329,540
91	Bakersfield, Calif.	329,271
92	Little Rock–North Little Rock, Ark.	323,296
93	Columbia, S.C.	322,880
94	Lancaster, Pa.	320,079
95	Beaumont–Port Arthur–Orange, Texas	317,572
96	Albuquerque, N. Mex.	315,774
97	Chattanooga, Tenn./Ga.	305,768
98	Trenton, N.J.	304,116

Table 1-1   (Cont.)

RANK	SMSA	1970 POPULATION
99	Charleston, S.C.	303,849
100	Binghamton, N.Y./Pa.	302,672
101	Greenville, S.C.	299,730
102	Reading, Pa.	296,382
103	Austin, Texas	295,516
104	Shreveport, La.	293,887
105	Newport News–Hampton, Va.	292,159
106	Madison, Wisc.	290,272
107	Stockton, Calif.	289,564
108	Spokane, Wash.	287,487
109	Des Moines, Iowa	286,130
110	Baton Rouge, La.	285,167
111	Corpus Christi, Texas	284,832
112	Fort Wayne, Ind.	280,455
113	South Bend, Ind.	280,031
114	Appleton–Oshkosh, Wisc.	276,948
115	Las Vegas, Nev.	273,288
116	Rockford, Ill.	272,063
117	Duluth–Superior, Minn./Wisc.	265,350
118	Santa Barbara, Calif.	264,324
119	Erie, Pa.	263,654
120	Johnstown, Pa.	262,822
121	Jackson, Miss.	258,906
122	Lorain–Elyria, Ohio	256,843
123	Huntington–Ashland, W. Va./Ky./Ohio	253,743
124	Augusta, Ga./S.C.	253,460
125	Vallejo–Napa, Calif.	251,129
126	Salinas–Monterey, Calif.	247,450
127	Pensacola, Fla.	243,075
128	Columbus, Ga./Ala.	238,584
129	Colorado Springs, Colo.	235,972
130	Scranton, Pa.	234,107
131	Ann Arbor, Mich.	234,103
132	Evansville, Ind./Ky.	232,775
133	Lawrence–Haverhill, Mass./N.H.	232,415
134	Charleston, W. Va.	229,515
135	Raleigh, N.C.	229,006
136	Huntsville, Ala.	228,239
137	Hamilton–Middletown, Ohio	226,207
138	Saginaw, Mich.	219,743
139	Eugene, Oreg.	215,401
140	Lowell, Mass.	212,860
141	Fayetteville, N.C.	212,042
142	Waterbury, Conn.	208,956
143	New London–Groton–Norwich, Conn.	208,718
144	Stamford, Conn.	206,419
145	Macon, Ga.	206,342
146	Santa Rosa, Calif.	204,885
147	Kalamazoo, Mich.	201,550

Table 1-1   (Cont.)

RANK	SMSA	1970 POPULATION
148	Montgomery, Ala.	201,451
149	Modesto, Calif.	194,506
150	Durham, N.C.	190,388
151	Brockton, Mass.	189,820
152	Savannah, Ga.	187,816
153	Salem, Oreg.	186,658
154	Wheeling, W. Va./Ohio	182,712
155	McAllen–Pharr–Edinburg, Texas	181,535
156	Roanoke, Va.	181,436
157	Lubbock, Texas	175,043
158	Terre Haute, Ind.	175,143
159	Atlantic City, N.J.	157,043
160	Lexington, Ky.	174,323
161	Lima, Ohio	171,472
162	Racine, Wisc.	170,838
163	Galveston–Texas City, Texas	169,812
164	Lincoln, Nebr.	167,972
165	Steubenville–Weirton, Ohio/W. Va.	165,627
166	Champaign–Urbana, Ill.	163,281
167	Cedar Rapids, Iowa	163,213
168	Springfield, Ill.	161,335
169	Fort Smith, Ark./Okla.	160,421
170	Green Bay, Wisc.	158,244
171	Muskegon–Muskegon Heights, Mich.	157,426
172	Springfield, Ohio	157,115
173	Topeka, Kans.	155,322
174	Springfield, Mo.	152,929
175	New Bedford, Mass.	152,642
176	Fall River, Mass./R.I.	149,976
177	Waco, Texas	147,553
178	Lake Charles, La.	145,415
179	New Britain, Conn.	145,269
180	Asheville, N.C.	145,056
181	Amarillo, Texas	144,396
182	Jackson, Mich.	143,274
183	Portland, Maine	141,625
184	Brownsville–Harlingen–San Benito, Texas	140,368
185	Anderson, Ind.	138,522
186	Provo–Orem, Utah	137,776
187	Altoona, Pa.	135,356
188	Biloxi–Gulfport, Miss.	134,582
189	Waterloo, Iowa	132,916
190	Mansfield, Ohio	129,997
191	Muncie, Ind.	129,219
192	Petersburg–Colonial Heights, Va.	128,809
193	Wichita Falls, Texas	126,322
194	Ogden, Utah	126,278
195	Decatur, Ill.	125,010
196	Lynchburg, Va.	123,474

Table 1-1 (Cont.)

RANK	SMSA	1970 POPULATION
197	Vineland–Millville–Bridgeton, N.J.	121,374
198	Reno, Nev.	121,068
199	Fargo–Moorhead, N. Dak./Minn.	120,261
200	Norwalk, Conn.	120,099

SOURCE: U.S. Department of Commerce, Bureau of the Census, *County and City Data Book, 1972* (Washington, D.C.: Government Printing Office, 1973), Appendix A.

approximately 75 percent of the nation's population lives in urban areas.[1] Much more meaningful is the concept of *urbanized area*, which is defined as including at least one city of 50,000 inhabitants plus adjacent closely settled areas. According to this definition, which will be the one used throughout this volume, approximately 60 percent of the nation's population is classified as urban.

The definition of SMSA raises other problems. A central city is defined in terms of its political boundaries, but how does one define a metropolitan area? For example, where does Baltimore's metropolitan area end and Washington's begin? The usual definition considers any adjoining population center as part of a central city's metropolitan area. It is obvious that Westchester County, New York (long an enclave of white, upper-income residents), usually considered part of New York's metropolitan area, is as vastly different from the heart of New York City as is Mt. Lebanon, Pennsylvania (a suburb with high-income residents), from Pittsburgh's central city. The problem of defining population areas must be carefully considered, because the physical proximity of suburban areas to the central city does not imply that those areas share the characteristics of the central city. On the other hand, citizens who reside far from the central city may in fact be greatly influenced by the events that take place there, whether they be corporate economic decisions or political decisions.

Central cities and metropolitan areas are important to the economic growth of the nation. New York City's Wall Street is thought of as the financial center of the Western world, if not the entire world, and the importance of Chicago in world agricultural trade, Pittsburgh in ferrous metals, New Orleans in shipping, Houston in petrochemicals, and Omaha in meat production cannot be overlooked. Just as New York City is a world trade center, Denver is the financial hub of the Rocky Mountain area, and decisions made in Seattle influence the entire Northwest. Despite the recent emphasis on the productivity of the agricultural areas in the United States, the nation is indeed a composite of metropolitan areas that set national standards of dress, behavior, and consumption and often strongly influence national economic, social, and political structures. This statement does not deny the importance of smaller communities in American life; it simply emphasizes that an appreciation of the relative importance of the 200 metropolitan areas is necessary for accurate policy comparisons and successful policy formulation.

Perhaps one of the most overlooked aspects of the snapshot description of contemporary urban America is the political significance of the cities included in the metropolitan areas listed in Table 1-1. Some are state capitals (Denver, St. Paul, Boston, and Salt Lake City), but most of the others dominate politics in their state and often exert considerable influence on national political decision-making. Statewide candidates, whether they are seeking the position of governor, United States senator, or President, often concentrate their political efforts in metropolitan areas. These candidates must consider their policy positions vis-à-vis voter blocs and attitudes in these areas. Again the point is clear: metropolitan America will continue to have a significant impact on the nation's political future.

Finally, America's urban centers also play a dominant role in the intellectual and cultural life of the nation. Its great museums, legitimate theaters, musical organizations, and libraries are concentrated in the largest population centers. In addition, artists and patrons are often attracted to an urban area because of the presence of these cultural assets, and thus increase the concentration of intellectual and cultural resources in that area. Thus metropolitan areas, as depositories of these strengths, are often leaders in producing new art forms and ideas.

For all of these reasons, central cities and metropolitan areas have become central to the future growth of the United States and the improvement of the life styles of its citizens. This does not mean that life for the inhabitants of smaller cities, towns, and rural areas is empty or meaningless, but that these 200 metropolitan areas will be the center of political, social, and economic developments, and that the decisions reached in them will set the stage for the future.

However, the snapshot view must be qualified in several significant ways. This is done most easily by considering metropolitan America in terms of the motion picture perspective, which combines a variety of historical and comparative views. This perspective is presented in Tables 1-2 to 1-4.

Table 1-2   Growth of Metropolitan Population and Land Use, 1950–1970

YEAR	NONMETROPOLITAN		METROPOLITAN	
	POPULATION (IN MILLIONS)	% OF LAND AREA	POPULATION (IN MILLIONS)	% OF LAND AREA
1950	66.5	94.1	84.9	5.9
1960	66.5	91.2	112.9	8.8
1970	64.0	89.0	139.4	11.0

SOURCE: U.S. Department of Commerce, Bureau of the Census, *Statistical Abstract of the United States, 1974* (Washington, D.C.: Government Printing Office, 1974), pp. 864–865.

Table 1-2 provides a historical view of urban growth and metropolitan land use in the United States during the past 20 years.[2] Note that the number of persons living in metropolitan areas increased by nearly 55 million in these 20 years whereas the non-SMSA population declined by 2.5 million during the same period. This supports the contention that the growth of the United States has been characterized by a shift from a rural to an urban society and that this shift is accelerating as the nation enters its third century.

Table 1-2 also challenges another widely held belief—that America is becoming one large metropolitan center. Note that the metropolitan population, even with the tremendous growth it experienced from 1950 to 1970, still occupies only 11 percent of the land. Even when the uninhabitable land is excluded, substantial amounts of land are still available for urban growth. The important point about land use patterns to be gained from Table 1-2 is that the growth of the metropolitan population in the United States has occurred on a relatively limited amount of the available land.

Table 1-3 Distribution of United States Population, 1950–1970 (in millions; percentage given in parentheses)

AREA	1950		1960		1970	
SMSAs						
Inside central cities	53.7	(36)	59.9	(34)	63.8	(31)
Outside central cities	40.9	(27)	59.6	(33)	75.6	(38)
Nonmetropolitan areas (outside SMSAs)	56.7	(37)	59.7	(33)	63.8	(31)
Total	151.3	(100.0)	179.2	(100.0)	203.2	(100.0)

SOURCE: U.S. Department of Commerce, Bureau of the Census, *Statistical Abstract of the United States, 1974* (Washington, D.C.: Government Printing Office, 1974), p. 17.

Table 1-3 indicates that in 1970 in SMSAs, more people resided in areas outside central cities (75.6 million) than in the central cities themselves (63.8 million). This is a continuation of the trend that began when improvements in transportation technology resulted in the establishment of public and private transit systems that enabled individuals to work in the city and reside elsewhere. The first two rows of Table 1-3 can be interpreted in various ways. Areas outside central cities are experiencing more rapid rates of growth than other areas; this appears to have been the dominant trend between 1960 and 1970. In the same period, the total populations of central cities, areas outside the central cities but within the SMSAs, and nonmetropolitan areas increased. The population of the nonmetropolitan areas increased at a slightly greater rate (6.8 percent) than the population inside central cities (6.5 percent). This does not indicate that central cities are no longer attracting people, but that during the 1960s, larger numbers of people were attracted to areas around the central cities than to the central cities themselves. Thus, any analysis of urban America must take into account the areas where people are presently residing and the trends of mobility and settlement. If the trend that began in the 1920s and 1930s continues, it is likely that metropolitan areas will continue to grow in terms of both population and land area, while increasing or maintaining their population density (that is, the number of people per square mile). The significant point, however, is that in terms of population, the central city, although it is still the largest single unit within a particular metropolitan area, will not be as dominant as it was in the past. The implication of this for land use policies will be investigated in Chapter 7.

Table 1-4 compares the racial and economic composition of metropolitan and nonmetropolitan areas. Race must be considered in any discussion of metropolitan and nonmetropolitan populations. Nearly three-fourths of the black population lives within SMSAs (17 million of 23 million) and more than 57 percent (13 million) of the black population lives within central cities, whereas slightly less than 68 percent (120 million of 177 million) of the white population lives within SMSAs and only 28 percent (49 million of 177 million) of the white population resides within the central city. The conclusion is inescapable: any policy designed to aid the majority of blacks will have to concentrate on the metropolitan areas, where their numbers are greatest. Another inescapable fact is that, except in a few cities (best exemplified by Gary, Indiana; Newark, New Jersey; and Washington, D.C.), blacks are in the minority, and do not have the numerical strength necessary to dominate local politics. The reason is that, even with the exodus of many whites from the city, whites still constitute 79 percent of the inside central city population and 95 percent of the outside central city population. Thus political strategy and proposals for change must take into account this set of conditions. This point will be returned to in later chapters.

A comparison of the data found in rows three to eight of Table 1-4 indicates that families residing in SMSAs but outside central cities with populations of more than one million have the highest median incomes. The differences in median income between those families residing outside the central cities, but within SMSAs, and those families residing in the central cities and in the nonmetropolitan areas (outside the SMSAs) are the greatest. For instance, a higher-than-average percentage of families residing inside central cities (regardless of SMSA size) earned less than $4,000/year and a lower-than-average percentage of families residing in nonmetropolitan areas earned more than $12,000/year. Again, the conclusion is inescapable: economic differences characterize urban America, and any policy proposal must take into account the political significance of these differences. These points will be discussed more fully in subsequent chapters, but the racial and economic differences between metropolitan and nonmetropolitan areas should be noted here.

Table 1-4 Variations in Selected Socioeconomic Characteristics between Residents of Metropolitan and Nonmetropolitan Areas, 1970

AREA	RACE		MEDIAN ANNUAL FAMILY INCOME			
	WHITE	NEGRO	% UNDER $4,000	%$4,000–$12,000	%$12,000–$25,000	% OVER $25,000
All AMSAs						
Inside central cities	49,000,000(79%)	13,000,000(21%)				
Outside central cities	71,000,000(95%)	4,000,000(5%)				
Nonmetropolitan areas	57,000,000(90%)	6,000,000(10%)	15.7	49.5	30.4	4.4
United States as a whole	177,000,000(89%)	23,000,000(11%)	11.7	43.5	37.6	7.3
SMSAs over 1 million						
Inside central cities			13.3	44.4	35.2	7.1
Outside central cities			6.6	34.0	47.4	12.0
SMSAs under 1 million						
Inside central cities			13.4	44.3	35.6	6.7
Outside central cities			8.0	42.5	42.2	7.3

SOURCE: U.S. Department of Commerce, Bureau of the Census, Statistical Abstract of the United States, 1974 (Washington, D.C.: Government Printing Office, 1974), pp. 17, 48.

Table 1-4 does not show the extreme differentials that exist within the neighborhoods of any city. For instance, in the Near North Side of Chicago, there are high-rise apartment complexes owned or rented by individuals with high annual incomes, as well as some of the worst examples of public housing in the United States, whose occupants often earn less than $3,000/year. Yet in the aggregate data for Chicago the incomes are averaged, and a somewhat misleading picture of actual conditions is presented that totally disregards the extreme variations that may exist throughout the city.

Similarly, aggregate data may ignore or distort the differences that frequently exist among residents of areas outside central cities. Numerous examples can be cited of largely blue-collar, working-class suburbs in which the average annual family income is $8500, as well as affluent suburbs in which the average annual family income is in excess of $25,000. Again, in aggregate data these differences are averaged, and the results can be misleading. The point is clear: aggregate data must be interpreted cautiously and used even more cautiously because they can "mask" as many important facts as they reveal. The important contribution of aggregate data is that they usually enable us to detect trends and make comparisons more accurately than we could by using data on individuals; such trends and comparisons can be used to develop specific policies to deal with important deficiencies.

Before this section is concluded, one final point should be made. Urban America has been and continues to be characterized by constant and rapid change. This is especially true of cities in the South and West, which are experiencing substantial population growth in short periods, as well as older cities of the Midwest and Northeast, where population totals are declining or remaining constant. In the former, population growth takes a variety of forms, but is usually characterized by the arrival of new residents and their absorption into the social and political setting of the area. In the latter, the population of a specific urban area is likely to be undergoing substantial change also, but this is not reflected in the total population figures because it results from the replacement of one population group or groups by another. For instance, central cities in the Northeastern and North Central United States are rapidly becoming enclaves of older, non-white residents with little formal education, while their suburban areas tend to attract middle-income residents who have attained a higher level of education. This transfer of population, which often results in slight total population shifts, can and often does cause social, economic, and political problems as profound as those associated with rapid population growth. Both sets of problems need to be thoroughly considered and understood if policies, once decided upon, are to be given even a minimal chance to succeed.

Unresolved questions

Few attempts were made to plan for the growth and development of America's urban centers during the past 200 years, or to provide meaningful policy options for those making important governmental decisions. In fact, the opposite has usually been true: governments at all levels have tended to respond to the problems of an active private sector rather than anticipating them and planning to meet them. The private sector, of necessity, has utilized a variety of human and natural resources to strengthen itself. Thus there are a number of important policy problems that have not been clearly defined and that have changed little in recent years. These problems are likely to be the subject of future discussions that will attempt to determine the utility of various options. The problems will be briefly summarized here in order to provide the historical and theoretical background necessary for an understanding of their significance.

To begin with, there will continue to be considerable debate about the appropriate relationships that should exist among the national, state, and local levels of government. The Constitution of the United States is quite clear on this point: it establishes a two-tiered federal system in which specific powers are delegated to both national and state governments.[3] The Constitution does *not* specify any powers that should be delegated to or reserved by local governments.

This decision by the Founding Fathers to create a federal state has had important implications for American politics, and these implications have probably been greatest in the area of intergovernmental relations (relations among the national, state, and local governments). Consider for a moment the great constitutional crises and debates of the early 1800s, the Civil War era, and the Roosevelt New Deal years, and it becomes obvious that when the Founding Fathers established a federal system of government, they also created a dynamic system the working of which would be subject to differing interpretations as times and conditions changed. The result has been that intergovernmental relations in America have been constantly shifting and that there has been continual discussion about the exact nature of the constitutional and legal relationships that exist between the national and state governments. The debate has taken a variety of forms.

Probably most common is the continuing struggle between the states-rightists and the centralists, those who maintain that the national government has broad powers. States-rightists insist that the constitutional powers given to the national government are clearly spelled out and that those not specified in the Constitution are indeed "reserved" to the states and to the people.[4] Thus, unless the Constitution specifically permits or empowers the national government to perform a task, the strict interpretationist maintains that the national government lacks the constitutional authority to do so. On the other hand, others have asserted that the Constitution delegates certain "implied" powers to the national government and that these powers may be utilized when it is clear that the task in question should be performed by the national government even though the Constitution does not specifically state that it has the power to do so.

This has been a major theme of the debate over the nature of American federalism, and the debate has not taken place in a policy vacuum. Two useful examples of these differing interpretations are Presidential actions and Supreme Court decisions. President Abraham Lincoln's decision to attempt to hold the Union together rather than permit the Confederate states to opt for secession reflected his view that the national government should be pre-eminent. Certainly Franklin D. Roosevelt's attempts to secure enactment of major new legislation to deal with the economic depression of the 1930s is another example of Presidential leadership based on a "national" interpretation of the Constitution. A frequently cited rationale for such action was that because the state governments failed to formulate policies aimed at alleviating the severe economic hardships affecting the nation, the responsibility for such action devolved upon the national government.

Similarly, judicial decisions have long been important in the debate over the nature of federalism in the United States. The Supreme Court renders the definitive judgment as to which actions of the national and state governments are in fact constitutional and which are not—that is, which actions violate the current Court's perception of constitutionality. Certainly the cases involving slavery, such as the Dred Scott case, and those involving the applicability to the states of the Fourteenth Amendment (due process and equal protection of rights) have had far-reaching implications for the nature of federalism in America. In the Dred Scott case, the Court limited the powers of Congress with regard to the states. However, after passage of the Fourteenth Amendment, the Supreme Court handed down frequent and often landmark decisions in the areas of civil rights and civil liberties in which it maintained that the due process and equal protection under the law clauses of that amendment were applicable to the states.

The intense debate about the nature of federalism that has continued throughout United States history has taken on even more significance in the last 25 years as a result of the discussion of the proper "roles" of national and state governments in the areas of public services, civil rights, and new programs designed to meet pressing social and economic needs. In the 1950s an interesting distinction was made by Morton Grodzins,[5] who argued that the study of federalism was too often concerned with determining which functions should most appropriately be performed at which level of government. According to Grodzins, this resulted in the view that the "top" layer was the national government and the "bottom" layer was the state governments. Thus the states could obtain power only when it was delegated from above. Grodzins maintained that the debate over which level was the appropriate one to perform a function frequently became oversimplified and too legalistic. He asserted that American federalism more nearly resembles a "marble cake," that both the national and state levels of government often perform similar functions, and that the emphasis should be on cooperation rather than competition between the various institutions at both levels.[6] Grodzins' emphasis on these aspects of federalism aroused interest in the field of intergovernmental relations as a subject area with specific emphasis on the interaction between national and state programs.

The nature of federalism in the United States remains an important issue in political debates, from school busing to proposed gun control legislation, and certainly any public policy recommendations must take this issue into consideration. A final point about federalism should be made.

Historically, the debate over the nature of American federalism has considered only the relationship between the national government and the state governments. The notion that states have legal control over the powers they may or may not grant to their units of local government has always been widely accepted. What this in fact means is that local units of government, including cities and counties, are dependent upon the states for constitutional and statutory authority in most areas. Thus, local governments are able to perform only the duties expressly delegated to them in their state constitutions and by their state legislatures. This is an important impediment barring the local units from developing significant policies to meet the problems confronting them. Since the customary practice has been for states to retain significant power, local units of government have often found it difficult to deal with many of the problems facing them without being granted much broader discretionary power.

Closely related to the issues of federalism and intergovernmental relations is the question of centralization versus decentralization. The determination of which level of government is best equipped to decide and implement policy matters is especially applicable to most metropolitan areas. For instance, should individual governments within the same metropolitan area independently decide what their air and water standards are to be, or is there a rationale for establishing a specific set of minimum standards that all units of government within that metropolitan area must accept and enforce? Similarly, should each unit be responsible for the transportation facilities within its boundaries, or should there be one areawide structure that provides service for the residents of all the local communities? The details of these possible policy choices will not be discussed here, but it should be clear that the decentralization versus centralization question has a number of aspects.

First, and perhaps most important, the qualitative effect of the division of governmental responsibility on living and life styles must be understood. Assume a decentralized system. It is possible, as a result of favorable prevailing wind patterns or river currents, for one unit of government to pollute air and water without suffering the direct harmful effects of such actions. In such a situation, environmental quality varies depending upon whether the area is upstream or downstream and whether it is upwind or downwind from the offending unit. Thus it would make little sense for the area doing the polluting to have stringent regulations if in fact the pollution were occurring elsewhere. Yet if the area being polluted lacked jurisdiction in the area where the waste actually entered the water or the air, it would be virtually powerless to control, reduce, or eliminate the pollution. In this particular example, the residents of the community being polluted would undoubtedly demand that some centralized authority take action, while those polluting would probably recommend that enforcement policies in these areas are best left to the local agencies. Again, depending upon where a person lived, the quality of his or her life would be affected either favorably or unfavorably by the enforcement policy decisions that were made.

Second, centralization, it has been argued, may result in economies of scale that reduce the overall costs of operating various programs. An economy of scale occurs when the cost of providing a service to a consumer decreases as the size of the unit increases and the quality of the service remains constant. For instance, if the same quality of police protection can be provided for 50,000 people at a rate of $6.75 per capita whereas it costs two jurisdictions of 25,000 each $7.75 per capita for the same services, an economy of scale exists. It is frequently argued that the cost of services that require expensive equipment and training is significantly reduced because centralization, with its elimination of duplication, results in increased purchasing power and operating efficiency and more effective planning. Numerous examples can be cited of the advantages of centralization in improving urban services, but perhaps the provision of adequate fire protection best illustrates the point. In a metropolitan area that includes one large central city and four suburban areas, it may be quite expensive for each of the local governments to hire and train fire personnel as well as to provide modern, sophisticated fire equipment. The contention is that it is more efficient for the various units of government to agree to provide fire service under a unified organization. The result could be decreased costs for equipment and training plus more efficient coordination of fire protection for the residents of all the communities. As is pointed out in the next paragraph, the resolution of these types of questions is not as easy or as simple as the preceding example suggests.

Finally, the answer to the centralization-decentralization question often hinges on important political matters, chief among them the final political composition of the centralized unit versus that of the decentralized units. Various groups may support or oppose centralization depending on what effect it will have on their political strength. For example, the leaders of many minorities, although they recognize the fiscal and economic benefits that may be gained from centralization, often oppose such proposals because, in many instances, they "dilute" a minority's political strength by decreasing the relative proportion of the minority's population vis-à-vis the entire population. Similarly, the residents of predominantly white suburbs frequently oppose centralization proposals because they are reluctant to relinquish control over their public schools or other services. Quite often proponents of centralization and decentralization fail to understand the importance of these political considerations to the groups involved. Clearly, the question of centralization versus decentralization often produces considerable tension and disagreement. It is given fuller consideration in Chapters 8 and 10.

Two other sets of questions are usually at the heart of all policy decisions, especially those applicable to urban America. The first concerns representation and democratic control; the second concerns the development of political institutions that will maximize the values deemed necessary for the maintenance and continuation of a democratic system. Both have important implications for the vitality and strength of any urban system of governance.

Certainly the question of representation is not unique to America's cities, but dominates any discussion concerned with achieving meaningful political control and organization. On the one hand, the emphasis must be on governmental responsiveness, which is usually thought to be maximized when representation is direct. The main justification for direct participation is that it increases the likelihood that governmental action will be responsive and in accord with citizen preferences. On the other hand, the complexity of today's urban society means that public leaders are frequently unable to utilize direct representational methods because of time constraints and the size of their respective constituencies. For instance, is it reasonable to expect a mayor of any city of more than 50,000 inhabitants to be accessible daily to any citizen who wishes to lodge a complaint, suggest a change in policy, or simply make a routine request? The need to reconcile these two positions demands the development of institutions that maximize governmental responsiveness and efficiency.

One of the most common solutions to this problem has been the representational system,[7] in which citizens do not directly participate in each and every decision affecting them, but choose others to represent them in the decision-making process. The rationale, assuming that the selection process is indeed open, is that the representatives will reflect the values and desires of their constituents. In other words, the chosen representative is a delegate of those who elected him; he simply acts in accordance with the dominant feeling of his constituents and not as an independent leader exercising discretion. The citizens have delegated to their representative the authority to make decisions affecting them and assume they will be well represented.

Contrasted with this system is the trustee system, in which representatives are "trusted" to reflect their constituents' interests as they interpret them, and are not required constantly to inquire about their constituents' views. The trustee system assumes that the representatives can in fact gauge the policy positions that will be in their constituents' best interests. However, in actuality the representatives' actions are frequently at variance with those desired by their constituents, and thus problems may be posed for both representatives and constituents.

This brief discussion has focused on the complexities involved in only two of the possible resolutions of the representational question. This basic problem of how to structure representation is often compounded by the economic, racial, and social diversity found in urban areas. For instance, the representative from an urban area comprised of constituents with similar backgrounds, values, and needs finds the task of accurately interpreting and reflecting constituents' interests and needs easier than does the representative from an urban area composed of diverse population groups with different concerns—regardless of whether the urban representatives are city council members, state legislators, or members of the United States House of Representatives. It is clear that careful thought must be given to the question of representation and the effectiveness of the mechanisms designed to bring it about if an urban political system is to be open, responsive, and democratic.

Certainly closely related to and directly affecting this question of representation is the question of the optimal size of an urban governmental unit.[8] This has been a hotly debated issue; the greater economy that results from increasing the size of the unit of government is contrasted with the improvement in the quality of representation that results from decreasing the size of America's urban areas. To some, the very size of a New York City makes effective democratic control virtually impossible, whereas others view its size as creating the possibility for the diversity that benefits a democratic system.[9]

Although the question of optimal size cannot be resolved, it must also be considered from another point of view. Several observers have argued that large cities, usually defined as having more than 250,000 inhabitants, are superior to small ones because of the economic gains that result from the increased efficiency, elimination of overlapping services, and other economies of scale associated with increased size. The economic benefits supposedly realized from such size outweigh the smaller units' ability to provide services and amenities on a more individual basis. Unfortunately, the advocates of this position fail to measure the political costs associated with increased size. For instance, if a particular characteristic such as race or economic class is shared by, say, 10 to 20 percent of the population within a particular political jurisdiction, the impact that group has on political decisions will be affected by changes in the size of the jurisdiction. If the size of the jurisdiction increases and if the total population increases without a corresponding increase in the size of the population sharing the characteristic, then the relative strength of the group will be lessened. The opposite occurs if there is an increase in the percentage of people with that characteristic. In either case, the political implications may be major, and those who advocate changes in city size should bear this in mind.

Certainly an excellent current example of this relationship is the debate over consolidation of the central city with its surrounding suburban areas. The usual contention is that such centralization will result in increased benefits for the residents of the central city while increasing the coordination and efficiency of services available to the entire area. The problem is that consolidation often means reducing the relative strength of one group, either in the central city or in the surrounding areas. The end result is that consolidation has not been widely adopted, nor is it likely to be in the future because of these political problems. Nevertheless, consolidation remains a favorite topic of those wishing to reform local government. It is considered more fully in Chapter 8.

Even if the question of overall size could be resolved, the appropriate division of the population into representative districts is also quite complicated and raises considerable problems. On the one hand, it is often argued that all representatives should be elected by the community at large rather than by specific districts. Representatives elected at large supposedly reflect the interest of the whole community, whereas representatives selected from districts are more likely to pursue policies and support programs that will aid their districts, perhaps at the expense of the community interest. In addition, the representative elected from a district is often considered to represent a more well-defined and narrowly based group of individuals and their interests than the representative in an at-large system. Obviously, these theoretical questions cannot be resolved here, but their importance in any discussion of the political organization of an urban jurisdiction should be quite clear. They will be considered in detail in subsequent chapters because they have specific significance for the policy choices presently available.

One last point about representation must be raised because it has become increasingly relevant as American urban society has become more complex. What should be the relationship between the average citizen and the expert, given the increasing complexity of urban life? Should citizens defer to the expert's judgment? Should they elect a qualified expert to represent them? Or should citizens remain skeptical of the elected or appointed expert's ability to solve technological and political problems?

An excellent case in point is the conflict generated by the War on Poverty in the 1960s and, in particular, the emphasis on citizen participation.[10] Should the citizens who are affected, in this case the poor, have the right to plan, participate in, and implement programs designed to reduce and eradicate their poverty, or should the programs be planned, administered, and controlled by "experts"? Certainly the governmental debate and the public discussion of this point made it quite clear that this dilemma is critical to the future of the cities. If it is decided that the urban expert is entitled to increased power because of his specialized knowledge, then the citizens' role

Table 1-5   Aspects of Political Representation

TYPE OF REPRESENTATION	SIZE	PARTICIPANT	INSTITUTIONS
Direct Emphasis on individual participation	Majority Implies relatively small numbers to permit individual interaction	Citizen competence on most subjects is assumed	Public hearings Community groups Contested elections
Indirect Emphasis on selection process and manner of representation	Minority Implies the possibility of larger groups in order to permit group interaction	Expert Required in complex society in order to reach rational choices	Formal technological bodies—regulatory functions Agencies insulated from public control

must be clearly defined. Are the citizens to set broad policy and let the expert administer it, or are the citizens expected to respond to the expert's recommendations? In a social, economic, and political setting that is becoming increasingly complicated, the resolution of these questions is quite important and may in fact hold the key to whether the quality of life in urban America can in fact be improved.

Table 1-5 summarizes the various points that were considered in the discussion of representation, and should make clear that the issue of representation is central to the policy-making process in America's urban centers.

The effectiveness of political institutions with regard to representation can be judged from a variety of perspectives, but probably the three most useful considerations are power, control, and responsiveness. By power is meant the amount of influence a person or political institution has—the more influence, the more powerful the person or institution. Thus, if a city charter provides the mayor with broad powers, then the mayor and local government officials will, in most instances, exert significant power in the city.

Control refers to the areas of authority over which a person or institution has jurisdiction and the relative amount of power they can exert. For instance, if city budgeting is the exclusive task of one institution, the amount of control that agency has over budgetary matters is vastly different than it would be if other, competing institutions shared that task.

Finally, responsiveness means that the institutions are meeting public needs, in a manner that is in accordance with public wishes. This is often the most difficult quality to develop, and specific programs frequently must be established to facilitate effective communication between average citizens and their political representatives. Responsiveness means not only meeting public needs, but doing so fairly and democratically.

This discussion is intended as background for much of the discussion in the later chapters about the appropriate political institutions needed to enable policy-makers to choose among a variety of policy alternatives. Power, control, and responsiveness are necessary considerations in the attempt to organize any political system, but they are even more important given the complexities of urban problems. Although it can be argued that in the future, policy choices will be bound only by theoretical concerns such as those just discussed, the role the city has played in history will doubtless also be an important consideration.

The historical legacy

In America the city has traditionally been viewed very negatively. The emphasis has usually been on the mistrust and on the seamy aspects of life that, according to the cities' critics, have existed there. It must be remembered that this reputation was not acquired only recently, but dates back to the time of the Founding Fathers. Suspicions of city dwellers were common, and Americans, most of whom were rurally oriented, tended to blame unfortunate financial or social developments on those living in the cities. Caricatures of the urban dweller dominated many political cartoons of the 1800s.

More importantly, cities were not granted legal recognition. As has been pointed out, the Constitution recognizes only states and the national government. In addition, most states tended either to ignore cities or to enact restrictive legislation that made them totally dependent upon the state legislatures. Thus cities often lacked the legal power to raise local revenues or to act decisively in areas affecting the quality of life of their citizens. Until the mid-1900s, the state legislatures of many states with large urban centers were dominated by rural interests, and urban areas often received less than adequate treatment. Reform advocates often overlook the role of institutions in bringing about change; in the area of urban reform, state legislatures have been and continue to be exceedingly important, as they control many facets of urban life.

In the tumultuous period of the late 1800s and early 1900s, demands for political reform began to be made, and much of the outcry was over the abuses many felt existed at the state and city levels of government. This movement, known as Progressivism, had a far-reaching effect at the urban level that took a variety of forms. First, considerable discussion ensued about the corruption in state politics and especially about the detrimental influence of political parties on the quality of urban governance. Efforts were made to weaken party allegiance as well as to increase the ability of the general public to control local officials and hold them responsible for their actions. Reforms such as shorter ballots (a ballot could not have as many items) and more stringent controls over the corruption that many felt dominated state legislatures were debated and, in some states, enacted.

Second, the cities themselves received considerable attention from many of the critics of the day, usually referred to as "muckrakers." Perhaps most significant was the activity of Lincoln Steffens, whose book *The Shame of the Cities*[11] is considered one of the leading statements made by the "good government" advocates of the Progressive Era. Steffens surveyed a variety of cities and described in great detail the incipient graft and corruption that he discovered. His contention was that these conditions were causing the deterioration of public services and would ultimately result in the deterioration of the city itself. Steffens was quite outspoken. He claimed that

> St. Louis, the fourth city in size in the United States, is making two announcements to the world: one that it is the worst-governed city in the land, . . . It isn't our worst-governed city; Philadelphia is that.[12]

Steffens' book became a guide for those advocating change in urban institutions, and the result was that proposals were forthcoming that called for a reduction in partisan politics and the influence of big city machines.

Interestingly, the emphasis was not only on changing human behavior, but on changing the institutions by means of which the city was governed. The two most important efforts at urban reform were the adoption of the nonpartisan ballot and of the city manager form of government.

Ballot reform was often stressed by the reformers of the Progressive Era, who apparently felt that partisan designations (the inclusion on the ballots of the names or symbols of political parties associated with candidates) would lead to uninformed and possibly "bloc" voting by the general public. Bear in mind that many voters in urban centers at this time were recently arrived immigrants with newly granted citizenship who understood little if any English and who often were unaware of for whom or for what they were voting. The party label often served as the appropriate "roadmap" for those seeking direction as to how their vote should be cast. For most it was difficult to know the pros and cons of voting for a particular candidate, so they found it easier simply to vote according to a party label. This is exactly what the reformers objected to, and consequently they attempted to remove the party label from the ballot, contending that the absence of the label would force the voter to learn about specific candidates and issues before voting. Thus the deserving candidate and not the party would be elected. According to this position, a vote was seen as a purely rational decision and not as something to be cast in ignorance. The most extensive use of the nonpartisan ballot at the local level has occurred in California.

Related to this attempt to eliminate party designation were the two objectives of eliminating corruption and increasing efficiency at the urban level. The basic aim here was to replace the elected mayor as the chief urban decision-maker with a well-trained professional city manager, appointed by the city council. The usual contention was that too many of the mayor's administrative decisions were based on political needs, when in fact these decisions could and should be more objective. It was argued that the costs of operating a city could be drastically reduced if a professional manager held the chief administrative post.

The city manager form of local government became quite popular and was adopted by a large number of cities. Many of the "new" cities of the Southwest and West adopted it when they formed their first governing organizations. The impact of the city manager form of government on urban politics is considered in Chapter 5, but the important point to be noted here is that the reformers, again reflecting the distrust of urban political activity, wanted to separate the popularly elected city decision-makers from the political aspects of decision-making. In sum, then, the reformers of the Progressive Era felt that cities could in fact be governed in a rational manner and, even more important, that they should be governed with as little direct political influence as possible. This legacy has directly affected most attitudes toward city government and, in the opinion of some, has kept cities from being organized in ways that make political, but not administrative, sense. The reformers of the Progressive Era had an impressive impact on city development and, until the 1960s, their recommendations and proposals may have had the most far-reaching implications for urban life of any group in American history.

In the 1960s, greater emphasis was placed on increased participation by a larger number of Americans and often resulted in direct governmental policies to increase individual citizen participation and subsequent group decision-making at the local level. Perhaps the best known of these policies was the War on Poverty launched during the Johnson administration. The Poverty Program, which is analyzed more fully in Chapter 6 allowed a new segment of lower-income Americans to participate in political and administrative decisions at the local level.[13]

After 1967, the original emphasis of the Poverty Program on direct citizen participation and control incurred the disfavor of most federal government officials, and its financial base slowly began to erode. By the beginning of President Nixon's first term in 1969, it had become obvious that the program's emphasis on direct participation by the poor was in fact being replaced by a greater emphasis on decentralization, which stressed the responsibility of the locally elected official in reaching important decisions about programs and their administration, rather than direct participation by those affected by those programs.

Perhaps the most important legacy of the Nixon administration's "new Federalism" was its emphasis on the ability of local officials to set priorities and to establish programs to meet them. The aid programs proposed and enacted during the Nixon years increased the discretion of the local officials and decreased the regulatory power of the federal government as well as the size of the local and federal administrative staffs needed to run programs that required federal funds. The Nixon plans seemed to assume that the local official indeed was responsive to the demands of the local citizenry.[14]

The future

Clearly, urban policy choices made in the future will be affected and, perhaps to some extent, even dictated by policy choices made in the past. Future choices will certainly have to deal with the basic theoretical and value-oriented questions that have been raised in this chapter. To begin any real discussion of contemporary urban America without a thorough analysis of these questions is to mislead and even to encourage the making of policy choices that neither reflect the basic values involved nor come to grips with their theoretical implications for the quality of urban life in America.

Although there is the continuing possibility of global war or an environmental disaster that could eliminate life as we know it, changes in the future are likely to be less dramatic and conclusive than they were in the past. As previously mentioned, there are a variety of constraints limiting the policy alternatives presently available to the decision-makers who formulate and administer urban policy. Unless these individuals are acutely aware of present trends and of the past as it influences the present and the future, policy choices are likely to be inappropriate and even detrimental to the quality of life in urban America. The next two chapters include a brief review of the available alternatives and the current limitations on their selection.

Notes to Chapter 1

1. For a full definition and discussion of SMSAs, see U.S. Department of Commerce, Bureau of the Census, *County and City Data Book, 1972* (Washington, D.C.: Government Printing Office, 1973), pp. xxi–xxv.
2. Totals for this and subsequent tables throughout the volume may not equal 100 percent because of rounding errors, and aggregate totals from various tables may not be the same because different base figures and definitions were used to compute the totals.
3. See the Constitution of the United States for the specifics of this arrangement. The Tenth Amendment is important because it reserves certain powers to the states. Obviously, the constitutional debate over this relationship has been lively and will doubtless continue.
4. This argument is based on the Tenth Amendment to the Constitution and subsequent legal and theoretical interpretations of it.
5. For a full discussion of his position, see Morton Grodzins, *The American System* (Chicago: Rand McNally, 1966). Other representative examples of contemporary contributors to the debate are M. J. C. Vile, *The Structure of American Federalism* (London: Oxford University Press, 1961); Daniel J. Elazar, *The American Partnership* (Chicago: University of Chicago Press, 1962); and Richard H. Leach, *American Federalism* (New York: Norton, 1970).
6. See Grodzins, *The American System*, pp. v–vi.
7. For a particularly stimulating discussion of representation, see Hanna Pitkin, *The Concept of Representation* (Berkeley: University of California Press, 1967).
8. For a lucid and important discussion of this point, see Robert A. Dahl, "The City in the Future of Democracy," *American Political Science Review* 61 (December 1967): 953–970. For a fuller discussion of this point that includes more empirical evidence, see Robert A. Dahl and Edward R. Tufte, *Size and Democracy* (Stanford, Calif.: Stanford University Press, 1973).
9. See Dahl, *op. cit.*, p. 965, for his argument that cities with populations of 50,000–200,000 offer the best opportunity for widespread civic participation.
10. For a variety of views on the War on Poverty and citizen participation, see: John C. Donovan, *The Politics of Poverty* (New York: Pegasus, 1967); Sar A. Levitan, *The Great Society's Poor Law* (Baltimore: The Johns Hopkins Uni-

versity Press, 1969); Daniel P. Moynihan, *Maximum Feasible Misunderstanding* (New York: Free Press, 1969); Ralph M. Kramer, *Participation of the Poor* (Englewood Cliffs, N.J.: Prentice-Hall, 1969); Richard L. Cole, *Citizen Participation and the Urban Policy Process* (Lexington, Mass.: Lexington Books, 1974).

11. Lincoln Steffens, *The Shame of the Cities* (New York: McClure, Phillips, 1904).

12. *Ibid.*, p. 19.

13. For an assessment of the effects of participation on the participants in these programs, see Richard L. Cole, *op. cit.*, pp. 99–138.

14. For a discussion of the "new Federalism," see Michael D. Reagan, *The New Federalism* (New York: Oxford University Press, 1972).

Chapter 2

The Contextual Setting of Contemporary Urban Politics

Introduction

Cities, especially American cities, have undergone significant changes in the 200 years since American independence. Despite these major changes, cities still are usually thought of as "sinful" places, and their residents have often been treated as second-class citizens by the state legislatures and by Congress. This practice is not new, nor is it likely to end in the near future. We can better understand the significance of this view for the city in America if we briefly consider the development of the city in history. One can argue that the Greek city-states were the earliest examples of democratic city life, or that the walled cities of Western Africa were essential to the development of the advanced civilizations that existed in that region prior to the development of Western Europe. For our purposes, the Renaissance period will serve as the starting point for a brief but necessary overview of nearly 700 years of historical development of the city and the subsequent impact of this period on urban development in the United States.

Development of cities in Western Europe

The Renaissance has long been considered one of the "golden ages" of Western civilization because during that period (usually considered to include the 300 years from the fourteenth to the sixteenth centuries), the art forms of music, painting, sculpture, and literature reached new creative peaks. The Renaissance marked the reawakening of the human spirit after the stagnation of the Dark Ages; generous public support was given to the imaginative and artistic talents of the individual.

Because the main emphasis was on art and cultural development, the fact is often overlooked that during this period cities developed first as major trade and commercial centers and, subsequently, as artistic centers. Probably the most notable group of cities in this regard was the tier of cities in Italy north of Rome that included Bologna, Milan, Venice, and Florence. All were rapidly developing trade, artistic, and educational centers that both created an atmosphere conducive to individual self-expression and creativity and provided the economic resources needed to support them. According to Jacob Burckhardt, who is considered by many to be the leading historian of the Renaissance period, in these cities the essential ingredient appears to have been a surge in the living standard of the merchant class and the development of substantial economic support for the arts.[1] The role of the city then is readily apparent: it provided the requisite business opportunities to develop the resources as well as the contact essential for support of the arts.

Cities were then, as they often are now, symbols not only of the creative genius of individuals but also of their more base and avaricious instincts. Thus from the Renaissance onward, Western man has had a dual outlook toward city living: it can be terribly exciting and rewarding for those able to afford it, but quite tedious and difficult for the vast majority who provide the services needed for the survival of the city and its well-to-do residents.

One of the more interesting developments of the Renaissance period was the appearance of political writers who offered very specific and practical advice on how those who governed could strengthen their position. Best known of these was Niccolò Machiavelli, who, in *The Prince* (1513), stressed the basic rules a leader should follow to gain and retain power. Included in his other writings are numerous essays on how a ruler should govern fairly, equitably, and openly, as well as advice for dealing with personal manipulation, stealth, and a basic disregard for individual rights.[2]

Certainly Machiavelli's writings were applicable to the times. Each of the Renaissance cities tended to be dominated by a few families whose struggles for power are legion in historical accounts of the period.[3] Stabbings, poisonings, and abduction were frequently part of the struggle to gain or maintain power in most of these city-states; an orderly succession of power was the exception and not the rule.

It was also during the Renaissance Era that city-states entered into political agreements with one another and with individual nations to ensure mutual defense or trade benefits.[4] These agreements were often subject to varying interpretations, and if circumstances changed, they were quickly denounced by the party who was in a position to lose the most. Thus the Renaissance in Northern Italy was characterized by political intrigue, personal cunning, and rapid change of rulers. This aura of corruption and manipulation influenced individual perceptions of urban life for some time to come.

During the substantial artistic development and political chaos that was taking place in Italy, the rest of Western Europe was experiencing the religious and political ferment of the Protestant Reformation and the accompanying struggle for personal freedom. From medieval days onward, it was obvious that to many individuals, cities were to be avoided because of the necessity to pay taxes there; because of the courts that symbolized authority; and because of the threat to personal health posed by the periodic epidemics of bubonic plague and other diseases that ravaged cities and decimated their populations. In short, the rapid growth of the other cities of Western Europe resulted largely from political and economic pressures and needs; thus these cities became centers of industry and commerce rather than of intellectual and cultural development.

Ferdinand Toennies, a German sociologist who developed various explanations of urban life in the late 1800s, maintained that the development of cities in fact signaled a basic shift in society types.[5] At the beginning of the Renaissance, according to Toennies, Western Europe was a Gemeinschaft society in which the nuclear family and familial self-sufficiency were of prime importance. The family produced all of its food and met its related needs with only minimal contact with the rest of society. This family self-reliance fostered intense feelings of loyalty among family members, which resulted in a very inward-oriented family group that stressed familial kinship ties.

With the development of specialized agricultural techniques and the beginning of the industrial revolution, Toennies maintains, European society began to evolve toward a Gesellschaft society,[6] which emphasized increased interdependence and specialization. Thus the farmer sold his wheat to a miller who sold the ground flour to a baker who sold the finished bread to the consumer. This increasing specialization led to a decline in the importance of the family, an increase in the need for cooperative efforts, and ultimately the breakdown of close interpersonal relationships, resulting in the fragmentation of the family. The end result was increased migration to the city and continued specialization. Although this description of the shift in the orientation of European society is necessarily oversimplified, it does accurately describe some of the changes that occurred in Europe from the Renaissance onward. These changes become more fascinating when viewed as the background of the development of cities in the United States.

Colonial and pre-Civil War America

America's cities played a pivotal role in the early settlement of the original thirteen colonies and the subsequent struggle for independence. Although some accounts of early American history tend to be highly romanticized, there is little doubt that throughout America's colonial period, cities served a variety of important functions. First, they were often the administrative centers for British rule and domination. Perhaps Boston best typifies this role; no one needs to be reminded of the significance of the "tea party" or the "massacre." Second, the cities were usually major trade centers regardless of whether they were located inland or on the coast. Charleston, South Carolina, was an important coastal port for the Southern colonies, while Pittsburgh, Pennsylvania, provided important trade services for the region immediately west of the Appalachians as a result of its location at the confluence of the Allegheny and Monongahela rivers. Third, cities were often centers of considerable anti-British sentiment and of important debate and political action. Again Boston is an excellent example. Samuel Adams and his followers opposed British domination, and the Stamp Act and the Townshend Act resulted in the Boston Massacre and the Boston Tea Party, which have become indelible and often-cited events of colonial history. There is no doubt that during the colonial period and shortly thereafter, American cities were in fact centers of intense unrest and were the headquarters of the political leaders who were mainly responsible for the ultimate success of the independence movement.

It is necessary to point out one major, but often ignored, aspect of the colonial and early American experience. Many who crossed the ocean to America were attracted by the inexpensive land and the freedom to pursue their own life style. Thus religious dissidents found a haven in the broad expanses of relatively virgin land that awaited them. In fact, the decision to take advantage of the availability of frontier land and of the opportunity to move on when conditions grew intolerable, a decision that could freely be reached by each individual, became a basic part of the early American experience. Perhaps the meaning of this freedom was most accurately described by Frederick Jackson Turner's "frontier" thesis of American history.[7]

Turner maintained that the opportunities offered by the United States were a reflection of the settlers' perceived availability of new land. When pressures and demands for change increased, dissidents could "move on" rather than being forced to challenge the basic organization of society or to give up their own personal beliefs and views. In addition, individuals who did not like to feel "crowded" could simply move on when they decided things were too crowded for them. Thus the availability of land provided not only the opportunity for individual ownership, but also an escape valve for those who were dissatisfied with conditions in their present location. Turner and most historians of that era ignored the costs to the American Indian of this pretext that unused land was available and felt that this ability to move on was a basic stabilizing factor in American history. Turner's most interesting inference concerned the impact that would be felt by society when the supply of land was exhausted.[8] Would the frustration created by the inability of dissidents to move on generate new and varied forms of political behavior that could be detrimental to American democracy? At the very least, it could be expected that the absence of new land might alter individual behavior.

As Turner and others pointed out, early settlement patterns were normally determined by the opening of new land to cultivation. Small farmers were common and formed the bulk of the Western migration, even when the term meant no more than movement past the Alleghenies or the Cumberland Mountains of the East into the valleys of the Kentucky, Ohio, and Tennessee rivers. As the farmers developed an area, small trading centers developed (almost always on a major river or lake) and flourished. Such areas (for example, Buffalo, Syracuse, Pittsburgh, Cleveland, Cincinnati, Louisville, Chicago, and St. Louis) were originally small but diversified trade centers that distributed the raw goods produced by the farmer and the skins brought in by the trapper, and also provided the supplies they needed. The importance of this trade function increased when first barge and then steamboat travel developed on the inland waterways, and canals were built that were part of the transportation infrastructure necessary for economic development. However, the drastic increase in the populations and importance of these emerging cities and others that were to develop in the United States was preceded by, and influenced by, two developments—one occurring prior to the Civil War and the other shortly thereafter.

In the early 1800s, major inventions were conceived that had far-reaching implications for America as well as for the world. Probably most important was the modern steam engine, which resulted in unheard-of transportation advances. The consequent expansion of the American railroad system was critical because it was basic to the industrial development of the United States. It was also significant because it caused hostility to develop between the farmers and the residents of America's cities. In addition, it increased the importance of the "middleman," whose role was to expedite shipments, but who also increased the cost of farm products to the urban consumer without increasing the rate of return to the farmer. The urban resident of those days, like his counterpart today, often incorrectly blamed the farmer for the increased costs. This dependence of the city resident on the middleman and, ultimately, on the farmer, for his food, and the suspicion that was subsequently engendered between the farmer and city resident played an important role in creating the hostility between urban and rural residents that frequently exists today. It also resulted in specific political conditions and coalitions that have influenced the quality of life in both urban and rural areas.

The railroad was the predominant invention of that time, but other inventions were also critical. The development of Whitney's cotton gin solidified the position of cotton as a basic cash crop in the South and continued the need for inexpensive labor, which slavery provided. Fulton's experiments with steam power also paved the way for the use of the steamboat on the inland waterways. There were numerous other inventions, and all were important in preparing the nation for the radical changes it experienced in the late 1800s. Many of the subsequent changes also increased the agricultural yield, which meant that fewer people could produce more food, thus enabling the agricultural sector to support a larger urban population. By the 1850s, the prerequisites for rapid urban growth and development were present, but such development had to await the Civil War and its aftermath.

Post-Civil War America and the industrial revolution

As the Civil War ended and the West was settled, the nation underwent a basic and dramatic transformation. The industrial development that was to symbolize American economic growth had begun, and burgeoned rapidly in a favorable environment. First, natural resources such as water and other energy sources were abundant in the United States. Second, new conditions called for new ways of meeting them, and the American people consistently developed new and often quite imaginative ways to improve the efficiency of business and industry. The telegraph and the railroads permitted rapid communication, and the assembly line fostered substantial economic savings and paved the way for mass production. The other key ingredient was the availability of inexpensive labor and the willingness of large industrial firms to use large numbers of employees without providing a fair return for their services. Coal companies created the company town concept, according to which the firm's employees were paid in script redeemable only through the company store. This system increased the probability of substantial profit, but even more important, it increased the dependency of the individual miner and his family on the coal company. The miners' mobility was reduced while their economic dependence increased.

The most significant result of the industrial revolution was the impetus it gave to urban development in the United States. Cities (especially those in the Northeastern and North Central states, such as Cleveland, Erie, Chicago, New Britain, and Baltimore) that formerly had been mainly service and trade centers became manufacturing centers if energy and raw materials were available. Pittsburgh, located amidst the plentiful bituminous coal fields of Pennsylvania, West Virginia, and Ohio, is an excellent example. Iron ore was shipped to Pittsburgh via the Great Lakes and was then transported by railroad to supply the other major ingredient necessary to produce steel. Various immigrant groups were brought into the area to maintain the railroads and to develop the mining industry.

The manufacturing plants also required inexpensive labor, and two sources of such labor began to develop. The first, and most commonly cited, source was immigrants from Western and Southern Europe. Large

Table 2-1 Immigration to the United States, 1850–1910

YEAR	LEADING FOUR COUNTRIES	NO. OF IMMIGRANTS
1850	Ireland	164,004
	Germany	78,896
	Great Britain	51,085
	Other Northwestern European countries	11,470
1880	Germany	84,638
	Great Britain	73,273
	Ireland	71,603
	Scandinavia	65,657
1910	Central Europe	258,737
	Italy	215,537
	U.S.S.R. and Baltic States	186,792
	Great Britain	68,941

SOURCE: U.S. Department of Commerce, Bureau of the Census, *Historical Statistics of the United States: Colonial Times to 1957* (Washington, D.C.: 1960), pp. 56–57.

numbers of Irish had arrived after the 1848 potato famine in Ireland, but from 1850 to 1910 the rate of immigration from Western and Southern Europe increased rapidly.[9] As shown in Table 2-1, immigration during this 60-year period underwent a shift in country of origin. In the early part of the period, the majority of immigrants came from Western Europe; toward the end of the period, the countries of Central and Southern Europe supplied most of the immigrants. Many left their home countries because of the adverse economic or political conditions that existed there or because of their desire to try and find the "American dream." Most of the newly arrived immigrants found that language and cultural differences delayed their integration into the larger society. The result was that most large cities became divided into sections along national and ethnic lines, and consequently political divisions and coalitions developed that could not and would not change for decades to come. The political significance of these developments will be discussed in Chapter 4, but for now it is sufficient to point out that industrial development, and the immigration accompanying it, resulted in rapid urban growth.

The second source of inexpensive labor was the Southern blacks, who began to move northward with the expectation that economic conditions were less severe and that political institutions were less repressive in the North than they were in the South. Since the end of Reconstruction in 1877, regular attempts had been made in the South to disenfranchise black people and to restrict their economic power. These practices ranged from "blacklisting" (not hiring "uppity" individuals) to overt physical intimidation and harm (illegal beatings and even murder). Harsh legal penalties were imposed on blacks found guilty of violating the law. In addition, white officials systematically denied constitutional rights to blacks by creating voting tests and institutional arrangements that guaranteed that the Democratic party of the South would be "pure" white. These abuses, along with a decline in the economy of many Southern rural areas, led to the beginning of a northward migration.

The same set of conditions—the same economic and political oppression—developed, at least initially, for the black migrants in their new locations. They were often forced to reside in deteriorating sections of the city and their wages were kept at subsistence level. In addition, they often paid higher prices for inferior products and were denied meaningful expression of their political rights because political parties were dominated by other urban ethnic and national groups. Thus these domestic migrants began to cluster in well-defined areas of the city and to develop institutions necessary for the continuation of their own familial, social, and cultural behavioral norms, just as had their foreign counterparts.

Despite the problems created by the rapid immigration and industrialization, America's cities thrived and frequently were exciting places in which to live. Certainly the diversity of the city began to be apparent; various art and food specialties characterized certain parts of the larger cities. In addition, cities began to develop their own "images"—New York as an important cosmopolitan world trade center, Pittsburgh as an incredibly productive basic producer of steel, and Chicago as the workingman's city, center of transportation and meat processing. The aim of this discussion is to point out not the peculiarities of each city, but rather the emerging importance of the American city as the symbol of dynamic change that was the industrial revolution.

However, it is crucial to point out that at this time, cities also began to receive their share of blame for the ills confronting American society. Urban planning was infrequent until the 1930s, and thus plans for provision of such public services as schools, transportation systems, police and fire protection, and sanitation were the exception and not the rule. Cities were left to grow with little consideration of aesthetics or of the implications of rapid growth for the health and safety of the community as a whole. Instead the emphasis was on private consumption, and this usually meant that a large segment of the population lacked basic services and amenities.

Certainly Lincoln Steffens and other muckrakers presented a very scathing account of the shortcomings of cities during this era.[10] The ills of the cities were compared with the virtues of rural life, and the cities were found wanting because of their high crime rates, physical deterioration, and growing social problems, not the least of which was the large number of "undesirables" who resided there. Even during this period, the often schizophrenic relationship between the city and the rest of society that was to become one of the dominant issues in urban politics in America began to emerge. Ironically, cities were becoming responsible for an increasing share of the economic development of the United States but were increasingly distrusted by large segments of society. Three critical developments oc-curred that influenced the next period of even more explosive urban growth. These developments are discussed in the next section.

The 1920s to the 1970s

It is important to note that of the three developments that were critical for the rapid growth of urban society during this period, one was the result of American technological ingenuity and the other two were caused by strong social and economic forces that were probably beyond the control of any one individual or group. The invention and subsequent mass marketing of the automobile, the Great Depression of the 1930s, and World War II all had important and far-reaching implications, not only for the city but also for American society and for the entire world.

The automobile has altered individual life styles in many ways, but primarily by encouraging mobility. Before the automobile, residents of cities either lived within walking distance of their place of employment or had to depend on some type of public transportation.[11] This increased residential density and encouraged interaction among city dwellers. The automobile facilitated outward movement from the city and rapid disper-sion of the population. One could drive to work in the city and enjoy the city's benefits without having to reside there if one owned an automobile.

Table 2-2 Automobile Sales and Registrations in the United States, 1910–1950

YEAR	SALES	REGISTRATIONS
1910	181,000	458,000
1920	1,906,000	8,131,000
1930	2,787,000	23,035,000
1940	3,717,000	27,466,000
1950	6,666,000	61,682,000

SOURCE: U.S. Department of Commerce, Bureau of the Census, *Statistical Abstract of the United States, 1974* (Washington, D.C.: Government Printing Office, 1974), p. 556.

As Table 2-2 indicates, the sale and registration of automobiles between 1910 and 1950 increased steadily, and one of the often-overlooked results was an increase in the number of suburban residents. In many respects, suburbia offered the best of both worlds—the city's business opportunities and the suburb's residential attractiveness. Robert Wood's book *Suburbia* describes some of the advantages of suburban living and explains that the growth of suburbia was largely due to the individual's desire for personal development.[12]

Every bit as important as the residential mobility the automobile encour-aged were its accompanying social costs. Roads had to be built and maintained, thus siphoning off funds that were badly needed for community development, and the quality of city air was threatened by another major pollutant. Perhaps the most important social cost was the subsequent out-migration of residents from the city at a time when cities needed to retain middle- and upper-class residents in order to have a minimal resource base.

This technological development was followed closely by the Great Depression. It is difficult to convey to readers who have not experienced the economic problems of the 1930s the personal costs that the Depression exacted from the American public. The American economy had been subject to periodic swings and occasional violent fluctuations, but the Great Depression was the most extreme. Few programs had been established that would compensate for the deficiencies that occurred in the private economic sector, and few preventive steps had been taken to ease the impact of financial chaos. The end result was the near-total collapse of the American economy and the threat of radical and violent domestic political change. Economic institutions that had been basic to American life for centuries, as well as the very precepts of democracy, were challenged.

Although excellent personal accounts of the hard times are available, it is difficult to assess the real and total impact of the Great Depression on the urban centers of the United States. Nevertheless, it is quite possible and indeed logical to conclude that the most important contribution of this era was the expanded role played by the national government—especially after Democrat Franklin D. Roosevelt was elected President in 1932—in providing preventive and rehabilitative services, including job opportunities, for those affected by the worsening economic conditions of the Depression. Even more significant than the programs sponsored by the federal government was its overriding concern that it not only had the right, but the obligation, to provide relief to the private sector. After the Depression, it became more acceptable to request and even demand increased national intervention, not only in economic, but also in other matters when local or state inaction or negative policy choices had exacerbated the situation.

The Great Depression, then, was important not only because of its negative aspects, but also because it helped to create the psychological climate necessary for the expansion of the activities of the national government in all areas—especially in areas that affected the cities. The national government became the initiator of projects and the appropriate government agency from which to seek response when conditions necessitated response; that is, there was a growing expectation that the national government would, could, and should intervene if the situation became serious enough or if the problems seemed to be matters of national importance.

The third event that helped to set the contemporary American urban scene was World War II, which created the demand for goods and services as well as the employment the economy needed. As a result, economic improvement slowly began, and by the early 1950s relative stability had returned. World War II fostered an increase in national pride and in the confidence of the American people that they could solve the pressing problems facing them. In addition, the war and its aftermath had two results that were of significance for urban development.

First, black migration to the cities increased sharply during the 1940s. According to Karl and Alma Taeuber, two of the leading experts on black migration, the black migration to the cities accelerated during World War I, "resumed at very high levels" in the 1940s, and accelerated between 1950 and 1960.[13] In their book, *Negroes in Cities*, the Taeubers conclude that between 1950 and 1960, "the North and West gained one and one-half million non-whites in the exchange of migrants with the South."[14] The vast majority of these migrants settled in the large urban centers of the North and in such specific areas as Chicago's South Side, New York's Harlem, Pittsburgh's "Hill," Cleveland's East Side, and Newark's Central Ward. Accompanying this in-migration was an out-migration of whites, which resulted in the continued predominance of whites and the virtual absence of blacks in the suburban areas. The national government had unwittingly ignored the "golden" opportunity that this internal migration presented to redress rights and alleviate or prevent serious racial problems. The failure to take advantage of this opportunity increased the probability of racial separation and conflict in the future and made fundamental change more difficult, if not impossible.

Second, the post-World War II period was marked by economic optimism and a high rate of consumption. Personal sacrifices that had been common as part of the Depression and the war effort were no longer made, and most citizens were reluctant to face the social and political problems then prevalent in the United States. The nation had undergone approximately 15 years of self-sacrifice and collective effort, and it was impossible to conclude that such dedication would continue unabated. The American people wanted to return to some degree of normalcy. World War II, the cold war, and the Korean War had diverted attention from the pressing domestic problems that have come to dominate contemporary urban politics. The result was a virtual dearth of policy decisions and a near-total absence of concern for the formulation of any meaningful policy to guide urban development in the United States.

Cities in contemporary America

As indicated in the discussion in Chapter 1, cities and their problems dominate contemporary America. The influence that cities have had on American life since 1950 needs to be thoroughly understood. Although there are numerous ways to measure that influence, perhaps a consideration of the city's present role in the three areas of economics and finance, culture, and politics will be most meaningful.

Economically, the major cities are the financial centers of America. Not only are the vast majority of corporate headquarters located in or near major cities, but the financial institutions in these cities have been responsible for most of the economic development of and the investment that has taken place in all American cities. The influence of these institutions has taken many forms.

On the one hand, large banks and insurance companies have played a direct part in financing the nation's housing industry. By making available large sums of capital, banks have often aided the developers of sizable tracts of land used for middle- and upper-income housing. The prime motivation of financial institutions has been to return a profit, and thus the large financial interests have not invested their funds with regularity in areas or for projects whose rates of return are questionable. The profit motive, basic to the capitalist system, has often dictated that areas deemed unprofitable be ignored or, alternatively, that the government underwrite the risks involved or supply the capital needed to build housing or other types of construction in such areas when the private sector cannot or does not. The discussion of housing and redevelopment in Chapter 6 makes clear that the nation's large financial institutions have been reluctant to risk investing their capital in unprofitable areas of most communities without this governmental protection.

These same institutions have also financed a sizable proportion of the vast investment that the private sector has diverted toward the expansion of professional and business office space in downtown and suburban areas in the form of "revitalized" business districts and shopping centers and malls, respectively. The appropriateness of the motivation for these plans is immaterial; the relevant point here is that large private financial institutions have had and will continue to have significant influence on the development of the urban centers of the United States.

These same institutions have also had a major and direct impact on the public sector of the American economy because of their role in debt and capital finance management. In many urban areas, long-term capital improvements (major buildings and equipment) are financed by the sale of municipal bonds. These bonds pay a guaranteed rate of return, and the city issuing them must repay not only the face amount of the bond but also the appropriate interest. The main advantage of this method of financing is that it permits a city to amortize or spread out its major money outlays over a longer period and provides tax incentives for the purchasers of the bonds. This, theoretically, should result in improved public services as well as a more stable tax rate over an extended period. If these large institutional investors were not available, most cities would find it very difficult to finance their large capital expenditures. Thus cities must make their financial setting attractive enough to encourage investment. The bond rating a city has frequently indicates its fiscal strength and the confidence held by the financial community in its stability.

Another indication of the city's importance in contemporary America is its cultural leadership. The great museums of America are found in the cities, as are the most impressive theatrical presentations. As previously mentioned, cities offer creative persons a dynamic environment that apparently encourages the finest expression of their talents. Cities have also traditionally been the main financial supporters of the arts, including ballet and opera companies, as well as symphony orchestras. Larger, more enthusiastic audiences are also found in cities, probably because many of the people who live in cities are interested in the arts.

The media play a major role in defining and influencing the values of the American public on both day-to-day and long-range issues. For instance, media coverage of the civil rights and Watergate events of the early 1960s and 1970s had a significant impact on the public debate of and ultimate resolution of these issues. The media may not change strongly held values, but they may in fact help to reinforce already existing ones or to provide a climate of opinion in which subsequent change is possible.

Finally, between 1950 and 1970 cities became important political forces. Mayors of large cities, such as Lawrence of Pittsburgh, Daley of Chicago, and Lindsay of New York, attracted national attention and began to influence national politics by advising, assisting, or otherwise encouraging those who were seeking the Presidency or by seeking higher political office themselves. They also made known their cities' needs, and the federal government responded by formulating broad national policies affecting such areas as housing, urban renewal, and poverty, as well as specific programs designed to alleviate a wide range of other urban problems. The specifics of many of these problems are discussed in later chapters, but it is important to note here that, despite the abundance of programs with specific urban emphasis, there has never been a comprehensive, coordinated urban policy or plan in the United States that has directed the growth of cities and metropolitan areas in an orderly manner. (By this is meant a specific set of regulations governing urban development, environmental protection, and the provision of public services, including welfare.) Instead, the emphasis has been on private development and a piecemeal approach with regard to standards and to the regulations governing that development.

It is difficult to assess all the motivations behind this approach and to explain the reasons for the lack of such a policy. But it is clear that policy-making in the United States, including urban policy-making, has tended to be reactive and incremental. By *reactive* is meant that decisions are usually made in response to situations or developments rather than in anticipation of them. *Incremental* means that the policies that have been adopted and implemented have not effected major changes, but have attempted gradually to adapt existing policies or practices to new situations or requirements. There have been signs that this approach may be changing—for example, the federal government's adoption of the "block grant" concept, according to which individual jurisdictions are provided with federal funds to be used for a variety of community development projects that are selected by local leaders. In addition, Congress continues to discuss various aspects of a national land use policy that would limit the number of persons moving to a particular region and curb land abuse. As indicated in Chapter 7, the likelihood that such legislation will be passed is remote, but the fact that it is being considered is an indication of a growing awareness on the part of the federal government that urban and metropolitan development in the United States may be best considered as part of an integrated policy rather than as one of many uncoordinated separate policies.

In many respects, this growing awareness of the need for an integrated national urban policy may well be the most promising development affecting the future of the cities. It confirms the growing political strength of the cities in demanding the more carefully formulated, innovative urban policy on which their survival depends. Thus major policy changes could be made in the coming decades that would be influenced by some of the historical events considered in this chapter.

Conclusion

These first two chapters provided a general overview of the historical development and the contemporary setting of American cities. The topics briefly raised in them will be considered in depth in the chapters that follow. The reader should be aware of the enthusiasm that pervades much of the discussion about contemporary urban America. New ideas abound, and there is the growing realization that innovative approaches must be considered and perhaps attempted if the present problems are to be alleviated, let alone solved.

The remaining chapters describe the range of problems facing contemporary urban America and assess the utility of various approaches that have been put forth to solve them. From these chapters it is hoped that the reader will gain a clear understanding of these problems, the various policy options available, and the consequences of those options. But there are no easy answers or quick solutions, for there is no reason to believe that the problems of America's cities will be less difficult or less important in the future than they were in the past. For better or for worse, the United States is a nation of cities, and policies affecting them must take into account past history as well as future possibilities.

Notes to Chapter 2

1. Jacob Burckhardt, *The Civilization of the Renaissance in Italy* (New York: Harper & Row, 1958), Vol. 1, pp. 51–106. See also Vol. 2.
2. See Niccolò Machiavelli, *The Prince* and *The Discourses*, trans. by Luigi Ricci

(New York: Modern Library, 1950); *The Letters of Machiavelli*, ed. and trans. by Allan Gilbert (New York: Capricorn, 1961); and Sheldon S. Wolin, *Politics and Vision* (Boston: Little, Brown, 1960), chap. 7.

3. For Burckhardt's discussion of the effect of these power struggles on the ruling strength of the Pope, see Burckhardt, *op. cit.*, pp. 120–142.

4. *Ibid.*, pp. 107–114.

5. Werner J. Cahnman and Rudolf Heberle, eds., *Ferdinand Toennies on Sociology: Pure, Applied and Empirical Selected Writings* (Chicago: University of Chicago Press, 1971), pp. 12–36, 62–74. For a fuller version, see Ferdinand Toennies, *Gemeinschaft and Gesellschaft* (Berlin: K. Curtius, 1926).

6. Cahnman and Heberle, pp. 62–74.

7. Frederick Jackson Turner, "The Significance of the Frontier in American History," *Frontier and Section* (Englewood Cliffs, N.J.: Prentice-Hall, 1961), pp. 37–62.

8. *Ibid.*

9. For various descriptions of this immigration, see Stanley Lieberson, *Ethnic Patterns in American Cities* (New York: Free Press, 1963); and Louis Wirth, *The Ghetto* (Chicago: University of Chicago Press, 1928).

10. Lincoln Steffens, *The Shame of the Cities* (New York: Hill and Wang, 1957).

11. For a discussion of the economics of transportation in the United States, see John R. Meyer, *The Economics of Competition in the Transportation Industries* (Cambridge, Mass.: Harvard University Press, 1959).

12. Robert C. Wood, *Suburbia: Its People and Their Politics* (Boston: Houghton Mifflin, 1958), pp. 259–302.

13. Karl E. Taeuber and Alma F. Taeuber, *Negroes in Cities: Residential Segregation and Neighborhood Change* (Chicago: Aldine, 1965), p. 13.

14. *Ibid.*

Chapter 3

The Folklore of Contemporary Urban America

The myths

Folklore has dominated many aspects of American life, and the urban folklore that has grown with the growth of the cities has frequently replaced reality. Although present urban problems may well be cause for alarm and for decisive public action if the quality of urban life is to be improved, such action must be based on fact rather than folklore and aimed at the basic causes of the problems rather than the bothersome symptoms that attract so much public attention. A discussion of the predominant myths and their background, frequently mentioned in any analysis of urban America, is thus in order.

The first myth is that America is becoming a nation of large cities, that these cities are rapidly expanding toward one another, and that megalopolises are beginning to develop in various regions. The best example of a megalopolis is the East Coast from Boston (some urban specialists would even include part of Maine) to the tidewater area of Virginia. This stretch includes the metropolitan areas of Boston, New York, Philadelphia, Washington, D.C., and Norfolk, Virginia, plus numerous other cities of major importance. Other examples are Los Angeles and San Diego in

Southern California; Dallas, Fort Worth, and Houston in East Central Texas; and the North Central belt of cities that begins with Milwaukee and runs south to Chicago, east through Indiana to Toledo, Ohio, then to Cleveland, and finally southeast to Pittsburgh, Pennsylvania. These are regional concentrations of major significance, but the populations comprising the metropolitan areas and the governments of each city are independent. The decisions reached in both the private and public sectors in any subunit are likely to have a "spillover" effect on other subunits in the same area. For instance, the problems of housing and pollution policy within any one particular jurisdiction may seem to be minimal, but the lack of housing or the failure to enforce environmental standards in that community could in fact affect not only its residents, but those of the surrounding areas as well. Thus the questions of political control and responsibility become central. Who has the authority to make relevant decisions that affect the entire area? Does anyone?

These questions lead to the logical conclusion, and second myth, that urban growth and development in the United States, as evidenced by these regional concentrations of government, have resulted in too great a fragmentation of power, and that this fragmentation has led to problems at the urban level. Critics of the present situation usually argue that there should be greater centralization of power and that this centralization should be achieved either by developing or increasing the power of regional governments or by increasing the power of the national government.[1] The argument is important and can be summarized as follows. There are too many governments in too many areas, and this situation frequently results in confusion and in conflicting policy decisions. Jurisdictional lines cutting across political boundaries should not be permitted to thwart necessary policy decisions beneficial to the entire area or to the national interest.

A third widely held myth is that all cities are experiencing severe and continuing financial difficulties and that, as political institutions, they lack the power to summon the economic resources needed to solve their pressing problems. According to this argument, local governments are the least able of all governmental units to protect themselves against economic swings.

First, they often lack the necessary revenue-raising measures to ensure the availability of adequate funds. Cities raise most of their revenues by means of an inelastic property tax, which combines assessed valuation and tax rate, the latter usually expressed either in mills (.1 of a cent) or in the number of dollars per hundred dollars of assessed value. The assessed valuation is usually based on the land and improvements (homes, buildings) and is some percentage of the actual market price. For instance, if the home and land it was on had a market value of $45,000, then the assessed valuation for property tax purposes would be some percentage of that value.[2] The property tax payable would be determined by the following formula:

$$\text{Assessed value} \times \text{Tax rate} = \text{Property tax}$$

Thus, if the prevailing tax rate was $6.50/$100 and the assessed value of the property and improvements was $15,000, the property tax would be:

$$\$6.50 \times 150 = \$975$$

This property tax would be paid to the appropriate local government and used to finance local services.

Second, cities are under tremendous financial and political pressure to expand and improve their services because their populations are constantly changing. However, at a time when the city's population requires the most in the way of services, the city is frequently unable to raise the needed revenues because its population cannot afford to pay increased taxes.

Third, cities do not receive adequate revenues from state and federal sources to permit them to provide quality services. Because of their more modern tax measures, the state and federal governments are better able to finance programs to meet urban needs. It is their obligation to then share those funds with the local governments that so desperately require them to survive.

Fourth, the inability to finance services (job training) leads to a cyclical situation that causes further deterioration in other areas (rise in crime rate) and in the general quality of city services.

A fourth myth that has developed is that politics in the city is indeed a "nasty and brutish" affair. Partly because of the inherent mistrust of the cities and partly because urban leadership conjures up images of smoke-filled rooms, graft, and overt corruption, urban political leaders are not viewed with great favor. In many cases, the images are inaccurate, but they are still widely accepted. Few urban leaders become prominent national leaders, and even a mayor as visible as John Lindsay had difficulty increasing his power in other parts of New York State or in national politics. Probably the best example of the general public's dislike for and distrust of many urban mayors is the apparent popular dissatisfaction with Mayor Richard Daley of Chicago.

Daley is reputedly the most powerful figure in the city, and supposedly has such tight political control over the local Democratic organization that he has the power not only to determine the outcome of the city elections, but to unduly influence statewide elections in Illinois as well. Some of his critics even contend that questionable things happened in Cook County, Illinois, in 1960 that eventually helped the state of Illinois cast its electoral ballots for John F. Kennedy and helped provide an important component of Kennedy's very narrow electoral margin over Richard M. Nixon.[3]

Although many might admire Daley's ability to use his power, few approve the tactics of his organization, allegedly dominated by loyalty based on personal patronage ranging from contract favoritism and cronyism to nepotism. Mike Royko has depicted the alleged abuses and misuses of power by the Daley organization.[4] Royko has contributed to Daley's poor public image by regularly challenging the decisions the mayor makes in administrating Chicago and by implying that political considerations are often the basis for these decisions. What makes the Mayor Daley example so fascinating is that despite the national disapproval frequently bestowed upon him and the critical evaluations of Chicago's progress under his leadership, he continues to be re-elected by margins that are large, even by Chicago standards. Although one could contend that this record is due only to the organizational strength of the Democratic party, there is little doubt that Richard J. Daley is quite popular and that many Chicagoans think he is doing a good job as mayor. Thus the paradox: a mayor is very popular in his own city, but receives little admiration from many Americans outside that city. Daley is the best example of this paradox. The reverse situation applied to former Mayor Lindsay of New York. He was generally thought of as being unpopular in New York City,[5] but was well received in the nation as a whole.

The reasons for city officials' lack of credibility, according to the myth, are basically that these officials are indeed in office only to protect their personal interests and to reward their followers. Exploitation of the citizenry by the elected official and his chief deputies is thus the only way for the political leaders to receive social, political, and economic benefits. Therefore, political corruption and personal dishonesty are bound to be found in any major city, and the citizens of that city are bound to pay higher taxes for inferior services and to be periodically exposed to scandals because of them.

The fifth myth is that cities are undesirable, unsafe places to live in or to visit. The media, especially television with its emphasis on detective and police activities in large cities, convey the impression that fear of personal harm inflicted by the deprived and deranged (murderers, rapists, arsonists, molesters, and thieves) pervades every city, and that individual citizens are not safe either on the streets or in their homes.

There are three reasons for this condition of human despair. First, according to the myth, the city provides the anonymity that encourages deviate behavior as well as a network for the marketing and distribution of habit-forming drugs, the most important of which is heroin. The heroin addict will engage in any activity from prostitution to murder in order to support the daily "habit." Right and wrong become meaningless when the body and mind demand physical and mental relief on a periodic basis. Thus, the urban streets become the stalking ground for the addict.

Because of its size, complexity, and innate corruption, the city is a perfect breeding ground for the hardened criminal and prostitute, who make a living by illegally satisfying the wants of others. Whether the person operates as part of a criminal organization or on an individual basis, he or she can effectively deal with local law enforcement officials who frequently would rather supplement their meager public salaries than enforce the laws. Thus, the city again provides the environment that breeds crime as well as the attitudes that foster it.

In addition, the legal process in large cities is often characterized by long delays, bureaucratic confusion, and, occasionally, illegal bribes. Thus, even if criminals are apprehended, chances are good that the severity of the penalties imposed on them will be lessened. This situation tends only to reinforce and encourage additional criminal activities.

The final myth about the cities is that many who are sickened by the declining morals and tired of living in fear flee the city. If possible, apartments are sublet, property and belongings are sold, and individuals and families relocate in more placid environments where the emphasis is on human dignity and a return to nature. Thus, the city is left to sink even further into the depths of despair because so few are willing to remain amidst the social and physical degradation. Because of the scarcity of reform- and civic-minded individuals, the city can only become an even less desirable place to live in the future. In sum, American cities have been abandoned by many of the very people critical to any revitalization effort and thus are "doomed."

The following list summarizes the previously discussed myths about urban America.

1.   The United States is becoming a nation of megalopolises.
2.   Fragmentation of power and local autonomy have contributed to current urban problems.
3.   Cities are experiencing severe and continuing financial difficulties from which they are unable to extract themselves.
4.   City politics is characterized by corruption, graft, and other unsavory practices.
5.   Cities are undesirable, unsafe places to live in or to visit.
6.   Most people who can, flee the cities, thus leaving them to individuals and groups incapable of governing them.

These myths convey a depressing picture. According to them the cities as they exist today are beyond help, and if substantial changes are not made, the future of the cities and hence the nation will be in jeopardy. The implications for public policy can be easily summarized.

Increased centralization of power at the local level, as well as at the regional level and within the metropolitan area, is absolutely necessary if the cities are to make a positive contribution to America's future. Without centralization, cities will continue to deteriorate. The problems of the cities, as well as the strategy by which they can be solved, are obvious. The strategy consists of implementing a rational governmental policy at the local level, and that is best done by a strong centralized authority.

Obviously, the preceding discussion of the myths and their implications must be taken with a certain grain of salt because these myths are highly subjective, yet often appealing, descriptions of urban life. If one reconsiders the various policy alternatives that were raised to deal with the urban problems of the decade 1964–1974 and the adjectives used to describe the situation that existed then, one is impressed by the apparent feeling of immediacy and urgency. Something had to be done quickly to eliminate poverty and to lower the crime rate. This was certainly not the time to stand idly by while others threw what they perceived to be water on the flames of urban problems. The order of the day appeared to be, "Don't just stand there, do something," the assumption being that any activity would be a marked improvement over inactivity. It will be obvious to the reader, after completing this volume, that action based on the best of motives, but based on misinformation or on a misunderstanding of how the political system operates, may be more dangerous and counterproductive for all concerned than inaction. This does not mean that a "do nothing" position is recommended; it simply means that there is danger in doing something for something's sake.

Perhaps the best example of this sense of urgency was the urban program pursued by the Nixon administration from 1968 to 1974 and continued by the Ford administration after President Nixon resigned in 1974. The Nixon domestic program, labeled the "new Federalism," had several main points. First, localities were provided with the federal funds they needed to meet pressing local problems. This resulted in a variety of new programs, such as general and special revenue sharing,[6] which are discussed in Chapters 7 and 8. Second, the power of local authorities to assess local priorities and establish local programs was increased—an interesting programmatic development. Strict federal controls over the programs and policies of the local governments were eliminated, and considerable autonomy and discretion were returned to local officials on the assumption that they would thus be more able to solve *their* problems in ways most suitable to *their* specific needs. Finally, welfare reform, which had been unsuccessful, was emphasized, and general and special revenue sharing replaced categorical grant assistance. In his 1971 and 1972 State of the Union Messages, President Nixon emphasized the "crisis" felt by the cities and American society and stressed the "urgency" of meaningful action.[7]

These examples illustrate the general acceptance of the myths that have been discussed. Conservative urban analysts, such as Edward C. Banfield, have contended that many of our present urban problems are insolvable by means of government action and that any government action is most likely to be dictated by what is politically acceptable rather than by what is a feasible alternative to alleviate or eliminate pressing social problems.[8] But such views oversimplify some very complex variables and fail to take into consideration an entire set of implications. Before these implications and their importance can be analyzed, a more balanced discussion of the myths previously presented is in order.

The reality

In this section the previously discussed myths are placed in a more realistic perspective. All of them have some applicability to contemporary urban politics, and are accurate to some degree. This does not mean that they are "correct"; in fact, quite often policy choices based on them could be misleading and could lead to major policy reversals and a reduction in the quality of urban life.

The first myth is that the United States is becoming a nation of megalopolises. The United States is not one big city at this point in time, nor is there a strong likelihood that it will become one in the future. However, there continues to be a population movement away from the farm and rural areas to cities of varying size. Table 3-1 shows the population shift that occurred in the United States from 1950 through 1970. Note

Table 3-1 Distribution of United States Population, 1950–1970 (percent)

AREA	1950	1960	1970
Urban areas of 2,500 or more	64.0	69.9	73.5
Urbanized areas of 50,000 or more	[45.8]	[53.5]	[58.3]
Central cities	(32.0)	(32.3)	(31.5)
Urban fringe	(13.8)	(21.2)	(26.8)
Other	[18.2]	[16.4]	[15.2]
Rural	36.0	30.1	26.5

SOURCE: U.S. Department of Commerce, Bureau of the Census, *Statistical Abstract of the United States, 1972* (Washington, D.C.: Government Printing Office, 1974), pp. 18, 20.

that during this period there has been a steady decrease in the percentage of Americans who reside in rural areas and a steady increase in the percentage of Americans who reside in urban areas of 2500 people or more and in urbanized areas of 50,000 or more. The result of this shift, which began in the early 1900s in the United States, was that a majority of the American population resided in urban areas by 1930. The shift reflects the economic attraction of urban life and the difficulties individual farmers have had competing in an industrialized and mechanized society. For many, economic realities have necessitated the abandonment of the farm and the move to the city.

As important as this shift has been, another shift is now occurring that could be even more significant. Note that within urbanized areas (areas with populations of 50,000 or more) between 1960 and 1970, there was a slight decline in the percentage of the population that resided in the central city compared with the percentage residing in the urban fringe. This clearly indicates that the percentage of the population living in the areas outside America's central cities is increasing, and that these areas may soon be as heavily populated as the central cities themselves in this size category. If this trend continues, as it appears to be, what is in fact happening is a decentralization of the population and a corresponding "spreading out" of the city. For this reason, the megalopolises of the future, predicted by the myth, may actually develop, but they will not resemble a New York or a Chicago, with their high population density and high-rise buildings. They are much more likely to resemble Denver or Los Angeles—dispersed populations connected by automobile or other means of transportation to manufacturing, business, and social activities. There is little doubt that Americans, at least a growing percentage of them, will opt for less dense living conditions, separated from, but within relatively easy access to, large urban centers and their amenities.

Those who contend that the megalopolis is the future pattern for urban areas are correct in pointing out the growing interdependence of cities within a particular region as well as the regional interrelationships that presently characterize national politics. For instance, the automobile industry was once largely confined to the Detroit, Michigan, area, but now the impact of auto sales is felt in Illinois, Indiana, Ohio, and Pennsylvania, as well as Michigan, as a result of the dispersion of assembly plants and of manufacturers responsible for component parts. Similar patterns can be found in other regions dominated by other industries. The implications of this trend toward regional growth and dispersion will be carefully considered in later chapters, but its existence should be acknowledged here. In many respects, the trend is a major justification for expanding planning and service delivery systems to the regional level, thereby avoiding the problems encountered within the specific jurisdictions.

Table 3-2 indicates that only 6 of the 20 largest central cities gained population between 1960 and 1970, but only the Boston and Pittsburgh metropolitan areas failed to gain population. This supports the general contention that metropolitanization has increased, but not as a result of the growth of the central city. There are many possible explanations for this.

Certainly individuals' perceptions of what residential living should be like are an interesting aspect of this movement away from the central city. In his book *Suburbia*, Robert Wood considers in detail the motivations of and rewards for those who seek to leave the city for the suburbs.[9] Wood's main point is that suburbs are often desired because they are viewed as "republics in miniature" that allow citizen participation in government and direct involvement in community affairs.[10] It should also be clear that for many leaving the city, concern about crime and a desire for educational and economic opportunities and personal self-fulfillment are decisive.

Table 3-2 Population Changes in the Twenty Largest Central Cities and Metropolitan Areas in the United States, 1960–1970

CITY	CENTRAL CITY		METROPOLITAN AREA	
	1960	1970	1960	1970
New York, N.Y.	7,782,000	7,895,563	9,540,000	11,575,740
Los Angeles–Long Beach, Calif.	2,479,000	2,809,813	6,039,000	7,040,697
Chicago, Ill.	3,550,000	3,369,357	6,221,000	6,977,611
Philadelphia, Pa.	2,003,000	1,949,996	4,343,000	4,882,245
Detroit, Mich.	1,670,000	1,513,601	3,950,000	4,203,548
San Francisco–Oakland, Calif.	740,000	715,674	2,649,000	3,108,026
Washington, D.C.	764,000	756,510	2,097,000	2,861,638
Boston, Mass.	697,000	641,071	3,109,000	2,753,500
Pittsburgh, Pa.	604,000	520,117	2,405,000	2,401,362
St. Louis, Mo.	750,000	622,236	2,144,000	2,363,346
Baltimore, Md.	939,000	905,787	1,804,000	2,071,016
Cleveland, Ohio	876,000	750,879	1,909,000	2,063,729
Houston, Texas	938,000	1,232,802	1,430,000	1,985,031
Newark, N.J.	405,000	381,930	1,833,000	1,895,096
Minneapolis–St. Paul, Minn.	483,000	434,400	1,598,000	1,813,587
Dallas, Texas	680,000	844,401	1,738,000	2,378,000
Seattle, Wash.	557,000	530,831	1,107,000	1,424,611
Anaheim–Santa Ana—Garden Grove, Calif.	104,000	166,408	704,000	1,420,676
Milwaukee, Wisc.	741,000	717,372	1,279,000	1,403,887
Atlanta, Ga.	478,000	497,421	1,169,000	1,390,247

SOURCES: 1960 figures from U.S. Department of Commerce, Bureau of the Census, *Statistical Abstract of the United States, 1974* (Washington, D.C.: Government Printing Office, 1974), pp. 20–25. 1970 figures from U.S. Department of Commerce, Bureau of the Census, *County and City Data Book, 1972* (Washington, D.C.: Government Printing Office, 1973), pp. 812, 814.

Most current discussions about growth outside the central city, but within the metropolitan area, overlook the fact that most American cities lack a coordinated growth policy. Cities have tended to develop in a helter-skelter fashion because of the specific needs, wants, and demands of a highly mobile population at a particular point in time, as well as the decentralized nature of planning decisions in most metropolitan areas. If a national, state, or metropolitan growth planning policy were formulated and then rigorously implemented, the probability of more orderly urban development would increase. Such a policy might not cause a change in settlement patterns, but, at the very least, it might be able to check the excesses that usually accompany suburban development, and it might even help control the urban sprawl that has characterized most American cities and their immediate environments. This is certainly an important policy decision and it will be considered more fully in Chapter 7.

The absence of coordinated growth policy is the best evidence in support of the second myth (that fragmentation of power and local autonomy have contributed to current urban problems).

The third common myth is that cities simply cannot meet the financial demands made upon them. As Table 3-3 indicates, the federal government is *not* a major contributor of revenue for local governments—the states are. However, cities raise more than one-third of their revenues by means of the local property tax.[11]

The problems with this type of financing are many and can be briefly summarized as follows.

1. The property tax does not tax economic growth and expansion as accurately as would a more elastic set of revenue-raising measures. The income tax is usually referred to as the most "elastic" revenue-raising alternative; that means that it will expand and contract as the general economy does with less of a lag than other tax systems. Since few cities utilize the income tax, they find it difficult to raise revenue, both when the

Table 3-3 Sources of Funds for All Local Governments, 1972–1973

SOURCE	PERCENTAGE OF LOCAL REVENUE
Intergovernmental revenues	40.4
State sources	[33.7]
Federal sources	[6.7]
Local sources	59.6
Taxes	[44.9]
Property	(37.2)
Other	(7.7)
Charges/other	[14.7]
Total	100.0

SOURCE: Calculated from U.S. Department of Commerce, Bureau of the Census, *Finances in Selected Metropolitan Areas and Large Counties, 1972–1973* (Washington, D.C.: Government Printing Office, 1974), p. 2.

economy is strong and when it is experiencing weakness, because inelastic property taxes do not reflect prosperity (except in the long run, as the area grows), and may prove quite harmful during recessions, for they usually remain constant despite a decline in the ability of individuals to pay them.

The demand for city services changes with fluctuations in economic conditions. During economically stagnant periods, such as 1974–1975, the demand for public services at the local level is likely to be at least equal to, and usually greater than, the demand for such services in prosperous times. Unemployment and sluggishness in the private sector often increase the demand for various public services. Thus, the need for services may be greatest exactly when the city has the least fiscal capability to raise the revenue needed to provide the services or to increase already existing services.

Certainly the fiscal crisis confronting New York City in mid-1975 is a prime example. New York City, with its extensive city employment roles and diverse services, was experiencing difficulty in meeting its payroll and other financial obligations and was faced with actual bankruptcy conditions. Mayor Abraham Beame was faced with a variety of alternatives, all of them unpleasant. After several unsuccessful attempts to obtain more revenue from both state and federal sources, and after publicly condemning the parties involved, Mayor Beame announced an austerity budget aimed at attracting investors to the bonds that were being sold by a new corporation.

The New York example has helped to affirm the myth of the continuous financial difficulty of cities in the mind of the public, and this acceptance has been reflected in the official word of many urban leaders. Moon Landrieu, mayor of New Orleans and a leader of the National League of Cities, typified this feeling in a statement to Congress in June 1974: ". . . current trends indicate that the fiscal crisis of the cities in deepening. . . . Inflation is having a devastating impact on municipal budgets. . . . We thus find ourselves being squeezed to a maximum. Expenditures are once again rapidly outstripping our ability to generate revenues."[12] The image of cities reducing services and eliminating jobs or understaffing agencies is prevalent in most accounts of city finance, and when a city actually makes drastic cuts in its labor force, as New York City did in late 1975 and early 1976, there is considerable public interest in the event.

2. The property's assessed valuation is subject to considerable fluctuation. If reassessments are not done regularly and if there is a high rate of inflation, it is possible that a city's tax base will not continue to increase, and the city will not be able to raise enough revenues to meet its financial needs.

3. The tax rate may also fluctuate drastically if the total assessed value of a community does not increase and if the demand by citizens for public services does. Thus, in any given year, the city may have to raise its tax rates substantially if it is to satisfy this increased demand. For example, if

during one year the city has a budget of $10,000, and during the following year it has a budget of $20,000, the city will have to double its tax rates to raise the needed revenues unless the city's assessed valuation has doubled. Thus the property tax is subject to swings as a result of fluctuations in both the service and the assessment variables.

4.   Assessment is not always an impartial economic procedure because it is frequently subject to political influence. In some cities in Massachusetts, for example, assessors are elected, and their assessment decisions often seem to be based on considerations other than purely economic ones.[13] Similarly, assessment practices in large cities are often challenged as favoring large real estate interests. Naturally, any assessor accused of partiality may take the position that it is in the city's best interest to increase the total assessment and that some favoritism is justified if such increased assessment attracts the industrial and commercial concerns responsible for increasing the total economic strength of a community.

5.   Many contend that property taxes in general fail because they often defeat their very purpose—there is no incentive to improve buildings or homes if such improvement will result in increased taxation. Similarly, the property tax is criticized as being inelastic. This means that it fails to respond to changes in the rate of general economic growth and decline. The homeowner pays the same property tax during both hard times and good times unless there is a change in assessed value or tax rates, but the *percentage* of income allocated to property taxes could fluctuate greatly, depending on his total income. For example, consider a semiskilled assembly line worker whose house and lot are valued at $25,000 and who pays $500/year in local property taxes. If he is unemployed for a long period, the total percentage of his income that goes to pay the property tax increases, whereas if he has earned substantial overtime pay, the percentage of his income that goes to pay the property tax decreases.

6.   Finally, the property tax is regressive in that everyone pays the same rate of tax regardless of ability to pay. The elderly, often on a fixed income unless there is an appropriate exemption (that is, a reduction in their property tax because of age), usually pay a higher percentage of their total income for property taxes than the working person who pays the same taxes. This inequity has resulted in a decrease in the number of retired persons who own their own homes and an increase in the number of retired persons who find home ownership financially impossible.

Those who assert that cities are financially handicapped usually contend that because the nonwhite and retirement-age segments of many urban populations are increasing, the cost of providing public services to these groups will continue to increase. The reasoning here is that the cost of providing educational services for a nonwhite child without a middle-class perspective is likely to be higher, and that the aged will need increased recreational and transportation opportunities that can be supplied only by

Table 3-4 Local Expenditures, 1972–1973 (percent)

PURPOSE	72 LARGEST SMSAs	ALL LOCAL GOVERNMENTS
Education	40.6	45.1
Local schools	[38.0]	[42.5]
Higher education	[2.6]	[2.6]
Public welfare	10.4	8.3
Health and hospitals	6.6	6.4
Police protection	5.7	5.0
Highways	4.4	5.7
Interest on general debt	4.1	3.7
Sewerage	3.4	3.2
Fire protection	2.7	2.4
Parks and recreation	2.7	2.3
Sanitation	1.7	1.5
Financial administration	1.2	1.3
Other	16.5	15.1
Total	100.0	100.0

SOURCE: U.S. Department of Commerce, Bureau of the Census, *Finances in Selected Metropolitan Areas and Large Counties, 1972–1973* (Washington, D.C.: Government Printing Office, 1974), p. 2.

*General debt includes all long-term credit obligations of the federal government and its agencies (exclusive of utility debt), and all interest-bearing short-term (that is, repayable within one year) credit obligations remaining unpaid at the close of the federal year. It includes judgments, mortgages, and "revenue" bonds as well as general obligation bonds, notes, and interest-bearing warranties. It excludes noninterest-bearing short-term obligations, interfund obligations, amounts owed in a trust or agency capacity, advances and contingent loans from other governments, and rights of individuals to benefit from employee-retirement or other social insurance funds.

the public sector. Table 3-4 summarizes the local expenditures of 72 of the nation's largest SMSAs and all local governments during 1972–1973. Note that education expenditures are the major item for both the SMSAs and all local governments. Also note the many other demands made on both categories of government. It is important to note that the 72 SMSAs spend a larger percentage of their revenues for services other than education than do all the local governments. This indicates the diversity of the governments in the SMSAs and the demand for services by the residents living there. Obviously, the employment, training, and equipment needs of public-safety (police and fire) personnel are vastly different and more expensive in an SMSA than in a smaller community. In the early 1970s, these differential spending patterns and the fiscal crisis confronting the larger cities were considered by policy-makers and the general public.[14]

The preceding points are often made by the nation's mayors when they request congressional support for a largely urban program. Testimony that cities do not receive a fair share of state and federal revenues obviously influenced the enactment of general revenue sharing, which will return nearly $30 billion to state and local governments by 1976. It is impossible to determine which position is the "correct" one, but it is apparent that another major policy alternative would be for the state and federal governments to assume an even larger share of the financial burden of the cities.

The last aspect of the urban financial picture to be discussed is the cyclical nature of the budgeting and finance processes at the local level. As has been pointed out in carefully documented research,[15] budgetary decisions are often bound by both fiscal and political restraints that vary with the economic and political realities of the community. Generalization about budgetary decision-making processes and policy is difficult because general changes may not have the desired effect on specific cities in all instances. For example, requiring an institutional change such as public hearings on budgetary matters may lead to a greater awareness by city officials of what people want, but it will not necessarily result in major substantive change or a reallocation of funds so that public expenditures will be forthcoming.

Closely related to this question of city fiscal affairs is the fourth myth, that cities are hopelessly corrupt and that local officials, for a variety of reasons, are on the "take" either directly or indirectly. This view is supported by descriptions of the politics of the Tweed regime in New York City in the late 1800s and early 1900s, as well as by descriptions of the indictment and conviction of contemporary city leaders for illegally obtaining profit by virtue of their positions of urban leadership.[16]

Perhaps the most detailed and most interesting account of political corruption at the urban level is George Washington Plunkitt's description of Tammany Hall politics in the late 1800s.[17] Plunkitt offered a series of recommendations for the reformers, whom he called "morning glories,"[18] and made a distinction between honest and dishonest graft. Dishonest graft occurred when an official committed an illegal act; honest graft occurred when an official used information to which he had access by virtue of his office to further his own economic gain. Thus, if city officials knew of city plans to purchase property, they could buy it from its original owner and then sell it to the city at a handsome profit.[19] A reading of Plunkitt's biography gives one the impression that he was not an evil person, but that he did typify the ward and precinct political types of his time, to whom personal gain and service to their constituents were important.

Plunkitt, the Tammany Hall politicians, and, many would argue, Mayor Daley, all endorse the power and authority of precinct and ward committee officials.[20] (A precinct is a geographical area with a polling place. In most cities, a precinct includes from 500 to several thousand voters. A ward is a collection of precincts and covers a much wider geographical area.) To be effective, political machines must maintain tight control over the precinct and ward organizations, and the leaders of these organizations should retain their positions as long as the "vote is delivered"—as long as the organization receives the electoral support it feels it needs from the jurisdiction.

What many critics of this philosophy often ignore is that machine politics is not a one-way process in which voters support the party in control of the machine. The party also provides benefits for the precinct and ward areas in the form of city services and perhaps even jobs for those who are considered reliable. Royko's account of Daley and the Democratic party machine in

Chicago clearly indicates that the return of services to the precincts and wards is an integral part of the machine philosophy.[21] Plunkitt also stressed this in his discussion of how he assisted those burned out of their homes as well as those in trouble with the "law."[22] The personal and direct appeal to the individual voter is to be maximized, for personal contact is the key to effective machine domination and political power.

Critics of the urban political machine contend that this leads to the worst type of inefficiency and waste. Those who may not be qualified are hired for city positions because they have political connections. Areas of the city that do not provide support for the machine may not receive equal or even adequate city services in comparison with the rest of the city. City contracts may be awarded to bidders because of their political connections rather than their overall merits. In short, according to these critics, the likelihood of gross inefficiency and corruption increases if a machine becomes well entrenched and dominates local politics.[23]

The important consideration is not the existence of corruption at the local level, but rather its extent and causes and its ultimate effect on the provision of services by the city government and on the quality of life in the city. Few would be naive enough to assume that questionable acts never occur in any city, but the institutionalization of such illegal acts is critical. For instance, in cities where outside contracts (that is, with a private firm) for a service such as snow removal are a regular occurrence, "favors" are frequently exchanged between the recipient of the contract and the person granting it. The question is whether this is an isolated example or a common practice that characterizes most or all contractual relationships between governmental and private interests.

Another aspect of corruption is its cause. Are people engaging in corrupt practices in order to receive large profits, or to ensure that they will receive any profits at all? Are they performing the illegal acts to gain an advantage, or are such acts mandatory if they wish to survive in a very competitive world? Obviously, the causes of corruption may differ a great deal, but they are important points to consider in assessing blame or measuring the ultimate impact of corruption. For instance, if, to receive city contracts, it is necessary to make campaign contributions, it would be unrealistic to expect private interests to go out of business rather than to compete on those terms for the contracts that are to be awarded.

In the final analysis, probably the most important aspect of corruption is the effect it has on the citizens of the community. They can be affected in numerous ways, but three are most common. First, if they receive inferior services or if they have to pay more for services because of corrupt practices (taxes increase in order to finance waste, inefficiency, and corruption), then they are suffering an economic hardship as a result of the corruption. Second, if the corruption permits or encourages violence, the citizen may be faced with physical danger. Certainly such threats have occurred throughout American history because local officials have chosen to ignore gambling, liquor, and prostitution statutes. Finally, if corruption becomes obvious and widespread in a community, the average citizen may lose confidence in his governmental officials, and that loss of confidence could make him mistrust government in general and adversely affect his business, family, and social relationships.

In his study of a medium-sized community in the Northeast that appeared outwardly calm, John Gardiner, a political scientist, found corruption in a variety of places.[24] In many instances officials who could have prevented the criminal action did not; instead they simply ignored the situation while others took a "piece of the action." Wincanton is probably not as atypical as many readers may think. If careful studies of corrupt practices in American cities were undertaken, they might reveal a pattern of questionable behavior on the part of some, but by no means all, elected officials, business executives, and ordinary citizens.

The fifth myth, that cities are shelters for undesirables and are therefore unsafe, is often believed by individuals who take a dim view of the ethnic heterogeneity that characterizes most American cities. They fail to consider the possibility that what appears to be a chaotic and often depressed area actually has a social, economic, and cultural vibrancy of its own. Physical deterioration does not mean automatic social, political, and cultural deterioration. The case against the city often emphasizes aggregate statistics on crime, which fail to convey the relative sense of security and safety of many of the city's middle- and upper-class residents.

Aggregate statistics on violent crime can be quite misleading for several other reasons. In the first place, violent crimes, even in large cities such as New York and smaller ones such as Omaha, Nebraska, tend to be concentrated in a relatively small section of the city's total geographical area. Thus a resident of that city who does not live in or visit that section is much less likely to be a victim of a violent crime than the aggregate statistics suggest. Second, drug and alcohol addiction are not confined to the inner city but are widely found in suburban areas with large concentrations of professionals and white-collar workers. Severe alcoholism may well be the nation's most chronic illness—as serious as, and perhaps more serious than, drug addiction. The use of amphetamines ("speed") and barbiturates ("downers"), as well as of hallucinogens such as lysergic acid diethylamide (LSD or "acid") by young people beginning in the 1960s was a nationwide phenomenon. It is therefore unfair to castigate city residents for moral degeneracy that is also prevalent in other areas.

The final myth is that the majority of the middle- and upper-income residents have abandoned the cities. Although there has been a considerable exodus of middle- and upper-income individuals from the cities, many individuals in those income categories have remained there. As Table 1-4 (p. 10) indicates, the suburban fringes of the SMSAs attract the largest percentage of residents with annual incomes of $12,000–$25,000 and over. But the table also indicates that more than 40 percent of the total population of central cities (regardless of population) have annual incomes of $12,000–$25,000 and over.

One last point needs to be made here. Data to support the generalizations made by many observers of the present urban scene are readily available, but unless the accuracy and reliability of those data are carefully scrutinized, they will yield a misleading and often seriously flawed picture of reality. In the concluding section of this chapter, the public's attitudes toward urban services, the quality of urban life, and the honesty of local officials are considered, and additional light is shed on the importance of the preceding myths and realities for the urban resident, decision-maker, and recommender of policy choices.

Public perceptions of urban America

Certainly the views of urban residents, especially on such urban problems as crime and education, are among the most quoted by the media. Nevertheless, there has not been any continuing research aimed at analyzing trends and shifts in the opinions of urban residents over an extended period. In an attempt to gauge these attitudes, the Kerner Commission, as part of its investigation of the civil disturbances of the mid-1960s, commissioned a variety of research projects designed to tap urban residents' attitudes about urban violence and race relationships.

In 1970, the Department of Housing and Urban Development (HUD) worked with the National League of Cities to implement an urban observatory program in 10 representative cities. The purposes of the urban observatory approach were many, but most important was the attempt to develop systematic and comparative data about all the cities in order to foster development and implementation of more meaningful programs. One of the results of this program was that an extensive survey research project was conducted in 1970 in the following participating urban observatory cities (figures in parentheses indicate the number of persons interviewed in each of the cities):[25]

Albuquerque, New Mexico	(471)
Atlanta, Georgia	(469)
Baltimore, Maryland	(500)
Boston, Massachusetts	(507)
Denver, Colorado	(357)
Kansas City, Kansas	(193)
Kansas City, Missouri	(383)
Milwaukee, Wisconsin	(443)
Nashville, Tennessee	(426)
San Diego, California	(517)
Total	(4266)

As the list indicates, the cities are quite diverse and in many respects are representative of a wide range of American cities. It is important, however, to note from the outset that, because of individual city differences and because these are 1970 figures, one must be cautious about drawing infer- ences, even from this carefully sampled and interviewed universe, and then attempting to apply them to other American cities.

Despite this caveat, the results of the research can be utilized to make some broad generalizations and to gauge the depth and range of urban citizens' feelings about their urban environments. In the following section, an attempt is made to draw conclusions from the responses of the citizens who participated that have applicability to cities in general. A more detailed analysis is made in Chapter 10.

Certainly urban citizens, despite their requests and demands for citizen participation, have been omitted from much of the debate over urban policy development in the United States. As has been pointed out elsewhere,[26] citizen participation and interaction may take a variety of forms, but it is a rare occurrence when such participation and interaction have a direct posi- tive benefit on the formulation of public policy. By utilizing available public opinion data, decision-makers may in fact be in a much better position to reach decisions that have wide-ranging implications for the quality of urban life and that are responsive to the public's perceptions of its needs.

Tables 3-5 through 3-9 summarize respondents' answers to 5 questions about urban life in their cities. Table 3-5 summarizes respondents' attitudes toward their city government in the past 5- to 10-year period (that is, 1965–1970 and 1960–1970). An efficient way to utilize this table and Tables 3-6–3-9 is to compare the views of citizens from each city with the views of all citizens interviewed, represented by the "Total" row. From Table 3-5, then, the following points are clear:

1. 42 percent of the citizens felt there had not been any noticeable change in their city government in the past 5 or 10 years. Kansas City, Kansas (61 percent), and San Diego (49 percent) have the largest percent- ages of citizens with this view; Atlanta (32 percent) and Nashville (36 percent) have the smallest percentages.

2. 28 percent of the respondents felt that their local government had indeed improved. Atlanta (42 percent) had the largest percentage of citizens with this opinion and Kansas City, Missouri (14 percent), had the smallest percentage.

3. Few people (22 percent) in the 10 cities felt that their local govern- ment was not as good now as it had been in the past; Kansas City, Missouri (33 percent), and San Diego (12 percent) were the two extremes.

4. *In general, it would appear that citizens did not perceive their cities as having rapidly deteriorated as a result of the urban crisis or a lack of political leadership.* In fact, most people interviewed thought that their local government had changed little, and that if it had changed at all, it had changed for the better.

Table 3-5 Citizens' Opinions of City Government in Past 5 or 10 Years

CITY	N	RESPONSE*							
		BETTER		SAME		NOT AS GOOD		OTHER	
		NO.	%	NO.	%	NO.	%	NO.	%
Albuquerque	471	(175)	37	(173)	37	(59)	13	(64)	13
Atlanta	469	(195)	42	(150)	32	(88)	19	(36)	7
Baltimore	500	(128)	26	(212)	42	(154)	31	(6)	1
Boston	507	(110)	22	(196)	38	(162)	32	(39)	8
Denver	357	(69)	19	(166)	46	(74)	22	(48)	13
Kansas City, Kans.	193	(33)	17	(117)	61	(32)	17	(11)	5
Kansas City, Mo.	383	(52)	14	(181)	47	(128)	33	(22)	6
Milwaukee	443	(138)	31	(181)	41	(98)	22	(26)	6
Nashville	426	(151)	35	(154)	36	(92)	22	(29)	7
San Diego	517	(136)	26	(253)	49	(62)	12	(66)	13
Total	4266	(1187)	28	(1783)	42	(949)	22	(347)	8

SOURCE: The Urban Observatory Program data tape, funded by the Department of Housing and Urban Development and administered by the National League of Cities and the United States Conference of Mayors Secretariat.

*The question asked was: "Over the past 5 or 10 years [1965–1970 or 1960–1970], do you think that local government here in (City) has gotten *better*, has stayed about the *same*, or do you think it is *not as good* as it used to be?"

Table 3-6 Citizens' Evaluations of Operation of City Government

CITY	N	RESPONSE* EXCELLENT		VERY GOOD		GOOD ENOUGH		NOT SO GOOD		NOT GOOD AT ALL		OTHER	
		NO.	%	NO.	%	NO.	%	NO.	%	NO.	%	NO.	%
Albuquerque	471	(15)	3	(103)	22	(215)	46	(99)	21	(16)	3	(23)	5
Atlanta	469	(14)	3	(123)	26	(177)	38	(126)	26	(12)	3	(17)	4
Baltimore	500	(8)	2	(48)	10	(199)	40	(189)	37	(50)	10	(6)	1
Boston	507	(6)	1	(28)	6	(149)	29	(224)	45	(68)	13	(32)	6
Denver	357	(6)	2	(70)	20	(175)	49	(80)	22	(8)	2	(18)	5
Kansas City, Kans.	193	(3)	2	(29)	15	(82)	42	(68)	35	(8)	4	(3)	2
Kansas City, Mo.	383	(6)	2	(33)	9	(122)	32	(181)	46	(29)	8	(12)	3
Milwaukee	443	(19)	4	(123)	28	(169)	38	(87)	20	(28)	6	(17)	4
Nashville	426	(4)	1	(79)	19	(175)	40	(130)	31	(24)	6	(14)	3
San Diego	517	(31)	6	(146)	28	(246)	47	(68)	13	(11)	2	(15)	4
Total	4266	(112)	3	(782)	18	(1709)	40	(1252)	29	(254)	6	(157)	4

SOURCE: The Urban Observatory Program data tape, funded by the Department of Housing and Urban Development and administered by the National League of Cities and the United States Conference of Mayors Secretariat.

*The question asked was: "And overall, how would you rate the way (city) is run?

5. An important reservation must be borne in mind when interpreting this table and Tables 3-6–3-9. Since the responses refer to only one point in time, it is impossible to trace specific trends or to develop comparisons over time. However, it is clear that the percentage of citizens who felt that their city government had deteriorated was not extremely high. On the other hand, the same conclusion can be reached about those who felt that their city government had improved.

Table 3-6 supplies information on urban citizens' evaluations of the operation of their government. The general positive tendency indicated by Table 3-5 is missing. For example:

1. The percentage of citizens who felt that their cities were run not so good (29 percent) and not good at all (6 percent) exceeded the percentage who felt that their cities were run in an excellent manner (3 percent) or very good (18 percent). Not only is the difference between the negative and positive outlook substantial (14 percent), the magnitude of the negative outlook cannot be ignored. *More than one-third of all the respondents had negative feelings about how their cities were being run.* If this finding could be proven to be symptomatic of an increasing trend, then the implications for governmental action should be obvious.

2. It is also important to note the disparities among cities. Boston (13 percent) and Baltimore (10 percent) had the highest percentage of citizens who felt that their local government was not run good at all. More than one-half of the respondents from Boston (58 percent) and Kansas City, Missouri (54 percent), had negative attitudes about the way their city was being run. In addition, more than one-third of the respondents from Baltimore (47 percent), Kansas City, Kansas (39 percent), and Nashville (37 percent) had negative feelings about the way their city was being run, and only in San Diego (34 percent) did more than one-third of the citizens hold positive attitudes about the way their city was being run.

3. *It is also important to note that in all but two cities, the most common response was that the city was being run "good enough."* Denver (49 percent) and Boston (29 percent) were the two extremes. *This implies that most citizens in these 10 cities accepted the way their government was being run.* The shifts in opinions over time had not, at least in 1970, reduced this favorable outlook. The variability of public opinion will be quite important in determining whether more citizens will move toward the "good enough" category or will move away from it and toward the positive and negative categories.

The preceding two tables provide an overview of citizen attitudes; the following three tables are based on several of the myths previously discussed in this chapter. Table 3-7 summarizes citizen attitudes toward the quality and quantity of services supplied relative to taxes paid. These responses can be construed as an assessment of the efficiency of local government, as one would expect most respondents in a well-run city to answer yes. The most interesting conclusions to be drawn from Table 3-7 are:

Table 3-7 Citizens' Opinions of Quality of Services Received Relative to Taxes Paid

CITY	N	RESPONSE*					
		YES		NO		OTHER	
		NO.	%	NO.	%	NO.	%
Albuquerque	471	(221)	47	(212)	45	(38)	8
Atlanta	469	(182)	39	(249)	53	(38)	8
Baltimore	500	(137)	27	(358)	72	(5)	1
Boston	507	(99)	20	(364)	72	(44)	8
Denver	357	(158)	44	(164)	46	(35)	10
Kansas City, Kans.	193	(50)	26	(121)	63	(22)	11
Kansas City, Mo.	383	(100)	26	(236)	62	(47)	12
Milwaukee	443	(154)	35	(245)	55	(44)	10
Nashville	426	(153)	36	(248)	58	(25)	6
San Diego	517	(328)	63	(150)	29	(39)	8
Total	4266	(1582)	37	(2347)	55	(337)	8

SOURCE: The Urban Observatory Program data tape, funded by the Department of Housing and Urban Development and administered by the National League of Cities and the United States Conference of Mayors Secretariat.

*The questions asked was: "Considering what people in (city) pay in local taxes, do you think the people generally get their money's worth?"

1. *Most respondents in most cities do not feel they are receiving the full benefit in city services in return for their tax dollars.* In 7 of the 10 cities, more than one-half of the citizens felt they were not receiving services commensurate with their taxes. These percentages ranged from 72 percent in Baltimore and Boston to 53 percent in Atlanta.

2. Of the two cities with more citizens responding yes than no to this question, San Diego (63 percent) was the only city where a majority adhered to this position; 47 percent of Albuquerque's citizens responded yes, 45 percent responded no. Except for San Diego, where nearly two-thirds of the respondents felt services were commensurate with taxes, most of the respondents did *not* feel they were receiving their money's worth in services.

3. Citizens frequently will have a positive opinion of city government when the question is fairly abstract, as indicated by the responses summarized in Tables 3-5 and 3-6, but they will be more negative when the question deals with a specific issue, as indicated by the responses summarized in Table 3-7. This implies, then, that *citizens, although their attitudes toward urban government are positive, may in fact have largely negative feelings about the specific policies of urban government.* The contradiction is difficult to explain, but perhaps it indicates the difficulties political leaders may have in solving urban problems.

Tables 3-8 and 3-9 also illustrate this contradiction. Table 3-8 summarizes the responses given when the citizens were asked to compare the honesty of people in government with the honesty of people in business. Note that 21 percent of all citizens feel that local government officials are less honest than business people, whereas only 6 percent feel they are more honest. Bear in mind that this question was asked prior to the debate over the honesty of public officials prompted by Watergate and other charges of corrupt practices that dominated the news between 1971 and 1974. Again, there is a great deal of variation among the cities. For instance, approximately one-third of the respondents in Baltimore (34 percent) and Boston (33 percent) felt that local government officials are less honest than business people, whereas only 12 percent of the respondents in San Diego held that opinion. With regard to the citizens who felt that local government officials are more honest than business people, the variation among the cities is quite slight: Milwaukee (9 percent) and San Diego (8 percent) had the highest percentage of citizens who expressed that opinion, and Kansas City, Kansas (2 percent), had the lowest percentage.

The implication is that, although 66 percent of all respondents feel that local government officials are as honest as business people, a sizable proportion of the urban population questions the integrity of local officials.

Table 3-9 supports this conclusion and also supports the contention that a specific question about illegal activity elicits a much higher negative response rate than does the more general question about the honesty of public officials.

Table 3–8 Citizen's Comparison of Honesty of City Government Officials and People in Business

CITY	N	RESPONSE*							
		MORE HONEST		SAME		LESS HONEST		OTHER	
		NO.	%	NO.	%	NO.	%	NO.	%
Albuquerque	471	(29)	6	(329)	70	(76)	16	(37)	8
Atlanta	469	(34)	7	(310)	67	(90)	19	(35)	7
Baltimore	500	(22)	4	(299)	60	(171)	34	(8)	2
Boston	507	(20)	4	(271)	53	(163)	33	(53)	10
Denver	357	(22)	6	(245)	69	(61)	17	(29)	8
Kansas City, Kans.	193	(4)	2	(120)	63	(53)	27	(16)	8
Kansas City, Mo.	383	(14)	4	(275)	72	(74)	19	(20)	5
Milwaukee	443	(40)	9	(290)	65	(79)	18	(34)	8
Nashville	426	(20)	5	(290)	67	(88)	21	(28)	7
San Diego	517	(40)	8	(372)	72	(63)	12	(42)	8
Total	4266	(245)	6	(2801)	66	(918)	21	(302)	7

SOURCE: The Urban Observatory Program data tape, funded by the Department of Housing and Urban Development and administered by the National League of Cities and the United States Conference of Mayors Secretariat.

*The question asked was: "On the whole, do you think local government officials are *more honest* on their jobs than most other people, say people in business, are about the *same*, or are they *less honest* than most other people?"

Table 3-9 Citizens' Estimates of Extent of Bribery and Other Illegal Activity in City Government

| CITY | N | RESPONSE* | | | | | | | | | |
| | | GREAT DEAL | | SOME | | A LITTLE | | ALMOST NONE | | OTHER | |
		NO.	%	NO.	%	NO.	%	NO.	%	NO.	%
Albuquerque	471	(51)	11	(176)	37	(94)	20	(66)	14	(84)	18
Atlanta	469	(116)	25	(202)	43	(73)	16	(20)	4	(58)	12
Baltimore	500	(172)	35	(155)	30	(108)	22	(14)	3	(51)	10
Boston	507	(172)	34	(182)	36	(62)	12	(21)	4	(70)	14
Denver	357	(27)	8	(145)	40	(73)	20	(38)	11	(74)	21
Kansas City, Kans.	193	(31)	16	(47)	24	(34)	18	(20)	10	(61)	32
Kansas City, Mo.	383	(64)	17	(153)	40	(53)	14	(33)	9	(80)	20
Milwaukee	443	(31)	7	(157)	35	(96)	22	(83)	19	(76)	17
Nashville	426	(91)	22	(158)	37	(89)	21	(24)	6	(64)	14
San Diego	517	(47)	9	(197)	38	(105)	21	(79)	15	(89)	17
Total	4266	(802)	19	(1572)	37	(787)	18	(398)	9	(707)	17

SOURCE: The Urban Observatory Program Data tape, funded by the Department of Housing and Urban Development and administered by the National League of Cities and the United States Conference of Mayors Secretariat.

*The question asked was: "In some cities, officials are said to take bribes and make money in other ways that are illegal. In other cities, such things almost never happen. How much of that sort of thing do you think goes on in (city)?"

More than one-half (56 percent) of the citizens responded that there was "some" to a "great deal" of illegal activity in the 10 cities. The highest percentages were: 68 percent of the respondents in Atlanta, 65 percent of those in Baltimore, 70 percent of those in Boston, 57 percent of those in Kansas City, Missouri, and 59 percent of those in Nashville. Even in cities where respondent outlook was more positive, percentages of respondents who felt there was "some" or a "great deal" of illegal activity often approached 50 percent: Albuquerque (48 percent), Denver (48 percent), Kansas City, Kansas (40 percent), Milwaukee (42 percent), and San Diego (47 percent). Only 27 percent of the citizens felt that illegal activities occurred only a little or almost never. This response was given by more than one-third of the citizens in Albuquerque (34 percent), Milwaukee (41 percent), and San Diego (36 percent).

Given these results, it would be interesting to repeat these questions today in order to see if the same results would be obtained. One can only surmise whether the public's responses to such questions would be different because of an increased public suspicion of and lack of trust in public officials in general.

Conclusion

In this chapter the basis has been provided for a meaningful investigation of public policy options and the general institutional and political forces that affect decision-making in urban America. In conclusion, several points should be emphasized.

First, it is useful to consider whether the generally held "myths" about urban America are true, and if so, whether they will be useful to policymakers in the future. If the myths can be shown to be either false or founded on a questionable set of assumptions, is it not then logical to conclude that any subsequent policy recommendations based on them might also be wrong or misguided? One of the essential points that was made in this chapter is that there is a need to critically evaluate and rethink the various "truths" about urban America. Different perspectives must be offered, and will be in the remaining chapters. Only then can the appropriate policy options be developed, discussed, and, it is hoped, acted upon.

Second, urban policy is not made in a vacuum. It is influenced by many complicated events and processes, but at some point it must be subjected to the test of pragmatism: Is it working? In other words, is it meeting the perceived needs or the problems it was intended to rectify in a relatively orderly and predictable way? All too often the policy is implemented without an earnest attempt to solicit citizen evaluation.[27] Throughout this book, the importance of increased citizen participation will be emphasized. As was indicated earlier in this chapter, citizens have strong feelings about urban governance that need to be fully recognized and considered. Although the public's position may be difficult to interpret, an attempt must be made to understand it and to consider it when making policy decisions.

Finally, it is important to note that policy decisions should be based on a realistic assessment of society's needs. Policy is often based on perceptions of what is thought to be needed rather than what is actually called for. Policy-makers must learn from past mistakes if future urban policy is to be meaningful and effective. The reader must decide whether the interplay of myth and reality in urban America tends to solve problems, delay them, or make them worse.

Notes to Chapter 3

1. For an excellent discussion of these reforms, see the Advisory Commission on Intergovernmental Relations, *Regional Governance: Promise and Performance* (Washington, D.C.: Government Printing Office, 1973); and Advisory Commission on Intergovernmental Relations, *Regional Decision-Making: New Strategies for Substate Districts* (Washington, D.C.: Government Printing Office, 1973).

2. The assessed value is usually between 20 and 40 percent of the property's actual market value. See Henry J. Aaron, *Who Pays the Property Tax?* (Washington, D.C.: The Brookings Institution, 1975).

3. For a discussion of Mayor Daley's role in the 1960 nominating and election process, see Theodore H. White, *The Making of the President 1960* (New York: Pocket Books, 1961), pp. 27, 149, 191, 200–230, 413–437.

4. Mike Royko, *Boss* (New York: Signet Books, 1971).

5. I recall a trip I made to New York City, during which I indulged in my favorite pastime—questioning cab drivers on the state of the city and its leaders. One such cab driver treated me to profanity and worse every time we hit a chuckhole or had to wait for a red light because the cabbie was convinced that each such obstacle was invented by Mayor Lindsay to personally harass the cab drivers of New York!

6. For a discussion of these programs, see David A. Caputo and Richard L. Cole, *Urban Politics and Decentralization: The Case of General Revenue Sharing* (Lexington, Mass.: D. C. Heath, 1974).

7. For the entire text of President Richard M. Nixon's 1971 and 1972 State of the Union Messages, see the 1971 and 1972 editions of *Congressional Quarterly Almanac*.

8. Edward C. Banfield, *The Unheavenly City* (Boston: Little, Brown, 1968), pp. 238–254.

9. Robert C. Wood, *Suburbia* (Boston: Houghton Mifflin, 1958).

10. *Ibid.*, pp. 3–19. For a different view of the role of the suburbs, see Anthony Downs, *Opening Up the Suburbs* (New Haven, Conn.: Yale University Press, 1973).

11. It is not possible to discuss in detail in this volume all aspects of urban finance. The interested reader may consult numerous other sources, two of

which are: Alan Campbell and Seymour Sacks, *Metropolitan America* (New York: Free Press, 1967); and James A. Maxwell, *Financing State and Local Governments* (Washington, D.C.: The Brookings Institution, 1969).

12. Mayor Moon Landrieu, Statement to the Senate Government Operations Subcommittee on Intergovernmental Relations, June 11, 1974, p. 15.

13. For a discussion of this point, see David A. Caputo, "The Normative and Empirical Implications of the Budgetary Processes in Four Medium-Size Cities"(unpublished Ph.D. dissertation, Yale University, 1970).

14. See Caputo and Cole, *op. cit.*, pp. 19–22, for a discussion of this fiscal crisis.

15. See Caputo, *op. cit.*; and John P. Crecine, *Government Problem-Solving* (Chicago: Rand McNally, 1969).

16. For some interesting accounts of urban corruption, see John A. Gardiner and David J. Olson, *Theft of the City* (Bloomington: Indiana University Press, 1974). For a discussion of New York politics during the Tweed days, see Seymour J. Mandelbaum, *Boss Tweed's New York* (New York: Wiley, 1965).

17. William L. Riordan, *Plunkitt of Tammany Hall* (New York: Dutton, 1963).

18. *Ibid.*, pp. 17–20.

19. *Ibid.*, pp. 3–6.

20. See Royko, *op. cit.*, pp. 65–85.

21. *Ibid.*

22. Riordan, *op. cit.*, pp. 90–98.

23. See Lincoln Steffens, *The Shame of the Cities* (New York: Hill and Wang, 1957), originally published in 1904.

24. John A. Gardiner, *The Politics of Corruption* (New York: Russell Sage, 1970).

25. I would like to express my appreciation to Lawrence Williams of the National League of Cities staff, who made the data tapes available to me. I alone am responsible for the analysis and interpretations that follow.

26. For a discussion of this point, see David A. Caputo, "Evaluating Urban Public Policy: A Developmental Model and Some Reservations," *Public Administration Review* 33 (March/April 1973): 113–119.

27. For a discussion of this point, see David A. Caputo, "The Citizen Component of Policy Evaluation," *Policy Studies Journal* 2 (Winter 1973): 92–97.

Chapter 4

Ethnicity, Class, and Race in Urban America

Introduction

Ethnicity, class, and race, singly and in combination, affect the lives of all Americans.[1] Ethnic characteristics have become part of the national identity of many Americans. However, America is a mobile society, and the uniqueness of each urban setting has often brought traits and customs into focus and sharpened the distinctions among individuals.

Perhaps most interesting are two questions, relating to (1) the possibility of separating ethnicity, class, and race; and (2) the relationship of these characteristics to specific behavioral patterns. It may well be impossible to separate politics into ethnic, class, and racial divisions because they often overlap and reinforce each other. For example, "WASP" (white Anglo-Saxon Protestant) denotes not just an individual's Anglo-Saxon heritage, but also that person's race and religion. Ethnic reference terms are not always explicit and informative because many attributes of a particular race, class, or ethnic group may be closely interrelated. Thus members of a particular racial or ethnic group may also belong to the same class. In this chapter it is assumed that, although the interrelationships are important to note, the three characteristics are in fact separable and deserve careful consideration because of the effect of each on the urban policy options available to decision-makers.

The answer to the question of whether these characteristics are directly linked to political behavior is less definite. In this chapter, reference is made to research that attempts to establish an association between culture and political behavior and institutions, as well as to research that offers evidence to refute that finding. The importance of this debate to the choice among policy will become obvious in subsequent chapters. Obviously, this is an important question in a nation composed of diverse groups, because if the specific characteristics of these groups can be linked to specific political behavior, future patterns and developments may be anticipated and perhaps even accurately predicted. The ability to predict the public's reaction to various policy alternatives will be useful in estimating the extent to which they can be successfully implemented to alleviate the pressing problems facing urban America.

Ethnicity and urban politics

Certainly the American people are among the most diverse of any country in the Western world—even when race is considered separately from ethnicity. For our purposes, ethnicity will be defined as *the identification an individual has with a group because of the concerns he or she shares with that group, or because of the traits he shares with others who also belong to that group.* Ethnicity is normally associated with specific nationalities that settled in the United States—usually the Europeans who immigrated to America at various points in its history. However, ethnicity is not common only to them.

The ethnic stereotypes and derogatory references are well known and have been popularized in songs and jokes. Ethnic jokes usually go through alternating periods—at one time they are popular, and at another they are considered in bad taste. It is interesting to note that the jokes frequently remain the same, but the name of the chief character changes to reflect a change in the status of an ethnic group, or increased popular interest in another ethnic group. Only the American Indian can claim never to have been an immigrant. An important debate centers on whether ethnicity has become less or more important in determining individual attitudes and outlooks in the United States. The role played by ethnicity in the historical process is important and requires consideration.

As indicated in Table 2-1, immigration to the United States reached a peak in the late 1800s and early 1900s. Figure 4-1 depicts the rate of immigration graphically. Since 1900, immigration laws have placed quotas on the number of immigrants arriving each year from any one country. The rapid immigration that occurred in the late nineteenth and early twen-

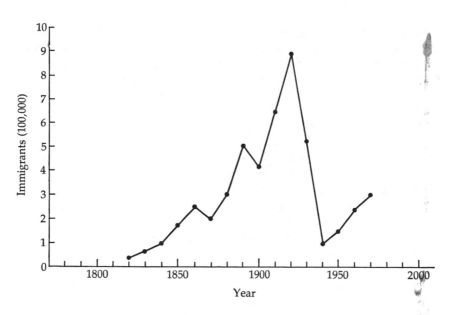

Figure 4-1 Immigration to the United States, 1820–1970

<small>SOURCE:</small> U.S. Department of Commerce, Bureau of the Census, *Statistical Abstract of the United States, 1973* (Washington, D.C.: Government Printing Office, 1974), p. 94.

tieth centuries severely tested American social, economic and political institutions. Bear in mind that the majority of the immigrants left their native countries because of religious, economic, or political problems. In addition, many lacked the attributes necessary for economic success in a new environment. Most of the immigrants gradually became acclimated to the way of life in the United States and to the political institutions and procedures they encountered in America's cities. The question that is still keenly debated among historians, anthropologists, and political scientists is whether the values of the immigrants were permanently changed by their American experience, or whether the immigrants were able to retain their identification with, and the practices associated with, their ethnic group. Several examples can be given in support of both conclusions.

Anyone who has lived in or even visited a city of any size is aware of the existence of ethnic neighborhoods. Thus most cities in the East have an Italian area, an Irish area, a Jewish area, and other areas predominantly settled by particular ethnic groups. Herbert Gans, in his study of urban renewal in Boston, discusses the specifics of ethnic group identity and living.[2] Gans stresses the fact that what the outsider considers a slum is in fact a neighborhood that sustains numerous important social relationships and often provides the sociopolitical environment necessary for individual improvement. The close proximity of the residents usually fosters considerable interaction and strong interpersonal relationships, as well as a heightened sense of neighborhood identity. The continual awareness of the group's heritage reinforces common religious, language, and cultural ties.

The strength of these ethnic groups is perhaps best illustrated by the various ethnic "days" celebrated by the different ethnic groups in New York City. A visitor to mid-Manhattan can view a variety of nationality day parades celebrating, for example, Steuben Day (German), St. Patrick's Day (Irish), and Columbus Day (Italian). These parades and other celebrations emphasizing ethnic identity effectively increase group awareness. Some observers would argue that the continuation of these ethnic celebrations and the obvious preference for settling in neighborhoods whose residents share common values clearly indicate that the members of these ethnic groups have neither given up nor rejected their ethnic identification, but have merely adapted their cultural traits to their American setting. In other words, members of these groups have been assimilated into the American social, economic, and political system, but have retained most of the unique and varied characteristics of their ethnic identification.

A counterexample can be given to show that assimilation of many ethnic groups has not occurred. In the early to mid-1800s, Western Massachusetts was settled by a variety of ethnic groups. French-Canadians immigrated southward from the St. Lawrence Valley to the area surrounding Springfield, Massachusetts, and a sizable number of Poles were brought into the area to assist in the building of several canals for the transportation of goods.[3] The ethnic identification of these groups remains quite strong. It is interesting to note that in one particular community of about 45,000 in this area, the Poles and French-Canadians each constitute approximately 40 percent of the voting public. The much smaller Irish population, approximately 12 percent of the voting public, has succeeded in controlling the mayor's office by joining with either the Poles or the French-Canadians and thus preventing both of them from monopolizing power. They have established a reputation for political leadership in the community, as have the Irish in many American cities.

Even more interesting is the intense dislike and rivalry that exists between the Poles and the French-Canadians. When a local politician of French-Canadian ancestry was interviewed, he remarked that

> You know, I married a Polish woman. I love her, but it has finished me in politics. My neighborhood accepts it, but I would never do well because of the animosity towards us both. In fact, it was several years till all the members of both families would speak to both of us. We are also concerned because we think it has affected our children. This is especially true in the treatment they receive in school and the nasty things the other children call them. It hasn't been easy.[4]

Although this may be an extreme case, the point is clear. In some areas, ethnic identification is still quite important and often structures social and political relationships among various groups. Too often ethnicity is dismissed as a thing of the past or regarded as something that is detrimental to the overall growth and strength of the American nation. During periods of international stress, the United States government has often punished those who have openly identified with and supported foreign countries with which they had ethnic ties. The treatment accorded the Japanese-Americans residing in California and other areas of the West Coast after the Pearl Harbor attack is an excellent example of government policy based on the belief that in some situations, ethnic ties take precedence over current citizenship.[5]

Thus the debate over whether the United States is in fact a "melting pot" has continued for several years. Many researchers have maintained that the United States has been successful in "Americanizing" the immigrants.[6] Usually the school system, with its emphasis on teaching the English language and establishing acceptable behavioral norms, is cited as the main socializing agent and the chief means of assimilating ethnic groups into the mainstream of American life. Other researchers have argued that many ethnic groups have not really given up the values and customs of their ethnic group, but have either adapted them to those of American society or alternate between two sets of values, depending upon which part of the community they are interacting with. This finding, if true, is important. If most ethnic ties are no longer strong, policy-makers may be free to attempt to implement a much wider array of policy options than they could if ethnicity did in fact set parameters for public policy decisions. The debate concerning the role and effect of ethnicity is inconclusive, but research conducted since 1960 concerning the influence of ethnic ties on urban political behavior deserves consideration.

Edward C. Banfield and James Q. Wilson have developed a concept of *political ethos*,[7] according to which urban residents have one of two outlooks, or world views. The public-regarding ethos is characterized by concern for the betterment of the entire community, the existence of personal relationships based on formal ties, and emphasis on efficiency and rationality. The private-regarding ethos, in contrast, is characterized by concern for the immediate geographical area or neighborhood in which one resides, personal relationships built on one-to-one contacts, and an emphasis on "getting things done" rather than how they get done.[8]

The contribution of Banfield and Wilson is additionally important because they made two other, related contentions. First, they linked the public-regarding ethos with older, more established groups, such as white Anglo-Saxon Protestants—the early immigrants from Northern and Western Europe.[9] They associated the private-regarding ethos with a wide variety of immigrant groups whose members usually had lower incomes and had attained a lower level of education—those who immigrated later from Southern and Eastern Europe. Second, they claimed that the ethos of a particular group may influence or even cause specific structural and institutional developments at the local level.[10] For instance, they maintained that the public-regarding ethos tends to be found in cities whose populations are predominantly middle class and white, and that these cities usually have a council-manager system of government, a nonpartisan ballot (on which party labels are not listed), and an elected city council comprised of representatives elected by all the voters of that city. On the other hand, the private-regarding ethos is most prevalent in cities whose populations are predominantly lower class and nonwhite. These cities have adopted the mayor-council form of government, partisan elections, and a city council comprised of representatives elected from distinct geographical districts rather than on an at-large basis.

The implication of their theory is clear: ethnicity has a direct effect on both governmental institutions and individual behavior. The political ethos theory provided a relatively easy way to explain the structures of government found in American cities as well as a rationale for the extent and manner of individual political participation in those cities. The private-regarding ethos requires the individual to base his decisions on what is best for his family and friends; the public-regarding ethos requires decisions to be reached on the basis of their contribution to the benefit of the entire community.

Although the later research by Banfield and Wilson[11] and others[12] led to refinement of the original ethos theory, such research has not resolved, at least for some, the question of whether ethnicity per se is related to or is a cause of specific types of political behavior. This question will be returned to in the concluding section of this chapter because it has important implications for the future of urban politics.

Class and urban politics

Most historians maintain that economic class has not been important in the history of American cities because American society is more fluid and offers greater opportunity to more people to create "new" wealth and to "succeed" than many countries of Western Europe, where historical traditions have restricted the individual's economic mobility. This position does not underestimate the importance of the drive for economic success; rather it asserts that life styles are vastly different in the United States because economic class lines have been and are less rigid.

Despite this general conclusion about American society, there are many indications that economic class may influence the political behavior of residents of urban areas and that it may be useful in predicting and measuring future patterns of urban political behavior. For our purposes, economic class is defined as *a set of characteristics usually associated with an individual's income.*

In the United States, economic class is usually defined in either of two ways. The first simply divides the populace into lower, middle, and upper classes on the basis of income: those with yearly incomes of $10,000 or less, $10,000 to $25,000, and more than $25,000 are placed in the lower class, middle class, and upper class, respectively. This is a relatively easy way to determine economic class, but one may question its accuracy. Table 4-1 summarizes the distribution of the American public into these three categories as well as the distribution of Americans living in rural areas and in SMSAs.

Table 4-1 Determination of Economic Class Distribution in 1972, Using Three-Tier Income System (percent)

AREA	LOWER CLASS ($10,000/YR)	MIDDLE CLASS ($10,000– 25,000/YR)	UPPER CLASS ($25,000+/YR)
SMSAs	39.1	52.2	8.7
Inside central cities	46.9	47.9	5.2
Outside central cities	32.8	56.8	10.4
Outside SMSAs	53.3	42.3	4.4
Farm	59.6	35.7	4.7
Nonfarm	52.5	43.2	4.3
Total, all families	43.7	49.1	7.2

SOURCE: Computed from Table 18 of U.S. Department of Commerce, Bureau of the Census, *Consumer Income*, Series P-60, No. 90 (Washington, D.C.: Government Printing Office, 1973), p. 48.

The bottom row of the table shows that most Americans are in the lower- and middle-income classes; only 7.2 percent of all families earn more than $25,000/year. A comparison of families residing in SMSAs with families residing outside SMSAs shows that (1) a larger percentage of the middle and upper classes resides in SMSAs than in areas outside SMSAs; (2) a higher percentage of those who earn more than $25,000/year resides in central cities than in farm or nonfarm areas; and (3) the highest percentage of low-income individuals is found in farm areas; the lowest percentage is found within SMSAs, but outside central cities.

Another important set of conclusions results from a comparison of the differentials within SMSAs. The highest percentage of individuals earning more than $25,000/year resides outside the central cities; less than one-third of the population of that area earns less than $10,000/year. The contrast between the class composition of the central cities and the areas outside central cities is marked and has important public policy implications that will be discussed later in this chapter.

Finally, note the differentiation of the class composition of areas outside SMSAs: the farm population is composed of a larger proportion of the low-income class than the nonfarm population, whereas the nonfarm population is composed of a higher percentage of the middle-income class than the farm population. Yet, the farm population has a higher proportion of those in the upper class than the nonfarm population.

Although Table 4-1 provides a useful overview, it does not show class distribution in specific urban areas. Thus, an analysis of the metropolitan areas of Detroit, Pittsburgh, or almost any other major American city would reveal that the percentage of low-income residents is higher in the central cities than in any of the surrounding areas. What has happened and is continuing to happen is that the central cities are losing middle-income residents and, in most cases, high-income residents, while low-income residents find it difficult to leave the central city and other low-income groups are attracted to the central city. Thus the population of areas outside the central city is becoming middle class while the population of the central cities is becoming more lower class. The reason is clear: the middle and upper classes, whenever possible, have left the central city and have left solution of its problems to the low-income groups.

Perhaps one of the best examples of this trend is Newark, New Jersey.[13] Newark has long been a stark reminder to policy-makers of what the urban future of many American cities may be if they fail to meet the many pressing problems facing them. Newark has experienced major civil unrest, the flight from the city of middle-income individuals who could escape, and the specific economic problems that result from dwindling tax resources. These problems caused city officials to try to use whatever federal assistance they could obtain to help defray the soaring property taxes that threatened to drive out many business and property owners. Newark exemplifies a city with an increased need for services as a result of an increase in its low-income population that coincided with a continued fiscal inability to provide those services. The situation has been so difficult that Newark was forced to use its first two years of general revenue-sharing funds (1972 and 1973) to meet current operating expenditures in the hope that the property tax, which fell mainly on the small property owner, would not have to be raised again.

The second way of defining class is to use a combination of variables such as income, education, and occupation. Even when this definition is used, the pattern outlined in Table 4-1 remains the same. Thus a large proportion of the populations of the SMSAs and especially the noncentral city areas of the SMSAs continues to belong to the middle and upper classes, while a large percentage of the population of the central city belongs to the lower class.

An additional point should be made about this definition of class. The proportion of the population that is included in each category may vary considerably from city to city. For instance, during normal economic times, a significant percentage of the populations of Detroit and Pittsburgh may belong to the middle class if that category is defined by income, but not by education or occupation, because of the high wages paid to semiskilled and skilled workers in the auto and ferrous metal industries. It is obvious that the common assumption that increased education leads to increased job opportunities and ultimately to increased income must be modified. In many instances, the power of the unions and the realities of the market place (the demand for certain skills has increased their value) have combined to alter effectively the normally expected class distribution. This tends to support the contention that the utility of a definition of class based solely on income may be somewhat limited.

There are several interpretations of the relationship between economic class and political power. One interesting and important argument contends that political power is often dominated by economic power. According to this argument, cities with large proportions of low-income residents do not receive any significant assistance from governments that draw their political power from and that are responsive to large vested economic interests. Government is thus seen as attempting to concentrate and isolate the lower class in the city and thus to perpetuate its existence. According to this position it is futile and even dangerous for those who desire change to look to the government for assistance because such help will ensure that government's eventual collapse, and therefore, by definition, cannot be forthcoming. The views of C. Wright Mills may be most representative of this position. In *The Power Elite*[14] Mills attempts to determine the basis of power of those in important positions in the United States and the ways in which this might influence future governmental action. Mills's concept is a somewhat Marxist and class-oriented concept of society as a whole, but a variation of it is applicable to urban areas. The variation considers the implications of decision-making for various socioeconomic groups in any particular urban center at any given time. The research conducted by Floyd Hunter in Atlanta, Georgia (Regional City was the name Hunter used for Atlanta in his writing), is usually cited as an example.[15] Hunter concluded that in the late 1940s an economic elite dominated Atlanta, including its political leaders, regardless of party.[16] Hunter also maintained that power in Atlanta was dispersed in a hierarchial manner by the few leaders at the top of the power structure.[17] These few leaders were not usually recognized by the general public as being the "leaders" of the community because they often used intermediaries to conduct their business and to represent them in the public forum.[18]

Although Hunter's research was sharply criticized by many, it found wide acceptance and generated extensive debate. Others expanded on it, and probably the most important contribution in this respect was made by Peter Bachrach and Morton S. Baratz, who countered many of the criticisms leveled at Hunter by pointing out that the study of decisions alone is not sufficient to uncover class bias.[19] Bachrach and Baratz maintained that a really powerful set of interests might even determine which items are brought up for discussion in a community.[20] In a sense this agenda-setting power is even more bothersome than open decision-making because such power is difficult to discover and prevents important issues from being raised. Like Hunter and Mills, Bachrach and Baratz maintained that classes tend to be pitted against one another in a conflict that only the upper classes can dominate and control. Thus it is pointless for the powerless to try to control or even influence decision-making because the system is effectively insulated from their efforts.

A second interpretation of the relationship between economic class and political power does not stress class bias, but asserts that the amount and type of economic resources at a person's disposal help to determine his ultimate impact on governmental decision-makers. The economically secure individual who can afford to devote time to politics or who has the requisite assets to influence decision-makers is more likely to enter politics than the individual who has a time-consuming, low-paying job. In addition, it is often argued that those with economic resources are more likely to participate in local politics because they have more at stake—increases in city expenditures and subsequent tax increases do in fact have a greater effect on such individuals. Thus, political conflict based on economic and class differences develops and affects the entire range of human interactions at the local level.

A counterargument points out that even the most economically disadvantaged have the vote. In his perceptive case study of politics in New Haven, Connecticut, Robert A. Dahl maintains that the vote is an essential resource for those who lack many of the economic resources necessary to influence public policy at the local level.[21] The vote is critical because those in the middle and lower classes vastly outnumber those in the upper class, and the vote of the former helps to offset the economic resources at the disposal of the latter.

Obviously, not all urban observers share Dahl's confidence in the vote; some maintain that it is at best an imperfect instrument for popular control. It should be quite clear that the mechanisms for direct and indirect participation are vastly different, and thus the consequences of their use may also be. The right to vote, a form of indirect participation, does not allow the individual the opportunity to influence specific policies or day-to-day decisions that would be available if the individual could participate directly as various decisions were being made.

A third interpretation focuses on the different views of poverty that have been prevalent during certain periods of American history. Many Americans have traditionally regarded the poor as less than desirable, and during most periods of American history the undesirable characteristics of the poor have been stressed. In the late 1800s and early 1900s, Social Darwinist thought justified the existence of the poor on the grounds that they were poor because they were unsuited to be rich.[22] In other words, the poor were relegated to living in squalor because of their failure to do well in the struggle for economic survival—not because society was being unfair or harsh. Social Darwinism was a very powerful justification for government inaction, and the failure of government to provide protection or services for clerical and assembly-line workers who were employed by large industrial concerns or who were physically incapacitated was often due to its acceptance of this position. A review of the statements of the proponents of Social Darwinism indicates their belief that society would benefit if the weak and less able to survive were permitted to perish or, at best, not be permitted to reproduce.

This general tendency toward governmental inaction in areas that were deemed the responsibility of the private individual continued until the Great Depression of the 1930s, when governmental policy shifted toward direct economic intervention. Even during that period, public programs aimed at providing employment were referred to as "make-work" and "boondoggles." Many Americans viewed the jobs created by the federal government as little more than handouts, and quite often recipients of federal assistance were subjected to harsh accusations concerning their character. Seldom has a series of governmental programs caused the public debate and clamor engendered by the policies of the New Deal. America was still seen by many as the land of opportunity; any self-respecting individual who wanted to work should be able to earn a living if he or she had any ambition. Obviously this argument was not popular among the millions of desperate unemployed Americans who watched their hopes for a meaningful life crumble as the economic situation worsened. There can be no doubt that the attitudes of many Americans today toward governmental employment programs and public welfare were formed during, or have been conditioned by accounts of, the events of the 1930s. If World War II had not provided the economic stimulus necessary to alleviate the nation's economic problems, increased demands for the adoption of competing economic systems might have been forthcoming. In any event, even today public attitudes are not very positive toward those receiving welfare or other economic relief. The receipt of such aid carries a stigma that many find onerous.

In recent years, the feeling has re-emerged that the poor possess certain characteristics that set them apart from the rest of American society. Probably the most interesting and carefully reasoned position on the subject of the poor is that of Edward C. Banfield. Banfield's contention, which has elicited a widespread and largely negative response from other experts on the subject, but which has not stimulated much serious discussion of his major points, is that the lower class will always exist because it lacks the ability to delay immediate gratification of its needs and to save for the future, and it is this "future" orientation that is essential to success in the American economic system.[23] The need for immediate gratification prevents the poor from planning for the future because it prevents them from furthering their education or saving for other goals.[24]

Banfield also makes important, but certainly debatable, points about governmental policy or action aimed at providing relief for the poor. He contends that such policy simply perpetuates their problems and may even worsen them because it is based on politically acceptable possibilities and therefore is really not feasible or even necessary.[25] As possible solutions, Banfield suggests the curtailment of many present programs and the adoption of new and controversial ones that stress individual initiative.[26]

Class is obviously important to Banfield. As implied in the discussion of ethos, the future-oriented concept is value laden; therefore it may not be as useful an explanation of the condition of the poor as Banfield would argue. Banfield, like the Social Darwinists, sees the lower class as undesirable, inferior, and detrimental to society—a group neither needing nor deserving governmental assistance.

In sum then, despite the supposed absence of class in America, class has existed throughout the nation's history. Before the important political attitudes and behavior associated with class are discussed, racial politics should be defined and considered.

Racial politics

Race is certainly a salient issue in urban America. The central cities of America are inhabited by a disproportionate number of racial minorities. In many cities racial separation is a way of life. Racial equality in the United States has been a topic of discussion throughout most of its history. One can trace the ambiguity over racial equality back to the Constitutional Convention, at which it was decided that, for purposes of representation in the lower house and direct taxation, three-fifths of the slaves of each state should be counted. Slavery, although it was beginning to disappear from some states, continued until the Civil War, which can be interpreted as a clash over racial equality as well as economic differences.

Table 4-2 lists the percentage of each state's population that is black, as well as the regional percentages. Certain patterns are discernible in this table, and conclusions can be drawn from them. First, blacks are not going to become a majority in the United States in the near future: only 11.1 percent of the total population is black. Second, the blacks are not as geographically concentrated as they were prior to the two World Wars, but are continuing to disperse throughout the nation.[27] The regional percentages clearly support this conclusion. Note that the South Atlantic, East South Central, and West South Central states have the largest percentages of black population, but even in those regions, the populations of only four states (Alabama, Georgia, Louisiana, and Mississippi) are more than 25 percent black. Note also that a relatively high percentage of the populations of the Middle Atlantic and East North Central states is black, but only in Illinois, Michigan, and New York is the percentage of the population that is black higher than the national average. The point should be clear: blacks are still concentrated in several well-defined areas of the United States and have

Table 4-2   Black Population in 1970, by Region and State (percent)

REGION/STATE	BLACK POPULATION
Northeast	3.3
Maine	0.3
New Hampshire	0.3
Vermont	0.2
Massachusetts	3.1
Rhode Island	2.7
Connecticut	6.0
Middle Atlantic	10.6
New York	11.9
New Jersey	10.7
Pennsylvania	8.6
East North Central	9.6
Ohio	9.1
Indiana	6.9
Illinois	12.8
Michigan	11.2
Wisconsin	2.9
West North Central	4.3
Minnesota	0.9
Iowa	1.2
Missouri	10.3
North Dakota	0.4
South Dakota	0.2
Nebraska	2.7
Kansas	4.8
South Atlantic	20.8
Delaware	14.3
Maryland	17.8
Washington, D.C.	71.1
Virginia	18.5
West Virginia	3.9
North Carolina	22.2
South Carolina	30.5
Georgia	25.9
Florida	15.3
East South Central	20.1
Kentucky	7.2
Tennessee	15.8
Alabama	26.2
Mississippi	36.8
West South Central	15.6
Arkansas	18.3
Louisiana	29.8
Oklahoma	6.7
Texas	12.5
Mountain	2.2
Montana	.3
Idaho	.3
Wyoming	.8
Colorado	3.0
New Mexico	1.9

Table 4-2 (Cont.)

REGION/STATE	BLACK POPULATION
Arizona	3.0
Utah	.6
Nevada	5.7
Pacific	5.7
Washington	2.1
Oregon	1.3
California	7.0
Alaska	3.0
Hawaii	1.0
United States	11.1

SOURCE: U.S. Department of Commerce, Bureau of the Census, *Statistical Abstract of the United States, 1974* (Washington, D.C.: Government Printing Office, 1974), Table 31, p. 29.

not migrated evenly throughout the nation. Thus attempts to deal with problems exacerbated by the racial problem must consider the peculiarities of the state and regional situations if proposed solutions are to be at all successful.

Although the black population is not dispersed evenly throughout the nation, it is clear that blacks have been and continue to be attracted to urban centers. As Table 1-4 indicated, 17 million of the 23 million black Americans reside within SMSAs, and 13 million reside within the central cities of the SMSAs. Table 4-3 indicates the black population in 35 representative American cities in 1970. It supports the contention that many major American cities are inhabited by a disproportionate percentage of the black population. Anyone familiar with the South Side of Chicago, northeast Washington, D.C., the Watts area of Los Angeles, or New York's Harlem can attest to the concentration of blacks in these cities. In three major cities (Washington, Atlanta, and Gary), blacks actually constitute the majority of the population. In some cities (Cleveland, Detroit, New Orleans, and St. Louis, for example), the black population is a major electoral force; in others (Albuquerque, Honolulu, Madison, Minneapolis, Portland, and Seattle, for example), the black population is only a small percentage of the total population. If we remember from Table 1-4 that 3 of every 4 Americans residing in central cities are white, the conclusion is inescapable: blacks will undoubtedly continue to play an important role in the elections in American cities, but they are not likely to gain control of the electoral process in the near future. Even in cities with large black populations, the age structure of those populations negates their numerical strength. In 1970 more than 9 million of the 23 million black Americans were under 18; of the 538,000 blacks residing in Washington, D. C., in that year, 197,000 or almost 40 percent, were under 18.[28] What these statistics indicate is not that blacks will have no electoral strength, but that that strength will be longer in developing and becoming an obvious force than has frequently been realized.

Table 4-3 Black Population in 35 Representative American Cities, 1970
          (percent)

CITY	BLACK POPULATION
Albuquerque, N. Mex.	2.2
Atlanta, Ga.	51.3
Boston, Mass.	16.3
Buffalo, N. Y.	20.4
Charlotte, N. C.	30.3
Chicago, Ill.	32.7
Cleveland, Ohio	38.3
Dallas, Texas	24.9
Denver, Colo.	9.1
Detroit, Mich.	43.7
Gary, Ind.	52.8
Honolulu, Hawaii	0.7
Indianapolis, Ind.	18.0
Jackson, Miss.	39.7
Kansas City, Kans.	22.1
Little Rock, Ark.	25.0
Los Angeles, Calif.	17.9
Madison, Wisc.	1.5
Miami, Fla.	22.7
Minneapolis, Minn.	4.4
Montgomery, Ala.	33.4
New Orleans, La.	45.0
New York, N.Y.	21.1
Norfolk, Va.	28.3
Oakland, Calif.	34.5
Omaha, Nebr.	9.9
Philadelphia, Pa.	33.6
Portland, Ore.	5.6
St. Louis, Miss.	40.9
San Antonio, Texas	7.6
Seattle, Wash.	7.1
Syracuse, N. Y.	10.8
Topeka, Kans.	8.4
Tucson, Ariz.	3.5
Washington, D. C.	71.7
All SMSA central cities	21.0

SOURCE: U.S. Department of Commerce, Bureau of the Census, *Statistical Abstract of the United States, 1974* (Washington, D.C.: Government Printing Office, 1974), Table 24, pp. 23–25.

After the extensive property and personal loss of the civil disorders of the 1960s, the Kerner Commission, appointed by President Lyndon B. Johnson, concluded that the United States was experiencing racial separation and would ultimately be two nations—one black and one white, separate and unequal.[29] This was a prophetic statement. The Commission went on to conclude that it was necessary to take steps to reduce the tensions brought on by racial separation. The Commission maintained that "the alternative is not blind repression or capitulation to lawlessness. It is the realization of common opportunities for all within a single society.

. . . What white Americans have never fully understood—but what the Negro can never forget—is that white society is deeply implicated in the ghetto. White institutions created it, white institutions maintain it, and white society condones it."[30] If the fact of racial separation is accepted (regardless of its past and present causes), then the problem becomes one of understanding the specific difficulties created by this separation.

First, there is documented evidence that the standard of living and general socioeconomic level of blacks is substantially below that of whites.[31] Supposedly, the gaps between the two groups are closing, but they still exist. Although illegal and subtle, discrimination in housing and employment is still a reality. In addition, local governments have been known to provide poorer services at less frequent intervals to the black residents of some areas, and some local government authorities consistently ignore requests for more equitable provision of better services to these areas. This often results in inadequate schools, police protection, sanitation, building code enforcement, and recreational facilities. For example, research has indicated that ghetto residents make regular, but often futile, requests for better police protection.[32] According to some criminologists, this lack of adequate police protection helps to account for the high rate of crime in these areas. Similar research on the provision of other services strengthens the conclusion that the basic services provided for areas where there is a high concentration of racial minorities are often inferior in quantity and quality to the services provided for other areas of the same city.

Thus the central political question is, how can racial minorities increase their share of services and the quality of those services? One view is that blacks cannot really hope to control the provision of services in a city until they have attained a numerical majority in that city. As Table 4-3 indicates, blacks have already attained this majority in some cities and have almost attained it in others. The difficulty with this strategy is that a *numerical majority* may not be an *electoral majority* because the residents may not be of voting age or may not be disposed to vote or to participate in political activity. There is evidence to indicate that participation rates of blacks are lower than participation rates of whites. If blacks are to increase their share of governmental services, they must realize the difficulties involved in such a process as well as the time required to implement major changes.

Gary, Indiana, a city of 150,000 just southeast of Chicago that is well known as the center of operations of United States Steel, is an excellent example of a city whose mayor found that a numerical majority is not necessarily an electoral majority. In 1967, Richard Hatcher, a Democrat and an effective and articulate leader of a coalition of blacks, was elected mayor of Gary. Since 1950, the black population of Gary has steadily increased. Even though Hatcher was considered a reform candidate and had popular support, he was not able to develop an effective political organization of his own until 1971. One observer has maintained that Mayor

Hatcher has been successful because he replaced a white machine with a black one.[33]

Despite his success in the 1971 mayoral election and his victory in a bitterly contested primary in 1975, Richard Hatcher has found that provision of more and better services for the residents of Gary is a difficult and often impossible job. He has faced many of the same problems encountered by other political leaders at the urban level, but the problems of Gary have been exacerbated by racial divisiveness and class differences. Thus the days when blacks can hope to control city government merely by attaining a numerical majority may be quite distant, and even when such political control is obtained, it may not result in a qualitative betterment of public services.[34]

If one accepts this limitation, then the question is, how can a group or groups, with limited power, influence the urban decision-making process? This question is both fascinating and perplexing and will be returned to in Chapters 9 and 10. It is sufficient to mention here that there are at least three basic strategies that can be combined and varied in numerous ways. First, racial minorities may try to isolate themselves and establish their own economic, social, and political system within the larger system. This is usually referred to as the separatist model and has numerous variations, depending on how separation is to occur. For the Black Muslims, who also emphasize the learning of basic religious teachings, the white man is the enemy and any contact with him must be avoided.[35]

Second, the minority community may strengthen its organization internally as a way to deal with and bargain with city officials. Most exemplary in many respects is the model advocated by Saul Alinsky, long considered a radical among social activists.[36] According to Alinsky, minority groups should develop a cohesive base so that they can then exert pressure on local institutions to meet their demands. The success of this strategy depends on the identification of mutual interests within the minority community and the translation of those interests into political power. This requires considerable and efficient organization and assumes the existence of a common set of goals that may in fact be lacking. The model varies according to the tactics used: violence may be used only under certain conditions, or passive nonviolence may be used only under certain conditions, or passive nonviolence may be the only acceptable behavior.

Third, the members of the minority community may feel that local institutions, officials, and programs are so biased against them that they must take the dispute into a larger arena if they are to have any chance of success. Thus, the civil rights movement has attempted to force federal intervention when states and localities failed to respond to its demands. Similarly, when some northern cities spent federal funds in a way that nonwhites felt was discriminatory, attempts were made to increase federal involvement, either by taking the issue to the courts or by lobbying to effect changes in the laws. This method of influencing the urban decision-making process, like the other two already discussed, has variations, but also like the other two can follow a pronounced and readily discernible pattern. The attempt to enlarge the arena of conflict has been discussed in the social science literature.[37] It has also been a cornerstone of the argument of most liberals who advocate federal government involvement to redress grievances or resolve problems that state and local governments have either ignored or handled unsatisfactorily.

The problems of access to decision-makers and insufficient provision of services are only two of the race-related problems presently confronting America—especially its urban areas. The basic question, the answer to which will determine their solution, is whether a democratic society can continue to exist if, over an extended period, a sizable minority group within that society does not receive adequate services merely because it is a minority. In other words, at what point do such practices become so intolerable and unjust that drastic changes in the economic and political systems are warranted? Two related questions are whether the members of the majority feel that minorities must be kept in this position of subservience and whether there is any possibility for substantial reallocation of resources or anything more than token racial integration. The theoretical questions raised here must be answered not only by the policy-makers, but also by every member of the general public.

Conclusion

This chapter has provided a brief but comprehensive view of ethnicity, class, and race in American politics, especially urban politics. The inter-relatedness of these three areas is critical. For instance, individuals may find themselves caught in a cross-pressured situation if they do not fit a consistent pattern. Blue-collar whites earning $15,000 to $20,000 a year by working on an assembly line may not be overly tolerant, but they probably will be more tolerant than if they earned less than $10,000 a year. Similarly, the black American earning $25,000 a year and residing in an integrated neighborhood may not be too interested in the attempts of other blacks to isolate themselves from the predominantly white society. The point is that all the members of a particular ethnic or racial group or economic class do not necessarily share the same feelings or desires for change. These overlapping pressures and points of common identification based on shared values and goals make the analysis of public policy very complex and the consideration of alternatives so important.

Also interrelated are ethnicity, race, class, and political participation. The stereotypes of the Irish politician and the black militant are just that: they fail to convey the complexities of political participation, including the lack of it, in American society. Since 1954, when the United States Supreme Court declared segregation in public schools to be unconstitutional,[38] forced busing to achieve integration in public schools has frequently resulted in open clashes between blacks and whites, and has brought many of them into the political arena for the first time. Whether in San Francisco or Boston, Pontiac, Michigan, or Richmond, Virginia, the controversy has been bitter, and members of the lower class have often found themselves in direct conflict with one another. Thus racial antagonism may delay or even prevent attainment of common objectives. This possibility must be taken into consideration by policy-makers, for it may circumscribe their efforts.

The reader should bear in mind these distinctions and be aware of their implications for the various policy choices that are discussed in the following chapters. Then the complexities surrounding any major policy change will become more clear, and the reader will have a better understanding of the difficulties of formulating and implementing comprehensive policies designed to improve the quality of urban life.

Notes to Chapter 4

1. Ethnicity, class, and race have been the subject of considerable research, not only by the social scientist investigating urban systems, but also by the interested layman. The following sources are suggested as logical starting points for the reader interested in further study.

    Ethnicity: Edward C. Banfield and James Q. Wilson, *City Politics* (Boston: Harvard University Press, 1963); Edward W. Bok, *The Americanization of Edward Bok* (New York: Scribners, 1921); William L. Riordan, *Plunkitt of Tammany Hall* (New York: Dutton, 1963); Stanley Lieberson, *Ethnic Patterns in American Cities* (New York: Free Press, 1963).

    Class: Hans Gerth and C. Wright Mills, *Character and Social Structure* (New York: Harcourt, Brace, 1953); Joseph A. Schumpeter, *Imperialism and Social Classes* (Clifton, N. J.: Augustus M. Kelley, 1951); and John Dollard, *Caste and Class in a Southern Town* (New York: Harper, 1950).

    Race: Ralph Ellison, *The Invisible Man* (New York: Random House, 1952); Claude Brown, *Manchild in the Promised Land* (New York: Macmillan, 1965); Stokely Carmichael and Charles V. Hamilton, *Black Power: The Politics of Liberation in America* (New York: Vintage Books, 1967); Malcolm X, *The Autobiography of Malcolm X* (New York: Grove Press, 1966); Gunnar Myrdal, *An American Dilemma* (New York: Harper and Brothers, 1944); and Matthew Holden, Jr., *The Politics of the Black "Nation"* (New York: Chandler, 1973).

2. Herbert Gans, *The Urban Villagers* (New York: Free Press, 1962).

3. L. L. Johnson, *Chicopee Illustrated* (Holyoke, Mass.: Transcript Publishing Co., 1896), p. 6.

4. Personal interview excerpt from the author's research for dissertation on municipal budgetary decision-making in four cities. For a more complete description of the role of ethnicity in this area, see David A. Caputo, "The

Normative and Empirical Implications of the Budgetary Processes of Four Medium-Size Cities" (unpublished doctoral dissertation, Yale University, 1970).

5. For two accounts of the treatment of Japanese-Americans during World War II, see Leonard Bloom and Ruth Reimer, *Removal and Return* (Berkeley: University of California Press, 1949); and Roger Daniels, *Concentration Camps, U.S.A.* (New York: Holt, Rinehart and Winston, 1971).

6. For a good discussion of this point, see Michael Parenti, "Ethnic Politics and the Persistence of Ethnic Identification," *American Political Science Review* 11 (September 1967): 717–726.

7. Edward C. Banfield and James Q. Wilson, *City Politics* (Boston: Harvard University Press, 1963); James Q. Wilson and Edward C. Banfield, "Public Regardingness as a Value Premise in Voting Behavior," *American Political Science Review* 58 (December 1964): 876–887; and James Q. Wilson and Edward C. Banfield, "Political Ethos Revisited," *American Political Science Review* 65 (December 1971): 1048–1062.

8. See *City Politics*, pp. 115–203, 329–346; and "Political Ethos Revisited," pp. 1050–1056.

9. See *City Politics*, pp. 42, 230.

10. See "Political Ethos Revisited," pp. 1048–1049.

11. See "Political Ethos Revisited."

12. Two excellent articles that summarize the opposing positions are Raymond E. Wolfinger and John Osgood Field, "Political Ethos and the Structure of City Government," *American Political Science Review* 60 (June 1966): 306–326; and Daniel N. Gordon, "Immigrants and Urban Governmental Form in American Cities, 1933–1960," *American Journal of Sociology* 74 (September 1968): 158–171. In addition, for a careful empirical consideration of this debate, see Robert L. Lineberry and Edmund P. Fowler, "Reformism and Public Policies in American Cities," *American Political Science Review* 61 (September 1967): 701–716.

13. Newark was the scene of one of the most violent and devastating civil disturbances of 1967. It has been besieged by serious problems and wracked by political scandal. The election of the city's first black mayor, Kenneth Gibson, has resulted in a climate of change and the provision of some new leadership, but serious problems still remain.

14. C. Wright Mills, *The Power Elite* (New York: Oxford University Press, 1956).

15. Floyd Hunter, *Community Power Structure* (New York: Doubleday, 1963). Hunter's research methods are discussed in Chapter 5.

16. *Ibid.*, pp. 107–111.

17. *Ibid.*

18. *Ibid.*, pp. 62–111.

19. For the best summary of their position, see Peter Bachrach and Morton S. Baratz, *Power and Poverty: Theory and Practice* (New York: Oxford University Press, 1970).

20. *Ibid.*, pp. 43–47.

21. Robert A. Dahl, *Who Governs?* (New Haven, Conn.: Yale University Press, 1961), pp. 58–86, 162–165.

22. People who held this view were deemed Social Darwinists because they were applying Darwin's "survival of the fittest" concept to economic class. See William G. Sumner, *Social Darwinism: Selected Essays* (Englewood Cliffs, N.J.: Prentice-Hall, 1963); and Richard Hofstadter, *Social Darwinism in American Thought* (New York: George Braziller, 1965).

23. See Edward C. Banfield, *The Unheavenly City* (Boston: Little, Brown, 1968); and Edward C. Banfield, *The Unheavenly City Revisited* (Boston: Little, Brown, 1974).

24. See *The Unheavenly City Revisited*, pp. 234–259.

25. *Ibid.*, pp. 260–287.

26. *Ibid.*, pp. 234–259.

27. For an excellent discussion of this point, see Charles Tilly, "Race and Migration to the American City," in James Q. Wilson, ed., *The Metropolitan Enigma* (New York: Doubleday, 1970), pp. 144–169.

28. Figures computed from Tables 38 and 39 of *Statistical Abstract of the United States, 1974* (Washington, D.C.: Government Printing Office, 1974), pp. 32–33.

29. *Report of the National Advisory Commission on Civil Disorders* (New York: Bantam Books, 1968), p. 2.

30. *Ibid.*, p. 3.

31. *Ibid.*, pp. 251–277.

32. *Ibid.*, pp. 307–312.

33. Anthony De Bonis, "The Myth and Reality of Machine Politics: Gary, Indiana, 1959–1971" (unpublished undergraduate honors thesis, Purdue University, 1972).

34. For a penetrating discussion of these and other problems that minorities may encounter, see the "Symposium on Minorities in Public Administration," *Public Administration Review* 34, No. 6 (November–December 1974): 519–563.

35. C. Eric Lincoln, *The Black Muslims in America* (Boston: Beacon Press, 1961).

36. Saul Alinsky, "Directing Urban Discontent," in Jim Chard and Jon York, eds., *Urban America: Crisis and Opportunity* (Belmont, Calif.: Dickenson, 1970). Also see Alinsky's *Reveille for Radicals* (Chicago: University of Chicago Press, 1946); and his *Rules for Radicals* (New York: Random House, 1971).

37. E. E. Schattschneider, *The Semi-Sovereign People* (New York: Holt, Rinehart and Winston, 1960).

38. *Brown v. Board of Education of Topeka*, 347 US 483 (1954).

Chapter 5

Participants in the Urban Policy-making Process

Introduction

Traditionally, analyses of the participants in the urban policy-making process have focused on the formal or institutional participants, such as the mayor, city manager, councilpersons, and other local officials. However, many informal, usually unofficial, groups also frequently play an integral role in any urban political policy-making process. Both formal and informal participants are discussed in this chapter, but first a brief discussion of the systems approach is necessary.

Social scientists have long discussed the structure of political systems and the relation of these systems to society. The importance of the systems approach has been acknowledged in the last decade. David Easton has argued that political analysis can be made more accurate and that the dynamic nature of the political process will be better understood if this approach is used.[1]

Figure 5-1 depicts the systems model as it applies to the urban political systems described in this book. Part *A* of the model represents some of the inputs into the political policy-making process—the needs, loyalties, and demands of the citizenry. For instance, if public services in a particular area of a city are inadequate, the citizens residing there may demand that they

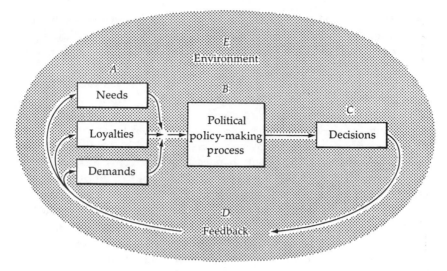

Figure 5-1 An Urban Systems Model

be improved, and if they are not, the citizens might register their dissatisfaction at the next election. Part C represents the decisions (considered
"outputs") reached by the decision-making institutions in the nation's
SMSAs during the political policy-making process (B). It is possible for no
decision to be reached because of official indifference or unwillingness or
inability due to lack of power. Part D is the feedback loop, by means of
which the decisions reached during the political policy-making process affect subsequent needs, loyalties, and demands of the citizenry. This is the
dynamic aspect of the systems approach, for it is the mechanism by which
change takes place. Again an example can be given to illustrate this process.
Assume that the residents of a particular area are concerned about the
traffic patterns in their neighborhood and request that the mayor's office,
the traffic department, and the city council adopt new ordinances that will
regulate the traffic flow. Once the decisions as to which policies will be
implemented have been reached, it is important to know what impact these
policies will have on the residents in that area and on other residents
throughout the city. This can be determined through the feedback loop. If
the residents are satisfied with the decisions, their demands will cease
because their needs have been met, and their political loyalties, in terms of
support for those responsible for the changes, will probably increase. On
the other hand, if the desired decisions are not forthcoming, it is quite
possible that the citizens might try to bring greater political pressure to
bear on the decision-makers to adopt and implement the desired policies.

Another possibility is that the residents of a particular area might suspect
that their demands were not met because a systematic bias existed against

them. Then the feedback loop would show growing alienation of the residents, or even apathetic withdrawal from participation in the political process because of the feeling that such participation was futile and perhaps even counterproductive.

This is exactly the point often made in respect to political participation in many American cities today. It is argued that many citizens have simply withdrawn from the political process because they are frustrated at not having their needs and demands met, and that often they do not receive adequate or fair consideration by public decision-makers because they lack the political clout to bring about changes in policy. This was one of the theories advanced to explain the civil disturbances of the 1960s; inner-city residents felt frustrated and alienated from their political systems and thus attempted to destroy them.[2] The causes of urban violence will be considered in Chapter 9, but it is important to point out here that the systems approach does permit one set of events to be linked to another by means of the feedback loop, which is the dynamic aspect of the systems approach.

Part *E*, the environment of the nation's urban centers, is the federal system, in which some power is delegated to the federal government, some is reserved for the states, and some is shared by both. This mix of governmental powers is important because not until recently have cities been considered important participants in the political policy-making process. The relative importance of urban programs vis-à-vis some of the other demands made upon the national government, especially with regard to fiscal matters, has finally been recognized. (It is unfortunate that so much time has been required for the cities to gain recognition.) Certainly, national defense has been and continues to be the federal government's major commitment, but since 1960 the commitment of the federal and state governments to programs dealing with urban problems has increased. This increased federal and state assistance has created a new environment for the urban political system. Even though the effectiveness of these programs is sometimes open to question, the tendency now is to request federal or state financial assistance before attempting to solve local problems at the local level by increasing local tax rates or by utilizing other methods to raise the required funds.

Part *B* of Figure 5-1, the political policy-making process, is the very core of any urban political system—the procedure by which needs and demands are transformed into decisions. In essence, the political policy-making process determines "who gets what, when, and how." In order to understand it and the range of its effects, one must be aware of both the formal and the informal participants and processes involved.

The foregoing will be considered more fully in the remainder of this chapter. In addition, three different views of the urban political policy-making process will be discussed, as well as their implications for urban political systems. The systems model is a useful way to view political systems because it permits the conceptualization of a very complex set of interactions and institutions. However, the many aspects of the urban political policy-making process cannot always be separated as easily or as conveniently as Figure 5-1 would seem to indicate. With this caveat in mind, let us consider the various participants, both formal and informal, in the political policy-making process.

Formal participants

Table 5-1 is a summary of the number of local governmental units in the United States in 1962 and 1972. The decline in the total number of such units is due largely to the consolidation of school districts in many rural areas that have seen consolidation as a way to gain the economic and educational advantages associated with increased size. An explanation of the types of governmental units listed in Table 5-1 might be helpful.

Except in most New England states and Louisiana, counties are the subdivisions most recognized and most frequently dealt with by state governments. Counties are usually general-purpose units of government (that is, they perform a variety of functions, including supplying services) that have revenue-raising (taxing) powers. The duties and responsibilities of county governments usually include building and maintenance of highways and provision of welfare services and police protection. In many areas of the country, local politics is dominated by people located at the county courthouse. V. O. Key's vivid and intriguing discussion of courthouse politics and politicians in the South provides a useful insight into both southern politics and courthouse politics.[3] Counties have not been the subject of much research in the past few years, even though recently counties in general have become more important in local decision-making and have been included as recipients of general revenue-sharing funds in both general and special revenue-sharing legislation.

Table 5-1 Number and Type of Local Governmental Units in the United States, 1962 and 1972

TYPE OF UNIT	1962	1972
Counties	3,043	3,044
Townships	17,144	16,991
Municipalities	17,997	18,517
Special districts	18,323	23,885
School districts	34,678	15,781
Total	91,185	78,218

SOURCES: 1962 totals from U.S. Department of Commerce, Bureau of the Census, *Census of Governments: 1962*, Volume I (Washington, D.C.: Government Printing Office, 1963), p. 1. 1972 totals from U.S. Department of Commerce, Bureau of the Census, *Statistical Abstract of the United States, 1973* (Washington, D.C.: Government Printing Office, 1973), p. 412.

Townships were once the basic unit of local government and are still important largely in New England and the Midwestern states. For the most part, townships, although usually classified as general-purpose units of government, provide a limited range of services and are being eliminated in many states. However, as Table 5-1 indicates, the process has been slow: from 1962 to 1972, only 153 failed to survive. Although the importance of townships may be declining, it is doubtful that there will be a significant reduction in their total number in the immediate future.

The number of special districts, on the other hand, has increased.[4] A special district usually performs only one function and is not accountable, except in an indirect way, to the general public. Special districts have legal powers, including the power to sue and to enter into contracts, but usually are established mainly to facilitate the delivery of a public service to one or more jurisdictions. The most common special district is the school district, which is discussed in the next paragraph, but special districts have also been created to serve transportation, housing, sanitation, and other functional needs. The main rationale for the special district is that it is the most functional type of organization because it can maximize the delivery of services while minimizing costs.[5] In addition, special districts may be more efficient because they are not directly controlled by elected officials and thus are not restricted by political considerations.

A unique type of special district is the school district. Existing in the legal sense to provide educational services, the number of school districts declined by more than 50 percent between 1962 and 1972. Before assuming that school districts are relatively unimportant, the reader should consider the importance of the Little Rock integration controversy of the mid-1950s and the South Boston integration conflict of 1974–1975. As will be indicated in Chapters 7 and 8, the schools often have been and continue to be the focal point of citizen interaction and public controversy in America because of the extension of the political, social, and economic crises confronting many urban centers to the schools. Add to this the fact that the mayors or city managers of many cities do not have direct control over their school systems, and it becomes clear that the problems of political access and accountability are quite central to any discussion of urban politics.

Note that there has been only a slight increase in the number of municipalities in this 10-year period. Of even more importance is that there were 407 cities with populations of 50,000 or more in 1970. It is these 407 cities, which represent the major urban concentrations in the nation, that are discussed in the following paragraphs.

The forms of government found in these 407 cities are listed in Table 5-2. It is important to note the often overlooked facts that more than 50 percent of all American cities with populations of more than 50,000 have a council-manager form of government and that the bulk of the remaining cities have a mayor-council form of government. It is also true that the council-manager form of government is rarely found in cities with popula-

Table 5-2 Form of Government in Cities with Populations of 50,000 or More, 1970

FORM OF GOVERNMENT	NUMBER OF CITIES	PERCENT OF CITIES
Mayor-council	164	40
Council-manager	212	52
Commission and other	31	8
Total	407	100

SOURCE: *Municipal Year Book, 1971* (Washington, D.C.: International City Management Association, 1971).

tions of more than 500,000. It is necessary to bear in mind that no particular city government conforms exactly with all the characteristics described in the following discussion. In fact, one of the more interesting aspects of American politics is that local government tends to be quite idiosyncratic; the politics and leadership styles of two cities with the same form of government may be distinctly different. Despite this general tendency, it is possible to develop some generalizations about the forms of government found in urban America.

Mayor-council form

Under this arrangement, which is particularly popular in the Northeast and the North Central states, the voting public elects the members of the city council and the mayor. The mayor is the chief executive and the council is the legislative body, and the expectation is that there will be interaction and cooperation between them. In practice, however, the mayor may exercise more power than the council because his is usually a full-time position, whereas council members usually have other full-time jobs and can devote only limited time to their council duties. Few city councils have a staff of professional experts to prepare alternative proposals to those put forth by the mayor. In addition, since the mayor is responsible to the voters of the entire city, he often claims to "speak" for the public interest, whereas it is often assumed that the members of the council represent only a small number of voters and vested interests. A mayor-council form of government is considered "strong" if the mayor has the following powers:

1. Veto ordinances passed by council.
2. Appoint and remove department heads without council approval.
3. Utilize funds to hire professional staff to assist the mayor.
4. Make budgetary recommendations and control spending programs.
5. Exercise general coordinating authority.

Possession of such formal powers does not guarantee a strong mayor, but it does increase the likelihood that the mayor will dominate the local political process. However, rarely is a mayor's authority based solely on these formal powers. For instance, Mayor Daley of Chicago derives a considerable amount of his power from his position as head of the Cook County Democratic organization. In his dual capacity as mayor (even though he lacks many of the formal powers just listed) and party leader, Richard Daley has established a considerable and effective power base and has thus become an important political leader not only in Chicago, but also in Illinois and in the nation.

Under a mayor-council system, the council enacts ordinances and legislation pertaining to budgetary matters. Council members may be elected from districts, on a citywide (at-large) basis, or by a combination of these two methods. Council members are frequently rather parochial and are district oriented rather than city oriented, and thus may be more popular and powerful within their own districts than in the city as a whole.

The debate over executive *vs.* legislative power currently being waged at the national level has a parallel at the local level. To some, it is logical that the mayor should assume increased power and responsibility because he is elected on a citywide basis and thus represents the general interest of the city. In addition, it is often maintained that the mayor is more visible to and therefore more accountable to the average voter. For these reasons, the mayor will supposedly be more interested in solutions to the problems of the entire city than in those of a small area of the city. The counterargument maintains that centralization of power around a strong mayor leads to the politicization of local decision-making; in other words, the possibility is increased that public policy may be beneficial only to those who have direct access to or control over the mayor. Other groups, such as economic, racial, or ethnic minorities, supposedly do not fare well under this system because they are represented by the council members elected from their neighborhoods, and the power of these officials would be lost or at least weakened if the council were made subservient to the mayor.

Regardless of the form of government, political considerations are bound to influence the decision-making process unless one defines politics in such a manner that all partisan influences are ignored. It was exactly this concern over the politicization of city decision-making and the belief that political decisions and governmental administration could and should be separated that led to the development of a second form of municipal government.

Council-manager form

Under the council-manager form of government, the voting public elects a city council, which in turn appoints a city manager, who is a qualified and highly trained professional and who will, it is hoped, administer the city in an efficient and objective manner. The council-manager form is quite popular in the South and West and in cities that do not have large heterogeneous populations. This form of government is a direct result of the reform movement of the early 1900s, which stressed rationality and a nonpolitical approach to the administration of municipalities.

The council appoints the manager, whose main job is to be responsible for the day-to-day administration of the city. The manager appoints and supervises the department heads and is assisted by a professional staff whose job is to ensure maximum planning and administrative efficiency. The council retains general legislative power, but often responds to specific requests and proposals (for example, budgetary matters and salaries) made by the manager. Under the council-manager system, the emphasis is on effective and efficient management and the provision of city services in the most orderly and economical manner.

In reality, the manager often becomes the dominant figure, because the duly elected mayor normally has very restricted powers and responsibilities. Most city managers have received extensive training in university programs established for that purpose and are considered professionals, not politicians. The International City Management Association (ICMA) was established to make available information concerning improved urban management techniques and provides a variety of technical and professional services for the city manager.[6]

Since managers serve at the pleasure of the city council, they must be mindful that their administrative policies and practices do not contravene the wishes of the council. Thus managers may adopt a variety of leadership styles, the two most common of which are the manager who attempts to maximize his term of office by seeking accommodation with political interests and the manager who attempts to lead those interests in order to bring about necessary innovation. The first style emphasizes cooperation and mutual agreement; the second requires active leadership on the part of the manager. Regardless of the style of leadership, the city's political climate will determine what the manager can and cannot accomplish.

Commission form

In the early 1900s, Galveston, Texas, was the first major city in the United States to adopt the commission form of government, and this type of government grew in popularity throughout the nation for some time, but as Table 5-2 indicates, in 1970 it was not widely used in cities with populations of 50,000 or more. Under the commission form, the voters elect an odd number of commissioners, who are responsible for both the legislative and the administrative functions of city government. One of the commissioners also serves as mayor, but his powers are largely ceremonial. In addition, each of the commissioners, including the mayor, becomes the chief administrative officer for a functional department (public safety, streets, sanitation) and administers policy in that area.

Probably the biggest disadvantage of the commission form is that power is highly decentralized, and coordination of policy is difficult if not impossible. In addition, because the same official is responsible for both formulating and administering policy, policy decisions are seldom reached in an impartial manner. Thus it should be obvious why the commission form of local government has had such limited popularity.

Implications of institutional choice

As discussed in Chapter 4, Banfield and Wilson contend that the type of government adopted by a city is closely related to the ethos of that city.[7] Thus the city with a large middle class tends to be more public-regarding oriented and will probably adopt the council-manager form of government. The city with a large lower class and a more private-regarding ethos will be more likely to adopt the mayor-council form of government.

In addition to the type of chief executive and administrative organization that exists at the local level, two other important variables merit consideration. The first is the type of election: nonpartisan or partisan (the party label or party name appears on the ballot). Those who wish to reform local politics and the electoral process have maintained and continue to maintain that the absence of party labels will increase the number of votes based on knowledge of the candidates and their positions on key issues and problems, rather than on party identification alone. Research on utilization of the nonpartisan ballot does not indicate that the absence of party labels increases voter knowledge of or interest in candidates' positions. It does indicate that candidates who have had extensive public exposure, not necessarily in public leadership positions, have an advantage over others who may not have had that exposure.[8]

The second variable is the method of electing council members. If council members are elected on an at-large basis, every voter in the city has the opportunity to vote for them, and they will be more likely to represent the interests of the entire community. If council members are elected from wards or districts, they will be more likely to respond to the needs and wishes of their constituents, even if they should conflict with the needs and wishes of the entire community. In sum, at-large elections may well increase the number of decisions made in the community's interest, but they may also deny minorities representation on the council. The district system increases the possibility of minority representation, but decreases the likelihood that the interest of the entire community will strongly influence decision-making.

The type and amount of reform in American cities with populations of more than 50,000 are shown in Table 5-3. Note that more than one-half of the cities have adopted the council-manager form of government (57 percent), at-large representation (68 percent), and the nonpartisan ballot (64

Table 5-3 Reform Characteristics and Degree of Reform in American Cities with Populations of More Than 50,000, by Region (1970)

REFORM CHARACTERISTIC	ALL CITIES		NORTHEAST*		NORTH CENTRAL*		SOUTH*		WEST*	
	%	NO.	%	NO.	%	NO.	%	NO.	%	NO.
Form of Government										
Mayor-council	43	(157)	75	(67)	55	(53)	30	(28)	10	(9)
Council-manager	57	(208)	25	(22)	45	(43)	70	(64)	90	(79)
	100	(365)	100	(89)	100	(96)	100	(92)	100	(88)
Method of Electing Council Members										
District or ward	32	(115)	59	(51)	37	(36)	23	(21)	8	(7)
At-large	68	(250)	41	(35)	63	(61)	67	(71)	92	(83)
	100	(365)	100	(86)	100	(97)	100	(92)	100	(90)
Type of Election										
Partisan ballot	36	(131)	63	(56)	39	(38)	28	(26)	12	(11)
Nonpartisan ballot	64	(238)	37	(33)	61	(60)	72	(67)	88	(78)
	100	(369)	100	(89)	100	(98)	100	(93)	100	(89)
DEGREE OF REFORM†										
0	44	(173)	13	(12)	36	(38)	50	(51)	78	(72)
1	23	(91)	19	(18)	26	(28)	30	(30)	16	(15)
2	20	(78)	41	(39)	20	(21)	15	(15)	4	(3)
3	13	(51)	27	(25)	18	(19)	5	(5)	2	(2)
	100	(393)	100	(94)	100	(106)	100	(101)	100	(92)

SOURCE: Author's computations from *Municipal Year Book, 1968, 1969, 1970* (Washington, D.C.: International City Management Association, 1971).

*Percentages for regional columns were computed by dividing total number of cities in the region into the appropriate number of cities reflecting the variable.

†Reform characteristics were considered to be council-manager form of government, at-large representation, and nonpartisan elections. Nonreform characteristics were mayor-council form of government, district representation, and partisan elections. A city received a 1 every time it had a nonreform characteristic and a 0 every time it did not. Thus a score of 3 indicates that a city had all three nonreform characteristics, whereas a score of 0 indicates that a city had all three reform characteristics. For two related uses of this research classification, see David A. Caputo and Richard L. Cole, *Urban Politics and Decentralization: The Case of General Revenue Sharing* (Lexington, Mass.: D. C. Heath, 1974), p. 171; and Robert L. Lineberry and Edmund P. Fowler, "Reformism and Public Policies in American Cities," *American Political Science Review* 61 (September 1967): 701–716.

percent). When regional variations are considered, a pattern becomes obvious. Cities in the Northeast are much more likely to have mayor-council forms of government than cities in the South or West, where the council-manager form predominates. If we analyze the regions from left to right, we see that the percentage of cities that have adopted nonpartisan ballots and at-large representation steadily increases.

The lower half of the table suggests two important conclusions. First, nearly one-half (44 percent) of all cities have all three of the characteristics associated with reform government. This means that the popular image that elections in American cities are still largely partisan is incorrect. Thus those who would argue for structural change as the way to bring about an improvement in the quality of urban life would do well to consider that most American cities already have a reform type of government. Second, an overwhelming proportion of the cities in the West (78 percent) and one-half of the cities in the South (50 percent) have all three reform characteristics, whereas 27 percent of the cities in the Northeast have all three nonreform characteristics. This indicates that the reformers who advocated institutional change as a first step toward effecting other changes in municipal government have, to a large degree, succeeded.

It has been shown that the governmental structures of American cities determine to some extent the nature of their policy decisions and programs. Whereas Banfield and Wilson analyzed the reasons for the adoption of various forms of government, Robert Lineberry and Edmund Fowler investigated the relationship between the governmental structure and the policy output of an urban political system.[9] They do not claim that the form of government "causes" a particular policy or program, but they do make a strong case to prove that specific forms of government are associated with specific public policies. At the same time they conclude that "cities with reformed and unreformed institutions are not markedly different in terms of demographic variables . . . political institutions seem to play an important role in the political process."[10]

These findings and other similar ones lead to the conclusion that the form of government apparently does influence policy-making, but not always as predicted. For instance, at-large council representation may decrease the effectiveness of minority groups in influencing policy or the election of a representative unless those groups are large and have an effective political organization. However, the evidence in support of these theories is not entirely conclusive. Wolfinger and Field, utilizing extensive aggregate data for American cities, conclude that ". . . there are so many factors bearing on political outcomes that the prevailing ethos in a city is not very important . . . the propositions of the ethos theory need to be modified to account for special circumstances that limit their validity."[11] Thus the debate concerning the influence of governmental structure on policy outcomes continues. In recent years, research has centered on the relationship between violence, innovation, and political structure.[12]

A large and diverse number of additional participants in the political policy-making process require consideration if the overview of the process is to be comprehensive. These informal participants are discussed in the next section.

Informal participants

The term "informal participants," as used in this section, means those individuals or groups that have only a limited formal role to play, but that have been very adept at gaining substantial leverage and influence as a result of their formal power, as well as those individuals or groups that play an active role in the urban policy-making process without being legally required to do so. A brief discussion of each of these is in order.

Elected party leaders

In many cities, the elected party leaders are not always the persons who hold public office or who the public recognizes as exercising the most leadership. Nevertheless, elected party leaders often do have significant power and influence policy-making in a variety of important ways. Probably most important is a leader's endorsement of a candidate for public office. If the political parties in a city are well organized, then it is critical to the electoral success of potential candidates to receive as much support as possible from elected party leaders because of the leaders' ability to secure the active help of the party organization.

In addition, party leaders are often the source of political favors and patronage. As pointed out in the earlier discussion of Plunkitt and the Tammany machine, there are many things elected party leaders such as precinct captains and ward bosses can accomplish besides providing a personal touch to local government. They can also readily supply a personal reference for anyone who needs a city job, and they are in a position to solicit favors from the bureaucracy.

For example, in most of the major cities in Indiana, regardless of their size or the amount of political reform they have achieved, a person must have the support of his precinct or ward leader in order to be considered for most city jobs; if the same party controls the ward or precinct as controls the state government then the same support is required if a person is to be considered for a state job. This makes it difficult for those who want to institute the merit system for city and state employees, but it also makes local politics more competitive because electoral victory and sustained party loyalty frequently result in tangible rewards (jobs). In addition, the county chairpersons of the state's large metropolitan counties (Allen, Delaware, Lake, Marion, St. Joseph, and Vanderburgh) exert substantial informal power in the state legislature. Many believe that passage of the governmental reform unifying the city of Indianapolis and Marion County, discussed in Chapter 8, was due primarily to the political influence and power of the local county chairpersons, who actively worked with the members of the state legislature to that end.

Party leaders also assist the parties in educating the voter and in getting out the vote. As a result of the party workers' organizational ability, many urban residents receive information (although it is often quite partisan and one-sided) that they probably would not have received, had the party leaders not canvassed their constituents. In addition, party leaders are expected to "deliver" their voters to the polls—that is, to encourage and, in some cases, to induce, those registered for a particular party to vote for the party candidate.

Finally, party leaders are important communication links between the general public and elected city officials. Since they usually have direct access to these officials because of their political ties, they are in a position to communicate the public's needs and wants to the leaders as well as to explain the rationale for various policy decisions to the public. In sum, the role played by elected party leaders should not be seen in a negative light, for in many ways they improve the efficiency of the policy-making process and make political parties more responsive to the needs and desires of the public.

Local bureaucrats and employee groups

Certainly any consideration of urban policy-making must include the various roles played by local bureaucrats and employee groups. The number of municipal employees has grown rapidly in recent years, and as a result of increasing unionization and organization these employees have had a substantial impact on local political processes.[13] In addition, the diversity of jobs performed by local organized employees is quite striking. Any city with more than 50,000 inhabitants is likely to have a substantial number of public-safety (police and fire) employees, as well as clerical, sanitation, parks and recreation, street maintenance, social welfare, and public health employees. The task of supervising and coordinating these employees is difficult and time-consuming, but is necessary to the smooth functioning of city government.

At this point a distinction between staff and line employees may be helpful. Line employees perform a certain function or are responsible for some aspect of a particular task. Most public employees, such as police officers, are line employees; their positions and responsibilities are relatively well defined and require specific skills and training. Advancement depends on both practical, on-the-job experience and additional training. Thus the required qualifications and abilities for each position and level can be precisely stated, and screening procedures can be devised to locate those who possess these attributes. This is the very purpose of the merit system, which rewards employees for their ability or meritorious service by promoting them, or increasing their salary, or both. In many cities the merit system is combined with the civil service system, both of which are designed to increase fairness and to decrease the partisan nature of municipal employment. Obviously, people interested in giving or receiving patronage dislike the merit-civil service system because it means that a person cannot receive a city job merely on the recommendation of a political leader.

As previously mentioned, in recent years there has been a marked increase in the unionization of the line employees in America's cities. In many large cities, teachers are represented by the American Federation of Teachers rather than by the more traditional representative group, the National Education Association. This increased organization has had two results. First, collective bargaining between city officials and union representatives has become a much more common and accepted practice. (Collective bargaining means that representatives of both the city and the union directly "bargain" and that the agreement reached must be mutually acceptable.) Most states have passed legislation prohibiting strikes by public employees. The result has been that whenever collective bargaining efforts seem to not be producing the results desired by the municipal employee group, "job" action takes place: employees reduce services or withhold them from the public—frequently by feigning illness (such as the "blue flu")—so that the city might be more inclined to satisfy their demands.

The second result of this increased unionization has been that unions are playing a more active role in the urban policy-making process. Not only do they attempt to have a direct say concerning the benefits their members should receive, but many also try to influence decisions that affect their general working conditions as well as other related matters such as appropriate class size (teachers), patrol tactics (policemen), and the specific tasks that an individual in a particular line position is expected to perform. The result has been an increase in the likelihood of direct interaction and even conflict between union members and city officials. In addition, the efforts of union groups to lobby for higher salaries and to support candidates sympathetic to their position have been more successful. A political leader who wants to have influence at the urban level must take into account the organizational strength and political power of these groups without appearing to be "captured" by them.

As the city line employees have become better organized, there has also been an increase in the number of staff officials. Staff positions are supervisory and administrative and are usually filled by individuals with prior experience. These are the individuals responsible for overseeing the daily activities of line employees and the effective performance of their services. Staff officials spend large amounts of time planning and organizing activities as well as solving problems and answering complaints. In addition, they establish general policy guidelines. For instance, the number of trash containers to be emptied per household seems of minor importance, but if a specific number is not set, the city must bear the cost of the resulting inefficiency. Sanitation employees will have to use their own discretion as to what number is "reasonable," and citizens will not know exactly what type of service to expect. To maximize efficiency and minimize fuel and labor costs, a staff official of the sanitation department plans the trash routes and estimates the number of trips needed to collect the allowable garbage.

Staff officials also play an integral role in the policy planning process—especially budgetary planning. Department heads are the chief spokespersons for their particular departments and are also the most active in securing political support for their departments' requests. This interaction has been the subject of numerous detailed case studies.[14] It is important to bear in mind that department heads often establish mutually rewarding relationships with specific citizen and political groups that result in public support for a department's policies and budgetary requests. The specifics of these relationships will be considered in the section on municipal budgeting later in this chapter.

One additional aspect of staff participation is the interaction between the department head, his subordinates, and his superior—whether city manager or mayor. As has already been discussed, a department head who can be removed by the mayor or manager is much more likely to be responsive to the requests of the mayor or manager than the department head who is appointed and removed by the council. The legal relationships that exist between the various staff officials and the chief executive greatly influence the daily interaction and informal personal relationships that exist between them.

Finally, when making administrative decisions, mayors and managers quite often find themselves in need of specific and highly technical information, and may lack the professional staff needed to gather that information and to provide a variety of policy recommendations. When Richard Hatcher was elected mayor of Gary, Indiana, in 1967, he found, much to his dismay, that the city budget did not permit him to hire a qualified professional staff. Since the city council was not sympathetic to his requests for additional funds, Hatcher had to secure the support of a private foundation to finance his professional staff. The lack of a qualified professional staff is a problem faced by the chief executives of many American cities, and frequently the result is that the mayor or manager must accept biased information supplied by those who favor specific policy decisions.

Participant public

For our purposes, the participant public will be divided into two groups: the voting public, and the organizations that are involved in the urban political policy-making process. The distinction between the two groups is important.

Despite the implications of the popular slogan that is supposedly applicable to most urban elections, "Vote early and often," the research on the how and why of urban voting has not been as careful or as sophisticated as the research on voting in national elections.[15] Much of the following discussion is based on some important research on urban elections of the early 1960s.[16] The findings and basic conclusions of Robert Alford and Eugene Lee are still applicable today, despite the changing nature of American politics.

Some figures on voter turnout may be useful. In the last three presidential elections, 62.1 percent (1964), 61.0 percent (1968), and 54.5 percent (1972) of the population of voting age voted.[17] Thus in not one of those three elections did the President represent a majority of all Americans because in each, approximately 30 percent of the public was not of voting age. Thus, some have contended that American politics is characterized by a relatively low level of public participation and involvement.[18]

Many factors determine voting participation at the urban level. Certainly one is whether the local election is held in conjunction with state or national elections. In many states, municipal elections are held at a separate time from other elections in order to reduce the spillover that the other elections might have. Research findings indicate that the scheduling of elections has an impact on both the number of individuals who register to vote and the number of individuals who actually vote. Alford and Lee found that voter registration rates were 46.9 percent and 59.0 percent and voting rates were 31.2 percent and 43.5 percent in cities that held separate and concurrent local elections, respectively.[19] This tends to support the contention that generally, for any number of reasons, most citizens show less interest in and participate less in local elections than in state and national elections.

Even more interesting and important is their conclusion that voter turnout is affected by a number of demographic and political structure variables: ". . . the average turnout among cities with high ethnicity, low education and low mobility is higher . . . than among cities with reverse characteristics."[20] This also leads to the next conclusion, that even when one controls for a wide variety of influences, ". . . partisan non-manager cities tend to command a larger turnout than non-partisan and manager cities."[21] Some interesting questions still remain: why are these findings applicable to America's urban centers and what is their significance?

Three theories can be advanced to explain low voter turnout. The first is that citizens simply do not think local elections are that important and therefore assume there is no compelling need for them to participate and no reward for their participation. Citizens think that if the situation ever arises in which they must participate or attempt to influence policy through the electoral process, they will and can do so. Thus it is wrong to interpret low participation rates as a sign of dissatisfaction; rather they signify an indifference resulting from the relative unimportance attached to city politics and especially elections.

A second theory takes the opposite view and maintains that low voter turnout is the result of the desire of those in power to retain their power. If there were to be widespread voter turnout, those in power would be threatened with a loss or diminution of their power, or at the very least, would be forced to be more responsive to the public's needs and wishes. Thus, those in power have a vested interest in keeping participation rates low and limiting participation to those who are likely to support them. This explains why elections are scheduled at different times, registration rules make it difficult to qualify for voting, and selected attempts are made to get out the vote.

The third theory contends that the low level of participation indicates that many citizens have become deeply alienated from local government and have decided to withdraw rather than participate in the electoral process because they have little control over its outcome and because they may be punished for their participation by direct reprisals (such as rigidly enforced local ordinances) or the denial of public services. Thus residents of a defiant neighborhood may prefer not to vote rather than to vote against a well-entrenched and powerful city official who could withdraw services from that area. An example is useful here. An excerpt from an interview conducted in the course of my research on urban budgeting is particularly appropriate.

Q. As mayor, how do you decide and set service priorities?
A. That's easy. I "encourage" my department heads to provide the first and best services in the neighborhoods which give me the most support. A good example is snow removal . . . . We get a lot of snow and when I get calls about how a neighborhood hasn't been plowed yet, I point out to the citizen that the city only has so many plows and that we will get to them as soon as possible. I don't tell them that I've asked the highway superintendent to be sure to plow my supporters' neighborhoods first, but I think they soon learn. After all, that's political reality.[22]

Obviously, which interpretation of the lack of public participation in urban electoral politics one chooses is linked to one's personal view of the urban system and American politics in general. The significance of each theory is readily apparent; if one accepts the first theory, the political system is responsive and working well; if one accepts the second theory, the political system is in need of drastic and far-reaching reforms. If one accepts the third theory, it would seem to be only a matter of time until major political change characterizes many American cities. Certainly these theories are applicable and important. They will be given greater attention in Chapters 6–9.

Many groups participate in the urban policy-making process in other ways, in addition to voting. These groups vary from city to city, but they usually include the municipal employee groups previously discussed, business groups such as the Chamber of Commerce, other merchant groups, civil rights and neighborhood groups, and specific-interest groups that represent the taxpayer, the poor, or other community groups. Some individuals may decide to participate actively because of a strong interest in or personal commitment to a particular issue or policy.

A variety of tactics are used by these groups. They may try to influence policy decisions indirectly by privately contacting decision-makers and indicating their preferences; they may try to influence them publicly by appearing at appropriate public meetings and making their position known; or they may launch a concerted campaign to achieve widespread public support for their position and thus increase public pressure on local decision-makers.

The success of these groups, like the success of individual voters, varies from city to city and according to the decision-makers involved. In Chapters 6, 8, and 9 the variables apparently associated with the effectiveness of these groups will be isolated so that their future role may be considered.

Illegal groups

Even though these groups are discussed in few texts on urban politics, they are important participants in the urban policy-making process, not because they might directly participate, but because so many urban decisions require that they be taken into consideration. For instance, drug addicts are an important problem for urban governments, not only because a larger police force and additional health and correctional facilities are needed to deal with them, but also because they increase the crime rate and create general apprehension.

Although films such as *Serpico* and other accounts of police and political corruption document the cooperation that has existed between organized criminal groups and urban governments, few generalizations are possible. It has been shown, however, that criminal organizations have in fact influenced the activities of police and other law enforcement officials attempting to control prostitution and gambling.[23] The reader cannot really understand the complexities of the urban political process without being aware of the possibility of, and the existence of documented evidence concerning, organized criminal activity aimed at influencing government policymaking.

The usual pattern is that the criminal organization obtains or "buys" selective enforcement of certain laws in order that their activities not be stopped. The most common activity thus protected is gambling, since it is relatively popular, is done by choice, and is difficult to prevent. Police forces usually remain honest and enforce the laws. This often means that court officials or other local officials must be induced to intervene on behalf of the criminal organization.

This does not mean that "Godfathers" run American cities or are the power behind the elected leaders. It does mean that whenever economic and political factors are favorable, organized criminal elements may attempt to influence the makers of public policy and the outcome of the policy-making process in order to gain a competitive edge.[24]

Urban gangs have been more active in most large cities since the early 1960s. Their activities are wide-ranging (petty theft, drug dealing, or providing expensive "protection" for merchants), but the goal is the same: financial gain.[25] In some instances, public agencies have dealt directly with gang leaders in an attempt to reduce hostility that might lead to violence. Any program or policy that concentrates on the inner city and its low-income residents must take into consideration the powers and activities of the urban gang.

The politics of municipal budgeting

The budgetary process is perhaps most representative of the complexities of the urban policy-making process. In the following discussion, frequent reference will be made to the box in Figure 5-1 labeled "Political policy-making process."

Budgetary decisions are important because they deal with the allocation of real and finite resources. In other words, a decision to spend x dollars for a particular function means that the same dollars cannot be used for another purpose. Since most cities have only limited funds and are faced with budgetary constraints, budgetary decisions often epitomize the difficulties raised by the question, "who gets what, when, and how?" It is possible to determine who "wins" and "loses" by analyzing the relative amounts of public funds allocated in municipal budgets to various programs and policies. The aim of this section is not to describe how most cities expend their funds, but rather to explain how budgetary decisions are reached. The discussion is based on a variety of case material.[26]

Municipal budgeting for any given budgetary cycle has three distinct stages: planning, decision, and implementation. The intriguing aspect of municipal budgeting is that participants in the budgetary process may "win" or "lose" during any of the three stages of that process and still not be dissatisfied with it. Municipal budgeting is characterized by a great deal of political uncertainty within the confines set by the economic constraints.

It is during the planning stage that initial and often critical decisions are reached. The city's chief executive (mayor or manager) and fiscal officer prepare an estimate of revenues expected during the forthcoming budget year. This estimate includes both local tax receipts and revenues from state and federal sources. Present and anticipated program costs, the tax rate, and a variety of political constraints are then considered in relationship to this forecast of revenues in order to obtain a preliminary working set of figures.

Once this initial set of "ballpark" figures has been agreed upon, the chief executive or the fiscal officer meets with individual department heads to discuss their specific departmental requests for funds for the ensuing fiscal year. Each department head normally tries to obtain as much money as possible for his department. He may do this by citing public need for improved or expanded service, or the benefits to be gained from increased financial support. The mayor or manager then decides which requests he will recommend, and which requests he will cut, and by how much, based on how closely the total requests agree with his preliminary figures and whether the city is able to raise the necessary additional funds. If the mayor or manager has decided on a certain percentage increase or decrease in the total city budget, this information soon filters down to the departmental heads, and they plan their requests accordingly. Normally, initial departmental requests will far exceed the limits the mayor or manager has set because most department heads assume their requests will be cut and thus ask for more than they expect to obtain, hoping that the final figure will be mutually acceptable. The final result of the planning process is the presentation of the budget by the chief executive to the legislative body for decision.

During the decision stage, citizens can influence policy by attending public hearings or through informal contact with the decision-makers. In cities where council members are chosen on a ward basis, the council focuses its attention on the specifics of the budget as they pertain to individual districts. For instance, if an amount is allocated for highway paving or sewer construction, the council will probably want to know which sections of the city will receive the benefits. Only if there are enough benefits for enough different sections of the city will the budget be received favorably by the council.

Recent research has indicated that public hearings apparently do affect how cities spend their resources.[27] If local groups or individuals muster enough support and organize effectively, the public hearing can be quite a useful vehicle for them. The public hearing gives groups and individuals the opportunity to ask probing questions and to seek justification for their requests, as well as to introduce new requests if their original ones have been ignored up to this point.

It is during the decision stage that the interaction between the mayor or manager and elected council members reaches a peak. A department head may promise better services in a council member's district in return for a vote, or the chief executive may agree to exchange a reduction in the amount of funds allocated to one department for an increase in the size of another. In the end, from the often intense and usually chaotic bargaining process a city budget emerges that determines the budgetary outlays for the ensuing year. Most department heads usually fail to get all the money they request, but most get enough to continue to function. It is obvious that an axiom applicable to budgetary politics is: if you don't succeed at first, don't give up, just try even harder in the next stage.

The final stage, implementation, is often overlooked by policy analysts. The programs funded by the budgetary decisions can be carried out in a variety of ways and can benefit various individuals and groups. Without misallocating his funds, a department head may be able to use them to achieve certain objectives that were not agreed upon during the budgetary discussions. Similarly, if the initial revenue forecasts were too high or too low, the chief executive may attempt, at some point during the budgetary year, either to "freeze" expenditures or to request supplementary appropriations in order to use the excess funds the city has received. The opportunity for individuals or groups to participate during the implementation stage is limited to attempting to bring pressure upon a department head in order to achieve a specific goal. Their chances of success will depend on the amount of political pressure they can muster.

Bear in mind that at any given point in time, three distinct budgetary processes are taking place. The first is implementation of the present budget; the second is making decisions affecting the next one; and the third is planning the budget for the forthcoming year. In addition, the budgetary cycle is continuous—that is, the implementation stage of one year often overlaps the planning and decision stages of the following year. Thus during each stage the participants are developing and adapting specific strategies in the hope of maximizing their gains.

In the preceding discussion it has been assumed that the urban policy-making process is relatively democratic and open—that is, that procedural norms guarantee basic rights and freedoms and that all who have the right to participate in the decision-making process can in fact participate.

In the next section an attempt is made to answer the question of who actually rules in urban centers.

Who actually rules?

The question of who actually rules America's cities is critical for the policy analyst who is interested in studying the possibility of bringing about basic changes or implementing new programs or policies. In the late 1950s and early 1960s, there was considerable controversy among social scientists as to who rules America's cities. This particular question is crucial, because if the power structure that exists in a particular community can be defined, it should then be possible to devise a strategy for implementing desired policy changes. Without such knowledge, the desired policy may never be implemented.

In recent years, there has been a marked tendency among political scientists in general, and specifically observers of American politics, to argue that American politics is dominated by an elite that is immune from public pressure and control. Thomas Dye and Harmon Zeigler state this point clearly in *The Irony of Democracy*.[28] They maintain that politics in America is dominated by the few, but that the values of these few are essentially democratic, whereas those of the masses are not.[29] Hence the irony that political control by a relatively small political elite permits the continuation of the democratic system in the United States.

Perhaps the best way to study the literature on community power is to divide it into three phases. Phase one includes the works of Robert and Helen Lynd and Floyd Hunter. These three sociologists were advocates of the stratification theory, which stresses the hierarchial organization of society. The Lynds did their research in the late 1920s and early 1930s in Muncie, Indiana (which they renamed Middletown), and concluded that the Ball family, manufacturer of canning jars, was the dominant economic interest in Middletown, and successfully controlled all aspects of community decision-making.[30]

Hunter conducted his research in Atlanta (Regional City) in the late 1940s and early 1950s.[31] It is important to analyze his research technique separately from his major findings. Hunter interviewed a representative cross section of community residents, and on the basis of these interviews compiled a list of community influentials. He then selected a small panel of community leaders whom he considered important and asked them to pick the most influential people on this list. When he combined the two sets of rankings he found that 14 people were generally acknowledged as being the most powerful and that all 14 were engaged in business and financial activities. Hunter concluded that the members of this economic elite, by controlling committees and influencing elected political officials, dominated public life in Atlanta to such an extent that it was impossible to implement any program or institute policy changes without their support.[32] In short, urban society in Atlanta was stratified and dominated by a small minority that ruled in its own self-interest. Hunter's findings have become known as the *elitist model* of community power, and his approach has become known as the *reputational method* of investigating community power.

In the late 1950s, Robert A. Dahl, with the assistance of a large group of Yale graduate students and substantial research funding, began an extensive analysis of politics in New Haven, Connecticut. This marked the beginning of, and is probably the best example of, phase two of the research on community power.[33] Dahl and Hunter differed as to what constitutes an elite. Dahl maintained that specific tasks must be completed before the existence of an elite is acknowledged. Most important among these was a thorough study of the decisions that were made in three issue areas affecting the city: educational policy, political nominations, and urban renewal.[34] By investigating who participated and why, in each decision made in each area, Dahl was able to discern several patterns of decision-making in New Haven. He ruled out a model of urban political organization based on either overt or covert leadership by an economic elite.[35] In fact, Dahl concluded that the business and financial leaders of New Haven were not as active in the making of most decisions as might be expected. He also found that the elected political leaders of the community (especially the mayor) and the party officials were important participants in most policy decisions.[36]

Dahl also concluded that politics in New Haven had changed since the city was founded (1784) because of the increasing number of new residents, whose numerical strength meant that their impact on politics was assured.[37] Dahl found that relatively few citizens exerted direct control over major decisions, but that many citizens, by exercising their right to vote, exerted substantial indirect control over the policy-making process. Dahl's basic findings have become known as the *pluralist model* of community power.

Dahl and other pluralists were quickly challenged by other social scientists, and this debate can be considered part of the third phase of the research on community power. Two basic criticisms were raised. First, the pluralists were criticized because of their research methods. For example, Peter Bachrach and Morton S. Baratz, building on prior theoretical arguments of the elitists, maintained that the pluralistic approach was to analyze the decisions that were reached and not the decision-making process, and thus might overlook situations in which a particular group was so strong that it controlled which topics were raised for public discussion.[38] Thus the study of overt decisions alone was said to reveal only who won or lost in debates over issues that a powerful few permitted to be brought up. Therefore, even the finding that a community is essentially pluralistic does not mean that it is an open political system unless attempts have been made to disprove the existence of agenda-setting by powerful vested interests and the existence of a systemic bias that prohibits certain policy questions from being debated publicly.[39]

Second, the pluralists were criticized because they failed to understand the theoretical significance of their own findings. In an interesting and provocative professional exchange between Dahl and Jack Walker,[40] Walker criticized Dahl and the pluralists for being too complacent about their finding that the amount of direct participation in urban policy-making was relatively slight and maintained that it was the responsibility of the political scientist to suggest specific ways in which direct citizen participation and influence could be increased.

This brief summary of the research on community power indicates that personal beliefs about the nature and organization of society influence how one interprets research findings. Dahl and Walker had access to the same information about New Haven, yet Dahl did not conclude that the lack of direct public participation in policy-making was necessarily bad whereas Walker thought that lack of it was a direct threat to democratic institutions and the democratic process.

Conclusion

This chapter included a discussion of the participants in the urban policy-making process, some of the influences on their behavior, and some of the dynamic aspects of urban decision-making. Several points need to be emphasized.

First, the urban policy-making process is quite complex, and analysis of it requires considerable time and effort if it is to be fully understood. The local newspaper is quite important to such analysis because it is the main source of information about local politics and the news behind the news. The electronic media are less influential because of the time limitations on the scope and depth of the news stories that are reported, but they do create more lasting impressions. If policy analysis is to be careful and meaningful, simplistic answers to the complicated political problems facing urban America must be avoided. The nation lacks many things, but it has an abundance of "experts" who are ready to sell their patent-medicine-type cures for these complex problems.

Second, the urban policy-making process is idiosyncratic, and thus generalizing from one example to another is almost impossible. This was a major criticism of both the Dahl and Hunter studies and has remained a point of contention in community studies even when they have included more than one city. A basic fact of life in urban America today is that few urban centers are affected by exactly the same institutional and political forces. Thus blanket generalizations should be avoided, and strategies must be tailored to the unique circumstances that exist in a community.

It is clear that the analysis of public policy and specifically of policy alternatives is important for the future of urban America. The past, present, and future policy options are considered in the remaining chapters of this volume.

Notes to Chapter 5

1. David Easton, *The Political System: An Inquiry into the State of Political Science* (New York: Knopf, 1953).
2. *Report of the National Advisory Commission on Civil Disorders* (New York: Bantam Books, 1968), pp. 1–2, 203–206.

3. V. O. Key, Jr., *Southern Politics* (New York: Vintage, 1949), pp. 62–69, 196–198, 273–274.

4. See John C. Bollens, *Special District Governments in the United States* (Berkeley: University of California Press, 1961), for an excellent discussion of the role of special districts.

5. *Ibid.*, pp. 1–2.

6. The International City Management Association has published numerous publications. One of the more important is James M. Banovetz, ed., *Managing the Modern City* (Washington, D. C.: International City Management Association, 1971).

7. Edward C. Banfield and James Q. Wilson, *City Politics* (Boston: Harvard University Press, 1963), pp. 33–46, 224–242.

8. For a fuller discussion of nonpartisanship, see Eugene C. Lee, *The Politics of Nonpartisanship* (Berkeley: University of California Press, 1960).

9. Robert L. Lineberry and Edmund P. Fowler, "Reformism and Public Policies in American Cities," *American Political Science Review* 61 (September 1967): 701–716. See also Richard L. Cole, "The Urban Policy Process: A Note on Structural and Regional Influences," *Social Science Quarterly* 52 (December 1971): 648–656, for a discussion of these points.

10. Lineberry and Fowler, *op. cit.*, p. 715.

11. Raymond E. Wolfinger and John Osgood Field, "Political Ethos and the Structure of City Government," *American Political Science Review* 60 (June 1966): 325.

12. See Michael Aiken and Robert R. Alford, "Community Structure and Innovation: The Case of Public Housing," *American Political Science Review* 64 (September 1970): 843–864; and Peter K. Eisinger, "The Conditions of Protest Behavior in American Cities," *American Political Science Review* 67 (March 1973): 11–28.

13. For considerations of this point, see: Jack Steiber, "Employee Representation in Municipal Government," *The Municipal Year Book* (Washington, D. C.: International City Management Association, 1969), pp. 31–57; and David T. Stanley, *Managing Local Government under Union Pressure* (Washington, D. C.: The Brookings Institution, 1972).

14. See John P. Crecine, *Governmental Problem-Solving* (Chicago: Rand McNally, 1969); and David A. Caputo, *Municipal Interest Group Strategies and Their Effects on Local Public Policy in Four New England Cities* (Storrs, Conn.: Institute of Urban Research, 1972).

15. See Lester W. Milbrath, *Political Participation* (Chicago: Rand McNally, 1965), for a general discussion of voting and other means of participation.

16. Robert R. Alford and Eugene C. Lee, "Voting Turnout in American Cities," *American Political Science Review* 67 (September 1968): 796–813.

17. David A. Caputo, *Politics and Public Policy in America: An Introduction* (Philadelphia: Lippincott, 1974), p. 24.

18. *Ibid.*, p. 23.

19. Alford and Lee, p. 803.

20. *Ibid.*, p. 807.

21. *Ibid.*, p. 808.

22. Author's personal interview transcripts, August 1968.

23. See especially John A. Gardiner, *The Politics of Corruption: Organized Crime in an American City* (New York: Russell Sage, 1970).

24. See David A. Caputo, *Organized Crime and American Politics* (Morristown, N. J.: General Learning Press, 1974).

25. For an excellent discussion of gang organization today, see R. Lincoln Keiser, *The Vice Lords* (New York: Holt, Rinehart and Winston, 1969).

26. See the works by Caputo and Crecine cited in footnote 14 as well as Aaron Wildavsky, *The Politics of the Budgetary Process* (Boston: Little, Brown, 1964); and Arnold J. Meltsner, *The Politics of City Revenue* (Berkeley: University of California Press, 1971).

27. See David A. Caputo and Richard L. Cole, *Urban Politics and Decentralization: The Case of General Revenue Sharing* (Lexington, Mass.: D. C. Heath, 1974), pp. 98–103, for a discussion of this point.

28. Thomas R. Dye and L. Harmon Zeigler, *The Irony of Democracy* (North Scituate, Mass.: Duxbury Press, 1975).

29. *Ibid.*, pp. 1–3.

30. Robert S. Lynd and Helen M. Lynd, *Middletown* (New York: Harcourt, Brace and World, 1929); and Robert S. Lynd and Helen M. Lynd, *Middletown in Transition* (New York: Harcourt, Brace and World, 1937).

31. Floyd Hunter, *Community Power Structure* (Garden City, N. Y.: Doubleday, 1963).

32. *Ibid.*, pp. 60–111.

33. Dahl's research findings are summarized in his *Who Governs?* (New Haven, Conn.: Yale University Press, 1961) and are only briefly summarized here. Another example is Raymond E. Wolfinger, *The Politics of Progress* (Englewood Cliffs, N. J.: Prentice-Hall, 1974).

34. Dahl, *op. cit.*, pp. 104–162.

35. *Ibid.*, p. 185.

36. *Ibid.*, pp. 190–220.

37. *Ibid.*, pp. 85–86.

38. For the most complete presentation of their position, see Peter Bachrach and Morton S. Baratz, *Power and Poverty: Theory and Practice* (New York: Oxford University Press, 1970).

39. *Ibid.*, pp. 12–16.

40. See Jack L. Walker, "A Critique of the Elitist Theory of Democracy," *American Political Science Review* 60 (June 1966): 285–295. See also Robert A. Dahl, "Further Reflections on 'The Elitist Theory of Democracy,' " *American Political Science Review* 60 (June 1966): 296–305.

Chapter 6

Prior Policy Choices

Introduction

In this chapter the results of past federal governmental involvement in three policy areas that have affected the nation's cities—housing, urban renewal, and the Poverty Program—are considered in detail. The action taken by the federal government in these two areas illustrates well the complexities of American federalism and the difficulties that have been encountered in attempting to solve the problems of the cities. Such a consideration may provide important lessons for the future and help to define future policy choices.

Categorical grant programs

It is important to be aware of the fundamental principles of each program and the patterns of policy choice that have sometimes been established. The programs considered in this chapter are excellent examples of the categorical grant or grant-in-aid approach,[1] which originated during the New Deal of the 1930s and was utilized almost exclusively until the early 1970s. A categorical grant is the granting of funds by the state government or, more commonly, the federal government, to an urban governmental jurisdiction to finance a particular program or to meet a specific objective. Thus the categorical grant can be seen as a redistributive device; the federal government earmarks part of its tax revenues for a specific function (say, sewer construction), and state and local jurisdictions then apply for the funds. It has been estimated that during the 1960s the number of categorical grant programs grew from 100 in 1960 to more than 600 by 1969, and from a total dollar amount of $7 billion to slightly less than $30 billion.[2] There is little doubt that these programs have had a considerable impact on America's urban centers. Their impact will be evaluated when the advantages and disadvantages of the categorical grant approach are analyzed in the concluding section of this chapter.

The administrative red tape that is frequently part of the application process has been criticized as a major negative aspect of the categorical grant approach. If a city wants to participate in the sewer construction program already mentioned, it must file a detailed application with the federal agency administering the program that requires specification of the location and size of, as well as the need for, the sewers. This application then goes through bureaucratic channels and, if it is approved and if funds are available, the city receives a specific amount of funds for sewer construction. The time that elapses from submission of the application to receipt of the funds might range from 3 to 18 months or even longer. Congress determines the legislative aspects of the categorical grant programs as well as the amount that is to be made available for a certain program during a specified period. Funds are usually appropriated on a yearly basis and quite often the legislation includes a stipulation as to how the funds are to be used or a limitation on the total amount any one city can receive.

A postaudit is usually made by the administering or another federal agency to ensure that the funds have been used as originally planned. Again, there is the possibility of administrative oversight, which, in turn, must be financed by public funds. One of the main results of the categorical grant program has been the growth of administrative staffs at both the local and the federal levels of government that prepare, review, evaluate, and revise programs. Ultimately these staffs are also responsible for implementation of the programs.

Some categorical grant programs first channel the federal funds, using a legislatively derived formula, to the states, which then allocate them to the smaller localities. Funds made available through crime-control legislation are usually distributed in this way. This adds another dimension to intergovernmental fiscal relationships in the United States and increases the need for additional state administrative workers to oversee the distribution and use of the funds.

In the final analysis, the major justification for the categorical grant approach is that it establishes minimum national standards. Recipient jurisdictions must meet certain legislative requirements in order to receive funds, and are checked by the postaudit. This does indeed increase the amount of indirect control exercised by the federal government because the availability of federal funds is usually an incentive for state and local governments to adopt policies that permit them to receive such funds.

The conservative maintains that the categorical grant approach is a form of centralization and therefore opposes it because such governmental assistance is really aid with "strings" and tends to weaken the ability of state and local governments to control their own future.

A counterargument is often made that the categorical grant approach is an effective way of increasing local responsiveness and that the establishment of minimum national standards does not overly involve the federal government in local planning and program administration.

An analysis of the three categorical aid programs is now in order.

Housing and urban renewal

In 1967 President Lyndon B. Johnson appointed a commission to investigate the housing situation in the United States and to indicate what role the federal government should play in replacing the deteriorating housing and in building new housing units. The Douglas Commission, officially known as the National Commission on Urban Problems but named for its chairman, Paul H. Douglas, a former United States senator from Illinois, issued an often quoted report[3] that called for a wide range of governmental actions to meet the need for housing in the United States. As is characteristic of most reports of this type, sweeping recommendations were made for policy changes, but few suggestions were made for specific programs to implement these policies. Four observations can be made concerning housing policy in the United States since the 1930s.

First, direct governmental involvement in the housing industry has been increasing since 1935, but there has not been any direct and massive governmental intervention to alter the supply or quality of housing. Rather, the emphasis has been on provision of incentives to private enterprise. As stated in the Douglas Commission Report,

> The nation has made a phenomenal record over the last two decades in building housing for the middle and affluent classes . . . . The efforts of private enterprise account for most of this construction, but Government policy has provided significant incentives and help through mortgage guarantees, secondary credit facilities, and Federal income tax deductions for interest payments and local property taxes.[4]

Second, housing policies have, at times, had unanticipated consequences that have not been beneficial to all residents of a particular urban area. For instance, the availability of land and homes outside central cities has frequently been an important reason for the out-migration of middle- and upper-income groups from those cities. This migration has made it difficult for the remaining citizens to raise sufficient revenues to maintain public services.

Third, although there has been much discussion of the benefits of federal housing and urban renewal programs, relatively few careful empirical investigations have been made of these benefits. Debate has frequently been prompted by political considerations, and public policy formulation has not always been preceded by careful deliberation.

Finally, federal housing and urban renewal policies offer an excellent opportunity to investigate the relationship between public agencies and policies and the private sector. Governmental policy has both a direct and an indirect impact upon the private sector. For instance, deficit government spending could result in an increased demand for private money to finance that spending. This could make investing in government obligations more financially rewarding for the nation's financial institutions, and the amount of private investment funds available for housing investment would thus be reduced. These four observations should be borne in mind because they will be useful in relating rather diverse points mentioned in the following discussion.

Housing

The federal government has intervened in two areas that affect housing. The first is public housing. The second, which is the most important and probably least understood federal program, is the guaranteeing of mortgage loans by the Federal Housing Authority (FHA).[5] The FHA was created in the midst of the Depression to provide what was then a necessary financial service for the housing industry. A mortgage is simply the loan of a stated sum of money for the purpose of building or buying a home; the loan is to be paid back, with accrued interest, within a specified number of years. (The most common repayment periods are 20, 25, and 30 years.) The home serves as collateral and is forfeited if payments cease. The FHA was established to guarantee repayment of mortgage loans extended to individuals who normally might be considered good risks (individuals who are responsible and have good credit records but who lack the funds necessary for a downpayment or require longer repayment periods than the bank allows), but who have difficulty qualifying for mortgage loans that are made available by commercial banks and savings and loan institutions. Thus if certain requirements are met, the FHA will guarantee repayment of the mortgage to a local bank (if the prospective homeowner defaults), which otherwise might be reluctant to carry the loan.

The FHA was viewed as an innovative way to increase the number of Americans who qualify for home ownership. The home building industry is important because it has a "multiplier" economic effect on the entire economy. As a result of each home start and subsequent completion, numerous jobs are created in related construction, trade, and supply industries. Thus the home industry, like the automobile industry, is a basic indicator of the strength of the nation's economy.

The policies and practices of the FHA have frequently been the subject of controversy, mainly because opinions differ as to the role the FHA should play. Prospective homeowners dislike the red tape and delay that often accompany an FHA application. Commercial bankers dislike the low interest rates set by the FHA and often add "points" to any FHA-supported mortgage. A "point" is 1 percent of the purchase price, and the adding of points helps to offset the administrative costs of the mortgage—particularly financing the property at an interest rate lower than the prevailing one, or assuming the risk of extending a loan to an applicant who would not normally receive it. Planners and reformers have been critical of FHA policies because preference is given to middle-income people and to those who wish to purchase or build single-family, detached dwellings. Table 6-1 shows that in 1965 the bulk of FHA mortgages were given to middle- and upper-middle-income families. Critics contend that many members of the lower class have been unable to obtain mortgage support. Quite often, the FHA has ignored low-income areas, and residents of those areas who were seeking financial support were induced to move elsewhere. It is also contended that the resultant increase in the number of single-family units has increased the depletion of the nonrenewable resources (natural resources as well as time and energy) utilized in housing construction and has led to serious depletion of the nation's natural resources. Finally, builders and developers in particular have been critical of the FHA, asserting that the various codes and requirements the authority has established for builders of FHA-financed units are unrealistic and reflect a general lack of knowledge of and concern for the problems faced by the builder.

In reality, the FHA is an excellent example of an incentive-oriented program in which the federal government does not build housing, but it

Table 6-1 Purchasers of FHA Homes in 1965, by Income Class

INCOME CLASS	INCOME RANGE	% OF FHA MORTGAGES
Poverty level and below	$ 4,000 and under	0.5
	$ 4,000–$ 5,000	2.9
Lower middle class	$ 5,000–$ 6,000	7.6
Middle and upper middle class	$ 6,000–$ 8,000	30.0
	$ 8,000–$10,000	26.0
	$10,000–$15,000	27.0
Well to do	$15,000 and over	6.0
Total		100.0

SOURCE: National Commission on Urban Problems, *Building the American City* (Washington, D.C.: Government Printing Office, 1968), Table 5, p. 100.

does indirectly influence the housing industry, and it does influence trends in the housing market.[6] Evaluation of the overall effectiveness of such a program is indeed difficult. Several other programs and policies of the federal government have encouraged or indirectly subsidized home builders and buyers. Some of them deserve mention.

Several key provisions of the income tax legislation apply to home buyers. First, the amount of a person's mortgage payment that is applied to interest is tax-deductible. This provision effectively lowers the actual interest rate and is thus an attractive feature for a person purchasing a home. Second, when a house is resold, the profit on the sale is taxable, but the tax can be deferred indefinitely if the seller purchases a more expensive home within a specified period. The last example shows the importance of the housing industry as an indicator of economic conditions in the nation. In 1975, Congress passed a tax-cut bill that included the potential of a $2,000 saving for individuals who purchased a home that was built but not yet occupied, or construction of which had begun before a certain date. (The bill was thus applicable to 1974 purchases.) The intention was to stimulate the housing industry by reducing the inventory of unoccupied homes; the anticipated result was an increase in new housing starts. Interestingly, few argued that this tax-credit plan was in fact special legislation for the housing industry. Passage of the provision clearly indicates the general acceptance of the importance to the economy of a strong housing industry.

Even with the special consideration given the housing industry, it is unlikely that the number of units needed in the future will be available, at a cost permitting their purchase by many Americans.[7] In addition, some critics have contended that federal policies, such as FHA policies and the tax provisions, have had two important unintended results that have complicated other aspects of urban life.

First, by encouraging the building of single-family homes, the FHA has encouraged the development of new residential areas on the outskirts of and in the suburbs surrounding central cities that have drawn large numbers of people away from those cities, and this has had two results: it has stripped the city of needed resources, and it has encouraged disorderly growth and subsequent fragmentation of urban areas. Second, and even more discouraging, the unavailability of mortgage guarantees for city residents who live in multiple-dwelling units has meant that the FHA has favored middle-income and white families to the virtual exclusion of low-income and nonwhite families. The cynical observer might conclude that this represents a conscious attempt to formulate a policy beneficial to only one group, but it could also be the result of unanticipated consequences, because the outcome of a particular policy may be far more complicated than was originally anticipated.

It is clear that even an indirect attempt by the federal government to affect housing policy can have a profound and wide-ranging impact on many aspects of urban life.

Public housing is a term that strikes fear into the hearts of many urban dwellers regardless of their race. When the public housing program was begun in the mid 1930s, it was seen as a useful and necessary way of providing low-income housing for those unable to secure adequate and safe housing without financial assistance. In short, it was intended to be a directly subsidized program that would provide an alternative to the dilapidated dwellings many low-income families had been forced into. However, the public housing program has been largely unsuccessful in meeting these aims. The reasons for this failure should be clearly understood.[8]

The normal operating procedure is for the federal Public Housing Authority to enter into contractual agreements with local housing authorities to plan, build, and maintain low-income housing. Families are provided housing if their income does not exceed a maximum figure, and their monthly rent is based on a proportion of their family income. This plan would seem to have potential benefits for society, but in reality it has had some undesirable consequences.

First, the housing projects have, to a large extent, become racially segregated. In many larger cities, blacks and other nonwhite groups are housed in one set of units and whites are housed in another (even though this is often no more than a continuation of prior settlement patterns). Since public housing has been concentrated in central cities, the amount of segregation in most SMSAs has increased.[9] In the last 10 years, there has been discussion of the desirability of scattering public housing units throughout the city and reducing the number of residents in each unit. Obviously, this suggestion has met organized and often intense opposition from many of the residents in the areas where the sites are to be located.

Second, the quality of life in public housing projects is generally inferior. The Cabrini-Green project in Chicago and the Pruitt-Igo project in St. Louis are excellent examples of public housing projects that failed to meet expectations. Perhaps the best and most illuminating study of life in a housing project is Lee Rainwater's *Behind Ghetto Walls*.[10] Rainwater, a Harvard sociologist, investigated life styles and conditions in the Pruitt-Igo project in St. Louis.

Pruitt-Igo had more than 20,000 residents and was considered one of the most unsatisfactory public housing projects in the United States. When the project was first occupied in 1954, there were 33 eleven-story buildings with a total of 2762 apartments. Rainwater feels that Pruitt-Igo is an example of a federal slum and that ". . . no other public housing project in the country approaches it in terms of vacancies, tenant concerns and anxieties, or physical deterioration."[11] Specifically, from the beginning Pruitt-Igo suffered from a variety of design problems. The elevator doors did not open at every floor, public restrooms were not provided, and construction materials were not of high quality. The project was situated near industrial and other polluters, and thus the physical environment was not conducive to constructive living. In addition, this project, like many others, was not well administered, and the relationship between the administrative staff (in this case employed by the city of St. Louis) and the residents was marked by controversy—primarily because routine maintenance was rare. Finally, the high percentage of women and children living in the project increased the danger of physical violence and robbery. In essence, Pruitt-Igo, as Rainwater states, ". . . condenses into one 57 acre tract all of the problems and difficulties that arise from race and poverty and all of the impotence, indifference, and hostility with which our society has so far dealt with these problems."[12]

To isolate public housing and to consider it apart from the wide range of difficulties associated with low-income status in the United States and of programs designed to alleviate them is to oversimplify a complex problem and to misunderstand its basic causes. This point will become clearer when poverty and the action that has been taken to eradicate it are discussed in the next section.

Although federal involvement in private housing has, to a large extent, been indirect, its impact has been major. The federal role in the urban renewal program has also been important, and again the results of such intervention have not been as anticipated.

Urban renewal

The extensive urban redevelopment projects that have been instituted since 1949 have resulted in dramatic and often major changes in many American cities.[13] Every major city has had at least one extensive renewal project, and several smaller and medium-sized communities have also been "made over." The extensive urban renewal that took place in New Haven, Connecticut, in the 1950s and 1960s is perhaps one of the best examples.[14] In addition, both the Gateway Arch area of St. Louis and the Golden Triangle area of Pittsburgh were high-density housing areas that were transformed into major sports and tourist attractions. Table 6-2 indicates the extent of urban renewal programs and summarizes the distribution of urban renewal funds by city population size. Cities in the 100,000 to 999,999 category received the bulk of approved projects; cities in this category and cities with populations of more than 1 million and in the 25,000 to 99,999 category received a percentage approximately equal to their percentage of the total urban population. The urban renewal program has been and continues to be a controversial subject, and illustrates well the incremental nature of policy-making in the United States.

Urban renewal was the result of a series of amendments made in 1954 to the 1949 Housing Act. The intention of the 1949 act was to provide adequate and decent housing for millions of Americans who lacked it. In addition, the legislation authorized the use of federal funds to redevelop or

Table 6-2   Distribution of Urban Renewal Grants, by City Population Size

CITY POPULATION SIZE	NO. OF LOCALITIES	% OF URBAN POPULATION	% OF TOTAL GRANTS APPROVED
More than 1 million inhabitants	5	15.4	15.3
500,000–999,000 inhabitants	16	8.8	14.5
250,000–499,999 inhabitants	29	8.6	15.6
100,000–249,999 inhabitants	68	9.0	17.6
25,000– 99,999 inhabitants	283	23.0	23.5

SOURCE: National Commission on Urban Problems, *Building the American City* (Washington, D.C.: Government Printing Office, 1968), p. 161.

build additional housing in areas from which substandard housing had been eliminated by the program. This was the beginning of the "site clearance" approach to urban redevelopment, which eliminated blight and deterioration by physically removing substandard housing. Subsequent legislation emphasized the renewal aspect. Buildings and housing that could still be utilized if improved were to be preserved rather than run over with a bulldozer.

Because the riverfront areas of many cities were the first to be settled and thus the first to be affected by out-migration, many of the most blighted areas were in close proximity to the riverfront and often included substantial parts of downtown business districts. The urban renewal legislation coincided with the building of metropolitan freeways, which made the commute from home to office faster and increased decentralization of businesses and employment from the central cities.[15] The result was that many communities made a determined effort to revamp and revitalize their central business districts. Many local financial institutions, such as banks and insurance companies, perceived investment in renewal projects as being quite worthwhile and frequently made funds available for the development of downtown shopping malls and office buildings. The financial arrangements often were quite complicated. Table 6-3 summarizes the financial arrangements of a "typical" urban renewal project. On the expenditure side, the local urban renewal agency (the city) was expected to plan the project, purchase the land included in the redeveloped area, help to relocate the residents presently residing there, and demolish or renew the area. The city was then expected to provide various services for the area. Of these, police and fire protection and education were seen as most important and were used most often in assessing the value of the city's contribution to the project.

The federal urban renewal program permitted some very interesting accounting methods to be used that significantly reduced the real cost to the city that was interested in renewal. Since the land was purchased by a governmental agency, eminent domain could be cited as justification for its purchase at a "fair market value." This meant that landowners had to sell their land; the city could then sell the rights to develop that land to a developer in the private sector and use the funds to replace those used for the purchase. In addition, as Table 6-3 indicates, cities were expected to pay approximately 25 percent of the total project cost, but they could meet this requirement by adding the costs of their services rather than by making direct cash contributions. For instance, if an area was already receiving police and fire protection and the city agreed to continue that protection after renewal, this was considered an acceptable portion of their share. This reduced the total dollar amount any particular city had to allocate to urban renewal and meant that many cities found that participation in the program was to their advantage. The federal share then often amounted to approximately 40 percent of the total project cost, but in reality, owing to the accounting techniques just mentioned, the federal share was much more likely to be in the neighborhood of 60 to 75 percent of the total project cost.

Table 6-3 Financial Arrangements of "Typical" Urban Renewal Project

FINANCES	% OF TOTAL PROJECT	AMOUNT (DOLLARS)
Costs		
Land purchase	75	15,000,000
Demolition	10	2,000,000
Moving of present residents	5	1,000,000
Provision of new services		
for renewal area	10	2,000,000
Total	100	20,000,000
Revenue		
Receipts from sale of		
renewal land	35	7,000,000
Local contribution or share*	25	5,000,000
Federal urban renewal grant	40	8,000,000
Total	100	20,000,000

*This could be in cash, services, or kind.

In addition to making available these financial advantages, the 1954 Housing Act and subsequent amendments placed greater emphasis on the role of the city in the planning and overall integration of redevelopment and renewal projects. In order to qualify for urban renewal funds, the city had first to develop a "workable" program. The workable program had to ". . . utilize appropriate private and public resources to eliminate, and prevent the development or spread of, slums and urban blight, to encourage needed urban rehabilitation, to provide for the redevelopment of blighted, deteriorated, or slum areas."[16] The result of the workable program approach was that cities turned to physical planners, and a large administrative unit of planning experts soon dominated many urban renewal agencies.

There has been and continues to be substantial disagreement over the ultimate usefulness of the urban renewal program for improving the quality of urban life. Table 6-4 summarizes the arguments in three areas of disagreement.

Table 6-4 Urban Renewal: The Controversy

AREA OF CONTENTION	PRO STATEMENTS	CON STATEMENTS
Housing	Substantially betters existing conditions Provides impetus for replacing substandard units Provides housing for middle- and upper-income residents within the city	Fails to replace low-cost housing with more low-cost housing Destroys many "natural" communities Results in increase in rate of deterioration of other housing
Business	Provides needed revitalization of central business area Permits urban center to survive Saves jobs and employment opportunities	Simply wages an orderly retreat in an unwinnable war Caters to large business interests Eliminates many semi-skilled and service jobs
Administration	Increases rationality of efforts by emphasizing planning Local contribution (usually 25%) is reasonable, thus encouraging local participation	Ignores social aspects of planning Creates too large a bureaucracy

A frequently heard criticism of housing, the first category, is that most urban renewal projects do not replace the units destroyed with low-cost housing. Developers cannot do this and still make the renewal projects attractive to the private investor who wants to maximize his profit. In fact, in some communities a result of forcing people to relocate in areas with limited housing is the deterioration of that housing because of overcrowding. New Haven, Connecticut, a city of 150,000 people, is a good example. The renewal project there replaced several very blighted areas with businesses and some low-cost housing, but not enough housing to replace that eliminated by renewal. Certainly this was a major reason for the dissatisfaction of many local residents whose expectations of new housing were not fulfilled. The cynic might interpret the result as another example of disregard of those without power and wealth; the developer might argue that in some instances, the economic realities of the market place make limited renewal a necessity if renewal projects are to be undertaken at all.

With regard to business, there is little doubt that business interests do in fact profit from renewal. The typical downtown project includes a shopping complex, at least one office building, a parking garage, and a modern hotel. In many communities the jobs these new businesses provide were of the white-collar type, and the result was a net loss of jobs for those without the necessary skills. In another type of renewal project, colleges, universities, and hospitals were built on the cleared land. Certainly the development implemented by the University of Chicago and Yale University created substantial controversy in their communities.[17] Herbert Gans, in his excellent and revealing case study of urban renewal in Boston's West End, maintains that the members of the Board of Overseers of Massachusetts General Hospital were instrumental in bringing about urban renewal in that area.[18] Others have contended that urban renewal is in reality a less than subtle attempt to remove black and low-income residents and to restore upper-income groups to areas they had previously dominated.[19]

Various questions began to be raised concerning the planning that necessarily preceded urban renewal projects, and these questions had implications not only for the urban renewal process itself, but also for the urban political process in general. Two of these questions deserve consideration.

First, for whom should planning be done, and who should do the planning? One obvious lesson of the urban renewal experience in general that is mentioned in Gans's study of Boston is that planners tend to ignore the social aspects of life and to concentrate solely on the physical aspects. Thus the number of people per housing unit and the efficiency of plumbing and other facilities, rather than the patterns of personal interaction, became the key determinants of policy decisions. Gans asserted that although in many ways Boston's West End physically resembled a slum, the planners were wrong in thinking that it was;[20] Gans concluded that planning is too often a tool used by those with power against those without it. A common view is that advocacy planning, in which groups that usually are not consulted in the planning process are given a voice, is necessary if planning is not to be used to the advantage of those in power. This view is supported by many excellent case studies of urban renewal in such cities as New Haven, New York, Chicago, Boston, and Newark.[21] The professional planner dominated the renewal process in these and most other cities. The recommendation of these studies was not that planning be eliminated, but that all points of view be represented in the policy-making process. Planners supply important information as to costs and benefits, but they also provide strong justification for a particular course of action, and they cannot be considered to be politically neutral.

Second, what about the unanticipated effects that planning may have in the future? In many cities, urban renewal projects were devised in steps, and different areas of the city were to be developed at different times in future years. If a neighborhood is included as part of the second 5 years of a 10-year plan for renewal, landowners in that neighborhood would logically choose not to improve or even to maintain existing property, realizing that funds invested for this purpose might not be recovered when renewal took place. This in fact happened in several cities, and often resulted in the more rapid deterioration of already marginal neighborhoods. Table 6-5 indicates

Table 6-5   Months Needed to Complete Major Urban Renewal Projects

% OF ACTIVITIES COMPLETED	STAGE				
	LAND ACQUI-SITION	RELO-CATION	DEMO-LITION	SITE IMPROVE-MENTS	LAND DISPO-SITION
100	48	54	54	126	132
75	32	35	36	80	122
50	16	26	27	52	75
25	10	15	19	42	57

SOURCE: National Commission on Urban Problems, *Building the American City* (Washington, D.C.: Government Printing Office, 1968), Table 13, p. 167.

the number of months required to complete major various urban renewal projects. There was often a considerable lag between initiation and completion of an urban renewal project. In some cases, substantial changes were made in the original urban renewal plans for a variety of reasons, and this may actually have contributed to a decline in the quality of life in that particular area because people were encouraged to make decisions based on assumptions that proved to be false.

The specific benefits and costs of urban renewal are best considered in a case-by-case analysis, but many of the problems discussed here are characteristic of most urban renewal projects. The urban renewal program has undergone periodic change during the more than 20 years since it was initiated. Legislation was frequently enacted to resolve the problems created by earlier legislation. Changes were also necessary because the initial planning often had unintended and unanticipated results.

Poverty programs

It is difficult in 1975 to understand the fervor and dedication of those who maintained that the War on Poverty would be the major domestic program of the 1960s.[22] President Lyndon B. Johnson chose poverty as the key domestic issue of his administration and made a determined effort to introduce basic policy changes and to initiate programs that would help the poor. The political consequences of these changes and programs have had a far-reaching effect on urban America. In order to understand the War on Poverty, one must understand the political forces that were responsible for it, the key legislative decisions that were reached in the process of establishing the program, and the results of the antipoverty legislation.

Political forces

Lyndon B. Johnson found himself in a unique position in early 1964. He had gained the office of President under tragic circumstances, in the midst of a national emergency. The nation and its leaders had not yet recovered from their shock and their sense of loss following the assassination of John F. Kennedy in Dallas, Texas, on November 22, 1963, and were, for a brief time, without Presidential leadership. Johnson, never an introvert, decided to pursue a policy of vigorous leadership. His long experience as a member and Majority Leader of the Senate had given him an insight into the working of Congress and the relationship between the executive and legislative branches of government. He was widely respected by the members of both houses of Congress. Knowing full well that the 1964 Presidential election was on the horizon, Johnson moved quickly and decisively to take charge of the government. He seized the policy initiative at a time when other Presidents, under more normal circumstances, would have been more slow to act. Because of the growing national concern about the problems of the poor, it was logical that one of the first of his decisions was to attack poverty.

In the course of United States history, the federal government has dealt with poverty in different ways. As Michael Harrington has pointed out, the poor in America have often been overlooked because of the general abundance and economic gains that have been enjoyed by most Americans.[23] Prior to the Great Depression of the 1930s, few government programs had as their aim the amelioration or elimination of poverty. Rather, this was seen as the primary responsibility of private individuals.

The Social Security Act of 1935 provided direct benefits to retired persons, the disabled, the blind, and families that had lost their breadwinners, but it was not aimed at alleviating the poverty of those unable to find jobs. Numerous classes of workers, such as farm laborers and domestics, were excluded from its coverage entirely. The jobs that had been created by the Work Projects Administration beginning in 1935 were curtailed in mid-1937, and since that time government job-creation programs have been viewed as something to be used only as a last resort.

Another reason for the lack of such programs was the widely held conviction that individuals could and should seize the economic opportunities available to them, which were largely a result of America's participation in the war effort. The economic upturn brought about by World War II strengthened the nation's belief in the American Dream and the possibility of self-made wealth. However, this confidence in individual initiative and the possibility of self-improvement made it difficult for those who, for whatever reasons, could not participate in the job market.

By the early 1960s, the nation was ready to wage a War on Poverty. America's growing middle class had become increasingly concerned with the problems of the poor for two reasons. First, the economy had recovered from the downswing of the late 1950s, and many Americans who had experienced the despair of the Great Depression now shared in the long-term economic advance. Suddenly they realized that they were more secure than they had been in previous years and that the economic fluctuations that had for so long characterized the American economy were becoming less severe. They could now become more aware of the problems of the less fortunate.

A second reason for this concern for the poor was that it was becoming increasingly "fashionable" to show an interest in the poor. Popular nonfiction, such as Michael Harrington's *The Other America*, focused public attention on the plight of the poor in America.[24] The thesis of this and similar works was basically the same: in a society where large numbers of individuals were financially secure, significant numbers, usually one-fifth to one-third of the total population, were locked in poverty and could not enjoy the economic benefits enjoyed by others.[25] During the 1960 presidential campaign, John F. Kennedy toured the Appalachian area and viewed with dismay the extreme poverty that existed there. His concern for these forgotten pockets of poverty, especially in West Virginia, increased public awareness and concern. The combination of the increasing public ability to be concerned with others and the availability of descriptive accounts of the impact of poverty increased pressure on federal officials to consider a new program to deal specifically with the problems of the poor.

Accompanying this increasing concern over poverty was an increased concern about the civil rights of black Americans. During the late 1950s, the civil rights movement became more visible, and the concerted efforts to remove existing legal and institutional barriers to desegregation increased. It was natural that those interested in promoting civil rights, the most vocal of whom were members of the educated middle class, should argue that any attempt to reduce poverty should be coordinated with integration efforts.

Several other governmental programs dealt with related aspects of poverty. The most important of these was the attempt by the federal government to define, understand the reasons for, and control juvenile delinquency. The 1950s saw an increasing awareness of juvenile delinquency and the fear that criminal activity on the part of the teenager would increase and continue to be socially disruptive. The wanton acts of violence and display of "machismo" of Marlon Brando and the Hell's Angels occupied the public's attention. Presidents Eisenhower and Kennedy established task forces to investigate the problem, its causes, and possible solutions.

Researchers and policy-makers agreed that the main reason for delinquent behavior was not that the individuals were inherently "bad," but that the economic system prevented them from obtaining what they desired in "normal" and acceptable ways.[26] The wants and needs of juvenile delinquents were not unique; delinquent youths merely had no clearly defined or socially acceptable way to satisfy them. Many youths who lacked the funds to purchase a car and whose parents could not or would not purchase one for them chose to steal one because they were prevented from successfully competing through normal economic channels to obtain it. Thus the solution was either to open present economic channels or to provide alternate channels, to prevent repetition of delinquent behavior in the future. As will be indicated in the next section, this theoretical base was also basic to the approach of the War on Poverty.

These political processes were at work when Lyndon Johnson declared "war" on poverty in January 1964, and the nation embarked on a new path. The results of Johnson's declaration were intense debate, partisan division, cynicism, and a program that has probably had some impact on poverty.

The legislation

There are a variety of excellent case studies that describe in detail the political and bureaucratic developments that accompanied preparation of the Economic Opportunity Act of 1964.[27] Lyndon Johnson instructed the task force he had assembled to formulate as soon as possible a comprehensive plan to deal with poverty. As John C. Donovan has pointed out, "once the President made the decision to declare war on poverty and to bring forth a new legislative proposal which would encompass a set of programs bearing a distinctly LBJ brand, the actual preparation of the bill became a major, all-consuming effort on the part of high-level executive staff people, most of whom were several layers removed from the President."[28] Thus the decisions pertaining to the scope and orientation of the program were concentrated in the executive branch, and there was little consultation with or interaction between the President and appropriate members of Congress or their staffs.

This point should not be overlooked because it may have some significance for the passage of urban legislation. One might well contend that the difficulties subsequently encountered during the War on Poverty might have been lessened if the President had consulted more frequently with both Congress and the bureaucracy during this early period. The national constituency to which the President is responsible is quite distinct from and broad in comparison with the constituencies represented by congressmen. This means that the President may seek a policy that is too broad in scope; its chances for success are lessened because it does not consider interstate differences. Such a distinction may explain why the legislative and executive branches emphasize different priorities, and it must be considered in any analysis of future policy choices and programs affecting urban society.

It is convenient to analyze three key aspects of the resulting antipoverty legislation. The first is the definition of poverty. The concept of poverty is seemingly simple, but poverty is not easy to define. If a relative measure such as the lower 20 percent of the population is utilized, then, by definition, that proportion of the society's population will always be poor when, in reality, the individuals in that category may not be poor when compared with individuals in other socieities. Similarly, if one uses an absolute measure, such as income level or caloric consumption, one has to establish minimums and maximums, and such a definition makes possible the "elimination" of poverty.

Those who planned the strategy of the War on Poverty decided that an absolute definition would suffice and that the poverty-level income would be $3200 to $4000 per year for a family of four. After adjustments were made for family size and location, it was found that more than 38 million Americans, nearly 20 percent of the total population, were below the poverty line in 1959. The leading states, in terms of the *percentage* of their population below the poverty line, were Alabama (42.5 percent), Arkansas (48.3 percent), Mississippi (54.5 percent), North Carolina (40.6 percent), and South Carolina (45.4 percent).[29] The states with the largest *number* of people below the poverty line were: California (2.2 million), Florida (1.4 million), Georgia (1.5 million), Illinois (1.4 million), New York (2.3 million), North Carolina (1.8 million), Ohio (1.5 million), Pennsylvania (1.9 million), and Texas (3.0 million).[30] The pattern is clear. Both the highest percentage and the largest number of the nation's poor lived in the Southern states and in the larger, more industrialized states of the North. In the South, poverty was most acute in the rural areas, whereas in the North, the condition of the inner-city poor was most critical. Thus the War on Poverty did *not* distribute benefits equally throughout the nation, but rather concentrated its resources in two geographic areas.

The second aspect is that the antipoverty legislation also depended quite heavily on several prior experiences and one key assumption. The critical assumption, similar to that discussed with regard to juvenile delinquency, was that the poor are not culturally different from the non-poor, nor are their values and beliefs essentially different. Instead, poverty was perceived as being cyclical. Persons born into poverty encounter obstacles that weaken their motivation, adversely affect their health, limit their opportunities to obtain educational training and restrict their mobility. The limited employment opportunities that result lead again to poverty.[31] Figure 6-1 illustrates the cyclical nature of poverty. Clearly, the individual's chances of "breaking out" of the poverty cycle are slim; furthermore, the closed nature of the cycle ensures that the next generation will also become trapped in it.

It is not difficult to conclude that if education and employment opportunities are made available to the poor, they will be more able to escape from the cycle. This explains why the War on Poverty concentrated so heavily on provision of job training and education.

Bear in mind that this approach is quite consistent with earlier attitudes toward differences in the values held by various groups in the United States. What this definition of the poor did was to deny that cultural traits are responsible for the poor being poor. In other words, it rejected the notion that the poor are poor because they do indeed have a different set of values and therefore lack the ambition and initiative necessary to succeed in a competitive society. This position, known as the culture of poverty view,

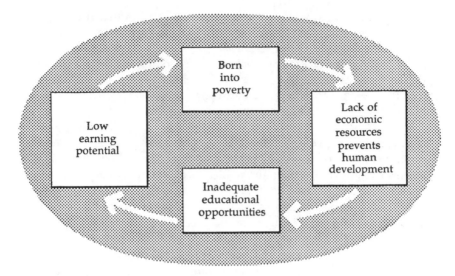

Figure 6-1   Cyclical Nature of Poverty

is well documented by the research of Oscar Lewis, an anthropologist who studied the poor in Mexico.[32] The view was popularized by Edward C. Banfield in his controversial book written in the late 1960s, *The Unheavenly City*,[33] and its revision, *The Unheavenly City Revisited*.[34] Banfield contends that "lower-class poverty . . . has as its proximate (but, as has been stressed, not its remote or ultimate) cause ways of thinking and behaving that are, in the adult, if not elements built into personality, at least more or less deeply ingrained habits."[35] Banfield contends that such poverty is "self-perpetuating," and "inwardly" caused, and that improvements in external circumstances are likely to affect it only gradually if at all.[36] This position, then, is counter to that of the architects of the War on Poverty: the poor are poor not because of a closed opportunity structure, but because they fail to hold the values that are necessary for their success.

The implications of the two positions should be clear. The closed opportunity structure position justifies vigorously pursuing a major effort to open the opportunity structure. The culture of poverty position justifies some attempt to ameliorate or make more tolerable the conditions in which the poor find themselves, but it does not justify initiation of massive federal programs to eliminate poverty. The former position implies the necessity of considerable government action to open the opportunity structure whereas the latter does not.

The emphasis of the War on Poverty was not on the cultural approach. In 1963 Elliot Liebow conducted a major study of unemployed street-corner men in Washington, D.C., and concluded that the values and behavioral patterns he discovered were in reality "shadow" values that the poor had adopted in their not-always-successful attempts to survive in a world with closed opportunity structures.[37]

After deciding on a basic philosophy, the program planners turned to the specific programs that were to be implemented as part of the War on Poverty. These programs were divided into two general categories: local initiative programs and national emphasis programs.

The local initiative programs covered the areas of employment, health, and education and were planned and administered by local community action agencies. The national emphasis programs focused on several major problems common to the poor and funded local attempts to deal with those problems. Certainly Head Start was one of the most important and successful national emphasis programs. It was based on evidence that indicated that children from poor families do not receive the necessary preschool training to prepare them to compete with other schoolchildren. The result was that they quickly fall behind, and by the third or fourth grade, if not sooner, they have learned to expect constant failure and thus refuse to try because they already know the outcome. Head Start was designed to introduce basic concepts (colors, numbers) to preschoolers and to provide them with a range of experiences and skills that would ease the transition to a structured classroom.

Other national emphasis programs included Upward Bound, which enabled promising high school students from poor families to spend the summer of their junior year attending special classes at a college or university in the hope that the experience would increase their desire for higher education; Legal Services, which provided legal advice to the poor; and the Youth Corps, which was designed to increase job opportunities for poor youths by removing them from their immediate environment to a Youth Corps training center in order to increase their work skills and upgrade their attitude toward work. All of these programs required substantial administrative expenditures and were often well staffed with professionals who sometimes received a disproportionate amount of the program's resources in return for their services.

Table 6-6 indicates the amount of money spent on these two types of program, the amount spent for the support of both programs, and the total amount spent from 1965 to 1969, the period when the War on Poverty was at its peak. The total of more than $3.4 billion spent in five years does indicate that a major effort was made to deal with the causes of poverty, but many would contend that the figure is too low in relation to the number of poor. Table 6-6 also indicates an interesting fact: by 1967, the national emphasis programs, which were more strongly controlled by federal bureaucrats and were less responsive to local initiatives, had begun to receive more funds than the local initiative programs, and this trend continued throughout the remainder of the decade. The reason for this shift is basically political and is related to the third aspect of the legislation—the

Table 6-6 Allocations for Poverty Programs 1965–1969 (millions of dollars)

TYPE OF PROGRAM	1965	1966	1967	1968	1969	TOTAL
Local initiative programs	115.2	274.6	275.5	323.3	330.8	1319.4
National emphasis programs	96.4	248.5	453.4	460.8	516.2	1775.3
Support programs	24.9	104.8	75.3	82.7	87.3	375.0
Total	236.5	627.9	804.2	866.8	934.3	3469.7

SOURCE: U.S. Office of Economic Opportunity.

specifics of the program's administration. As the controversy over administration of the program increased, congressional support for it decreased.

The legislation contained what appeared to be a very innocuous section that received little direct reaction from politicians or from the general public during its consideration by the legislators, but that was to have important and far-reaching implications for urban America. The legislation called for the establishment of community action agencies to plan and administer community action programs. The legislation defined a community action program as one

1. which mobilizes . . . resources, public or private, in an attack on poverty;
2. which provides services, assistance, and other activities . . . to give promise of progress toward elimination of poverty or a cause or causes of poverty . . . ;
3. which is developed, conducted, and administered with the *maximum feasible participation* [*emphasis added*] of residents of the areas and members of the groups served; and
4. which is conducted, administered, or coordinated by a public or private nonprofit agency (rather than a political party), or a combination thereof.[38]

This section of the legislation was the cause of many major disagreements. The problem was to determine which community groups (that is, business groups and other private groups) were to participate in the programs and, even more important, what was to be the exact role of the poor in formulating and implementing programs and policies intended to improve their condition. Determination of the role the group affected by a governmental policy is expected to play is important not only for policy development, but also for democratic rule. This topic will be discussed more fully in Chapters 9 and 10. "Maximum feasible participation" is subject to various interpretations, and the leaders of virtually every community action program spent considerable time debating the intended meaning.[39] The result was usually bitterness and mistrust.

Point (4) of the passage just cited also caused considerable public discussion and controversy. This provision created the possibility that community action programs might be outside the formal control of elected officials.

Table 6-7 Possible Institutional Arrangements for Poverty Programs

ADMINISTERING AGENCY	RECIPIENT OF FEDERAL FUNDS
Local government	Either publicly elected officials or officials appointed by publicly elected officials
Mix of private industry and public governmental agencies	Boards usually composed of both private and public officials
Private nonprofit	Officials chosen by the community or officials who had been successful in gaining support of federal authorities

If a group could convince the Office of Economic Opportunity that it was in fact the appropriate agency to administer a community action program, the question of whether it was controlled by city hall was immaterial. The ramifications of this possibility and of the policy decisions that would result from such a situation quickly became apparent to many urban political leaders. As shown in Table 6-7, substantial financial resources might go to agencies over which there was little or no direct public control. If you were an urban political leader, you might be concerned that groups beyond your control and influence might receive separate financial resources from another level of government. These questions of political power and power relationships dominated the early years of the community action programs until passage of the amendment introduced by Representative Edith Green (Dem., Oregon) that gave governors and mayors the power to certify which community action programs were to be recipients of federal funds.[40]

Outcomes

One of the outcomes of the War on Poverty was that it prompted considerable interest, concern, and action with regard to program evaluation and policy analysis in general. Social scientists became quite interested in assessing the success of the programs, measuring their impact on the participants, and determining whether they produced unintended harmful results. Evaluation of the effect of the War on Poverty is difficult, but some broad conclusions are possible.

First, few observers would agree that the War on Poverty succeeded in totally eliminating poverty in America. According to John Donovan, the number of poor in the United States declined from 39 million in 1959 to 24 million in 1969 while the total population increased, thus reducing the percentage of the population experiencing poverty from 22 percent to 12 percent.[41] The problem is to determine what part of that decrease is attributable to the War on Poverty and what the outcome might have been in the absence of concerted government action in this area. Donovan asserts that the ". . . programs authorized by the Economic Opportunity Act . . . were never funded at a level adequate to meet the universe of need to which they were directed."[42] Donovan indicates that the effort to reduce poverty made an important contribution to the decline in poverty, although he hedges a bit on this point. It can also be argued that the general economic growth of the 1960s and the Vietnam War, rather than the War on Poverty, made the main contribution to the decline in poverty. The Vietnam War created a demand for military goods, withdrew large numbers of young men from the work force, and provided a general stimulus to the entire economy.

Clearly, it is impossible to control for all contingencies when planning an attack on poverty. Even President Johnson commented that ". . . I did not know whether we would pass a single law or appropriate a single dollar. But one thing I did know: when I got through, no one in this country would be able to ignore the poverty in our midst."[43] The increased awareness of the existence, extent, and causes of poverty in America may have indirectly influenced many policy decisions. For these reasons it may be both unfair and unwise to conclude that the War on Poverty had little or no impact, just as it would be incorrect to conclude that the program was totally responsible for the partial or total elimination of poverty. Thus the program's specific effect on the incidence of poverty cannot be determined, but there is no doubt that the program did have some positive benefits.

Second, there is evidence to indicate that the local poverty agencies were often used as vehicles for political advancement. Howard Hallman, a member of a private research organization has concluded that one ". . . use of the new organizations by community leaders [was] to build a power base which is transferable to other arenas."[44] Hallman documents several instances of the successful use of the financial resources of community action programs by black and American Indian leaders to launch their political careers. This may have been a very beneficial result of the War on Poverty if one considers that recruitment of political leadership from within the poor community to be a desirable goal. In any event, participants in poverty programs often found that they provided the resources, opportunities, and exposure that were needed to begin their political careers.

It is difficult to reach any definite conclusion concerning the effect of the War on Poverty on the outlook of the poor. An argument can be made that promising to eradicate poverty and then ending the program before the task is completed is a guaranteed way to raise expectations and then lower trust. At the same time it can be argued that the efforts to end poverty had symbolic importance even if they were not completely successful, because they were clear evidence of the larger society's commitment to the poor and to the improvement of their condition. Unfortunately, although much has been written and assumed about the impact of the War on Poverty on the poor, and despite the tremendous research effort generated by the program, there is little documented evidence concerning their feelings about it. For instance, leaders of the North City Area Wide Council, Inc., of North Philadelphia have expressed their frustration and their displeasure with the lack of recognition and the unfair treatment they received from city officials.[45] Although they make a very convincing case against the Poverty Program and state cogent reasons why the poor can expect little assistance from governmental agencies, they fail to consider specifically the impact of their programs on the poor themselves.

An important exception is the research of political scientist Richard L. Cole. Cole investigated the impact of participation in poverty programs on those who participate in numerous poverty programs in the Midwest and combined his data with that from other surveys. His methods are too complex and his conclusions too numerous to be adequately summarized here, but it is important to note his conclusion that ". . . the merits of neighborhood participation . . . far outnumber its potential demerits. It has been shown that citizen participation can improve the delivery of goods and services to the neighborhood, can improve political trust, and can make at least some people more self-governing."[46] Assuming that Cole is correct, it becomes apparent that one of the most important legacies of the War on Poverty is the tradition of increased citizen concern, involvement, and organization. In the final analysis, increased citizen participation may have far greater significance for improvement of the conditions affecting the poor than any other result of the program. Citizen participation is explored further in Chapter 9.

Conclusion

Although the importance of the housing and urban renewal programs and the Poverty Program for urban America should not be overemphasized, it is difficult to find other areas where there is more interplay of politics and policy and where that interplay is more important. Housing and urban renewal policies have been debated in political circles for more than thirty years and the tone of the debate has often been strident. Certainly the discussion about the desirability of ending the War on Poverty that took place in the early 1970s, and the moves that were subsequently made to achieve that end, are a further example of this interplay.

Bear in mind that Johnson's initial success in gaining swift acceptance of the Poverty Program began to erode in the late 1960s and early 1970s as the American military and economic involvement in South Vietnam increased and the mood of the nation became more conservative. Increasing congressional opposition to the War on Poverty and the public's growing concern over rising governmental costs defined the limits of and to some extent determined the outcome of public policy debate and action.

It is clear from this discussion of two policy areas that government programs often have unintended benefits and results. Planning, no matter how carefully done, does not necessarily guarantee the successful implementation of major new programs. The lessons that have been learned and the problems that have resulted from these programs are discussed in the next chapter.

Notes to Chapter 6

1. For an extended discussion of the grant-in-aid approach, see Michael D. Reagan, *The New Federalism* (New York: Oxford University Press, 1972), pp. 54–88.
2. *Catalog of Federal Domestic Assistance: 1969* (Washington, D.C.: Government Printing Office, 1969).
3. The Report of the National Commission on Urban Problems, *Building the American City* (Washington, D.C.: Government Printing Office, 1968), is cited throughout this chapter.
4. *Ibid.*, p. 66.
5. *Ibid.*, pp. 94–103.
6. *Ibid.*, pp. 99–100.
7. *Ibid.*, pp. 66–93.
8. *Ibid.*, pp. 108–133.
9. *Ibid.*, pp. 122–124.
10. Lee Rainwater, *Behind Ghetto Walls* (Chicago: Aldine, 1970).
11. *Ibid.*, p. 9.
12. *Ibid.*
13. *Building the American City*, pp. 152–169.
14. *Ibid.*
15. John F. Kain, "The Distribution and Movement of Jobs and Industry," in James Q. Wilson, ed., *The Metropolitan Enigma* (New York: Anchor Books, 1970), pp. 1–43.
16. 68 Stat. 623, 624 (1954).
17. Peter H. Rossi and Robert A. Dentler, *The Politics of Urban Renewal* (Glencoe, Ill.: Free Press, 1961); and Raymond Wolfinger, *The Politics of Progress* (Englewood Cliffs, N.J.: Prentice-Hall, 1974).
18. Herbert Gans, *The Urban Villagers* (New York: Free Press, 1962), pp. 281–304.
19. Stokely Carmichael and Charles V. Hamilton, *Black Power* (New York: Vintage, 1967), pp. 155–157.
20. *The Urban Villagers*, pp. 305–335.
21. For instance, see Lawrence M. Friedman, *Government and Slum Housing* (Chicago: Rand McNally, 1968); Harold Kaplan, *Urban Renewal Politics* (New York: Columbia University Press, 1963); Herbert Gans, *op. cit.*; and Raymond Wolfinger, *op. cit.*
22. For some descriptive analyses of the War on Poverty, see John C. Donovan, *The Politics of Poverty* (Indianapolis: Bobbs-Merrill, 1973); Sar A. Levitan, *The Great Society's Poor Law* (Baltimore: The Johns Hopkins University Press, 1969); Daniel P. Moynihan, *Maximum Feasible Misunderstanding* (New York: Free Press, 1969); and Richard Blumenthal, "The Bureaucracy:

Antipoverty and the Community Action Program," in Allan P. Sindler, ed., *American Political Institutions and Public Policy* (Boston: Little, Brown, 1969), pp. 128–179. For an interesting discussion of a closely related program, Model Cities, see Edward C. Banfield, "Making a New Federal Program: Model Cities, 1964–1968," in Allan P. Sindler, ed., *Policy and Politics in America: Six Case Studies* (Boston: Little, Brown, 1973), pp. 124–158.

23. Michael Harrington, *The Other America* (Baltimore: Penguin Books, 1963).

24. *Ibid.*

25. *Ibid.*, pp. 9–24, 155–170.

26. U.S. Department of Health, Education, and Welfare, *Report to the Congress on Juvenile Delinquency* (Washington, D.C.: Government Printing Office, 1960).

27. *The Politics of Poverty*, pp. 17–38. See also other sources cited in footnote 22.

28. *Ibid.*, p. 28.

29. *Ibid.*, p. 170.

30. *Ibid.*

31. For a discussion of this point, see Daniel P. Moynihan, "The Professors and the Poor," in Daniel Moynihan, ed., *On Understanding Poverty* (New York: Basic Books, 1968), pp. 3–35.

32. Oscar Lewis, *The Children of Sanchez* (New York: Random House, 1961); Oscar Lewis, *La Vida* (New York: Random House, 1966).

33. Edward C. Banfield, *The Unheavenly City* (Boston: Little, Brown, 1970).

34. Edward C. Banfield, *The Unheavenly City Revisited* (Boston: Little, Brown, 1974).

35. *Ibid.*, p. 143.

36. *Ibid.*

37. Elliot Liebow, *Tally's Corner* (Boston: Little, Brown, 1967), pp. 208–231. Liebow's findings could be interpreted to support a culture-of-poverty approach.

38. As quoted in Sar A. Levitan, "The Community Action Program: A Strategy to Fight Poverty," in *The Annals* 385 (September 1969): 64.

39. See Moynihan, *Maximum Feasible Misunderstanding*, pp. 128–166; and Kenneth Clark and Jeannette Hopkins *A Relevant War Against Poverty* (New York: Metropolitan Applied Research Center, 1968).

40. *The Politics of Poverty*, pp. 150–151.

41. *Ibid.*, p. 170.

42. *Ibid.*, p. 178.

43. Lyndon Baines Johnson, *The Vantage Point* (New York: Popular Library, 1971), p. 72.

44. Howard Hallman, "Citizen Participation in Urban Community Development" in *Urban Community Development Strategies* (Washington, D.C.: Center for Governmental Studies, 1972), p. 46.

45. "Maximum Feasible Manipulation," as told to Sherry R. Arnstein, in *Public Administration Review* 32 (September 1972): 377–389.

46. Richard L. Cole, *Citizen Participation and the Urban Policy Process* (Lexington, Mass.: D.C. Heath, 1974), p. 137.

Chapter 7

Present Policy Choices

Introduction

The preceding chapter focused on public programs that have been in existence for a number of years. This chapter is concerned with more recent
urban phenomena: the debate over the amount and type of federal aid to
the cities; the policy on school desegregation being implemented by the
courts; and the debate over the important environmental question of land
use in the United States. Each of these examples is important because of its
unique contribution to our understanding of the dynamics of urban public
policy, but taken together they offer insights into the following:

1. the importance and effectiveness of the various interest groups
   active in attempting to influence federal policy toward cities;
2. the incremental nature of policy-making;
3. the political forces at work which set the stage for urban
   policy-making;
4. the types of conflicts and disagreements that are likely to bring
   about changes in public policies and to create political controversy in the future.

Before considering each of these points, it is necessary to define the concept of *incrementalism*. Incrementalism means to make policy changes gradually over a long period. Thus policies often evolve as a result of present needs and prior experiences. An excellent example is the housing legislation adopted in 1949, which has been amended periodically since then by the Congress, but always with certain basic concepts remaining the same.

Incrementalism can also refer to the decision-making style or technique used in reaching decisions. This style differs from the opposite decision-making style, referred to as the *synoptic approach*, which includes a careful review of all possible alternatives and available options.[1] According to the incremental model, the decision-maker will choose an option that is perceived to maximize the likelihood of attaining the particular goal that is important at a given time. The decision-maker, because of the limited time he has in which to act and the consequent inability to obtain information on all other possibilities, will not consider all possible alternatives, but will concentrate on those few that are considered to be acceptable.

An example is a police chief confronted with rising crime rates. He might decide that something needs to be done and then .earch for possibilities. It should be clear that his options are many. The chief can try to increase the efficiency of the force by reassigning officers or changing patrol tactics; requesting additional funds in order to hire more police; blaming legal officials for the increase by stressing how "soft" judges and other officials are on criminals; concentrating on reducing the crime he finds most serious and not enforcing other regulations as vigorously; or doing nothing, on the assumption that the situation will eventually change for the better. Using the incremental approach, the police chief is likely to select the option that he perceives to be consistent with past policy choices and that will most likely achieve the objective of a reduced crime rate. The chief is under a time constraint and therefore cannot perform an exhaustive investigation of every available alternative.

Time is often overlooked in many studies of decision-making. If officials do not have sufficient time to make a decision, they may adopt short-run policies that allow them the opportunity to search for the other, longer-term policies that they want.[2] When decision-makers are confronted with the necessity to make rapid decisions affecting a large number of people, their decisions often differ from those that they would have made had there been more time to reach those decisions.

Rapid and major change is unlikely to be found in a policy area previously characterized by incremental change. Taken collectively, the incremental changes may result in major change, but each separate policy change could not be interpreted as being a major change. It is incorrect to assume that policy-makers and public policies change rapidly or that policy-makers always make a complete review of all the alternatives before reaching a decision. The realities of decision-making simply prevent this from happening.

The usual constraints on the public decision-maker (time, ability to absorb material, range of competence) are complicated and intensified by basic political constraints. In making a decision, the elected official weighs the political costs of each alternative; in addition, the official may be subject to substantial pressure by various groups. Given the realities of this situation, is it not realistic to expect policy decisions to result in minimal change?

In this chapter, the three examples of recent policy decisions, as well as the discussion of revenue sharing, considered by some to be a "revolutionary" new program, illustrate the results of incremental decision-making. Although incrementalism has frequently been criticized by many observers of American society, it is a byproduct of the group participation that characterizes American politics.

Revenue sharing

Background

In October 1972, President Richard M. Nixon signed into law the 1972 State and Local Fiscal Assistance Act, which has become commonly known as the general revenue-sharing act. The signing culminated a long process of political interaction and bargaining and is a most interesting and enlightening example of urban policy-making and intergovernmental relations in the United States.[3]

The general revenue-sharing legislation was to return more than $30 billion in federal revenues to state and local governments by 1976. This meant that the more than 37,000 units of local government would receive general revenue-sharing funds on a regular basis. Table 7-1 is a summary of the recipient units of government and the amount of revenue they received in 1972. The proportion will be the same for the duration of the general revenue sharing program, which expires on December 31, 1976, unless renewed by Congress. Note that one-third of the funds is to be given to the states and two-thirds are to be given to the local governmental units. In addition, the nation's municipalities receive 35 percent of the total available funds while counties receive 24 percent of the total funds.

Under the provisions of the legislation, states may spend their funds for any normal and customary purpose, whereas local units of government are required to spend their funds for "priority expenditures" and "necessary and ordinary capital" expenditures.[4] Priority expenditures include public safety (police and fire), environmental protection, public transportation, health and hospitals, recreation and culture, libraries, financial administration, and social services for the poor and aged. These categories are quite broad, and the local units of government have been given considerable discretion in defining the various services that belong in each category. The

Table 7-1 Distribution of General Revenue Sharing, 1972

JURISDICTION	NO. OF RECIPIENT UNITS	AMOUNT RECEIVED (BILLIONS OF DOLLARS)	% OF TOTAL AMOUNT
States	50	1.8	33
Counties	3,047	1.3	24
Municipalities	18,055	1.9	35
Townships	16,255	.3	6
Indian tribes	323	.1	2
Total	37,730	5.4	100

SOURCE: U.S. Treasury Department.

priority expenditure requirement has not created a great deal of difficulty for most localities, and they have not been prevented from spending the money for local projects. The other restrictions in the legislation are few: recipient units cannot use the funds as part of their local contribution to match other federal revenues, the funds cannot be used for discriminatory purposes, the local governments must follow simplified administrative procedures for recording and reporting the use of the funds, and local units must abide by existing federal labor regulations.

In order to understand why enactment of this legislation was possible, it is necessary to understand the climate that prevailed at the time. The late 1960s was a time of tremendous social unrest—even widespread violence—in many American cities. In addition, the costs of the Vietnam War made it increasingly difficult for the national government to continue to provide large amounts of money, under the various categorical grant programs previously discussed, without further inflating an already inflated economy. After the election of Richard Nixon in 1968, an attempt was made to bring the federal budget under tighter control and to reduce spending to less inflationary levels. The cities continued their plea for federal funds, and by late 1969 and early 1970, the press and electronic media were warning of the impending fiscal collapse of many major American cities. According to these accounts, soaring tax rates and increased demands for more and better public services made it impossible for the cities to meet their obligations, and it appeared that only massive federal aid would alleviate the crisis.

In the midst of this controversy, President Nixon proposed general revenue sharing as a cornerstone of his New Federalism, which was designed to return a significant amount of power and responsibility to state and local governments. The Nixon proposal, first formally made in August of 1969, had been changed considerably by the time the State and Local Fiscal Assistance Act was passed in 1972. According to Nixon, revenue sharing was to be a key aspect of the second American revolution; the state and local governments would be provided with the fiscal resources they needed to meet and, it was hoped, solve their pressing problems.[5]

An often overlooked aspect of the enactment of revenue-sharing legislation was the political situation that helped to bring it about. Certainly the intense lobbying efforts of various national public interest groups and state and local officials (for example, the National Governor's Conference, the National Association of Counties, and the National League of Cities) were extremely important.[6] In addition, the debate over the legislation became mixed with Presidential politics in 1972, and it became difficult for announced candidates not to be for general revenue sharing, since opposition implied a distrust of the decision-making process at the local level. In addition, organized labor and civil rights groups, which opposed the legislation, did not press their objections too strongly, nor did they attempt to organize the public against the legislation. Opponents of the legislation found themselves poorly organized and unable to mount an effective effort against the formidable political coalition that had formed. An indication of the general favorable attitude that prevailed toward general revenue sharing was that even when the House and Senate had approved different formulas for the distribution of the funds, compromise was reached by permitting each state to select the formula that maximized the return to that particular state.[7]

The significance of general revenue sharing was that it was a new and unique concept. It had been widely discussed for nearly a decade and was advocated by both Republicans, such as Melvin Laird when he was a United States Representative from Wisconsin, and Democrats, such as Walter Heller when he was an economic adviser to President Kennedy. Heller, a noted liberal economist, was important in conceptualizing the program.[8] According to him, the federal government, because of its income taxing capability, would have a budgetary surplus at the conclusion of the Vietnam War, whereas state and local governments would continue to have considerable difficulties meeting their financial responsibilities because of an inadequate resource base and the unavailability of the tax mechanisms (especially the income tax) necessary to raise funds. Heller advocated that the federal government "share" a portion of the revenue it received from income taxes with the states and localities and permit these localities to decide how to spend the funds and what additional resources they would need to meet their needs. The Heller proposal assumes the existence of a three-tiered federal system consisting of national, state, and local levels of government as well as the availability to the local governments of the necessary resources.

This approach contrasts sharply with the categorical grant approach discussed in Chapter 6. Michael Reagan, in *The New Federalism*, makes a strong case for the categorical grant program. He emphasizes the importance of first meeting national priorities and of mandating that certain requirements be met by recipients prior to receiving funds and as conditions for continued receipt of funds.[9] The categorical grant approach does increase the amount of federal supervision of local decision-making and may, according to one's perspective, result in increased compliance with national goals. For instance, under the urban renewal legislation, a city was required to have a comprehensive plan for future renewal and development. This required most cities to increase the size of their planning staffs, which they probably would not have done otherwise.

A problem with categorical grants is that substantial numbers of federal, state, and local bureaucrats are often required to supervise the distribution of funds, thus reducing the total amount of funds being distributed. In addition, the funds can be used only for specific purposes and their use is carefully monitored. If a city has a water-quality problem, but is ineligible for categorical grants to improve water quality, it cannot use the funds it might receive under another federal categorical program for that purpose. This shortcoming, according to critics of the categorical grant approach, often makes states and localities too dependent on the federal government, whereas general revenue sharing results in increased local control but limited federal accountability.

The categorical grant approach was popular until the late 1960s, when increasing dissatisfaction with it from a wide variety of sources made change inevitable. The interesting thing about general revenue sharing, both the debate over it and its subsequent implementation, is that it means a variety of things to its supporters. The liberal sees it as a way to increase the resources available to state and local governments; the conservative sees it as a way to decrease federal involvement and increase local autonomy. The urban taxpayer often perceives it as a way to reduce local property taxes. Community groups view it as a source of largely unrestricted funds for which they can compete.

Now that general revenue sharing has been in effect for more than three years, it is possible to assess its impact.

Outcome

Although some have contended that the impact of general revenue sharing is impossible to measure, several major empirical research projects with this aim are currently under way. This author and Richard L. Cole of George Washington University made a three-year study of the impact of general revenue sharing on cities with populations of more than 50,000.[10] The Brookings Institution and several other organizations have also conducted extensive research on the effects of general revenue sharing.[11] The results to date make possible the following conclusions.

1. Cities are spending their general revenue-sharing funds in virtually the same ways that they spent other funds in the past. For instance, in 1973 and 1974, the cities responding to the Caputo-Cole research spent an average of 60 percent of their general revenue-sharing funds for law enforcement, fire prevention, environmental protection, street and road repair, and parks and recreation. In 1971, the sums spent by these same cities for these categories amounted to slightly more than 50 percent of their total

expenditures.[12] Thus it would appear that, for a variety of reasons, the general revenue-sharing funds are being spent in about the same proportion for the same items as previously.

2. Although the Caputo-Cole research and the Brookings study apparently differ on the validity of this conclusion, the funds apparently are *not* being used to initiate innovative programs, but to expand or improve already existing ones—and to reduce taxes or stabilize the present tax situation. The Brookings study found that 57.5 percent of the local shared revenue was being spent for new programs, whereas the Caputo-Cole research indicated that 70 percent of the funds was being used for existing programs.[13] Although the funds have frequently been used to initiate new programs, general revenue sharing has also made possible the continuation and improvement of existing programs.

3. The general revenue-sharing funds are being distributed among the economic and racial minorities that benefited from the past categorical grant programs. According to official Treasury Department reports, a small percentage of the total general revenue-sharing funds is being used for health/hospitals and social service programs.[14] Although one cannot conclude that economic and racial minorities have not benefited from general revenue sharing, it appears that they have not received substantial benefits and that their opposition to any attempt to expand or renew general revenue sharing can be expected. In April 1975, representatives of these groups made a statement to the General Revenue Sharing Subcommittee of the Senate Finance Committee that was strongly critical of the program and recommended that major changes be made if the legislation were renewed.[15]

4. One important result of general revenue sharing has been that it has helped to stabilize local tax rates. Table 7-2 indicates the amount of shared revenue received by 20 of the nation's 50 largest cities in 1972 and the percentage of their local expenditures represented by general revenue sharing funds. Note that the program's impact varied greatly from city to city. Washington, D.C., having the smallest percentage (2.7 percent) of its city expenditures of the cities in the table, reflected in general revenue sharing and El Paso, Texas, the largest (17.2 percent). Note that for many cities, general revenue sharing funds are equivalent to the revenue that would result from a small to medium local tax increase, and thus it appears that, as several of the studies indicate, general revenue sharing has indeed been responsible for postponing local tax increases or reducing the amount of any tax increase needed to meet governmental needs.

An interesting question in this area is whether inflation has limited the cities' ability to provide public services. New York City's serious financial problems brought that city close to bankruptcy in late 1975.[16] The causes of the cities' fiscal problems are many and varied, but certainly the ability of all cities to provide public services has been affected by inflation. The increased need for supplies and equipment has further increased costs dur-

Table 7-2 Amount of General Revenue Sharing Funds Received in 1972 by 20 of America's 50 Largest Cities as Percentage of Local Expenditures

CITY	AMOUNT RECEIVED	% OF CITY EXPENDITURES
New York	$247,524,126	3.1
Chicago	69,477,799	9.1
Los Angeles	35,422,819	5.9
Philadelphia	43,758,115	6.3
Detroit	36,530,556	8.5
Houston	15,029,925	9.3
Baltimore	23,881,944	3.6
Dallas	9,699,255	5.9
Washington, D.C.	23,647,564	2.7
San Antonio	7,785,895	12.2
Boston	17,753,054	4.1
St. Louis	12,702,004	7.9
New Orleans	14,744,411	12.7
Phoenix	9,280,433	10.2
Pittsburgh	11,679,788	12.0
Denver	12,189,871	6.9
Kansas City, Mo.	10,222,903	7.8
Atlanta	4,583,171	2.8
Honolulu	12,542,903	8.4
El Paso	5,473,903	17.2

SOURCES: Joint Committee on Internal Revenue Taxation; U.S. Department of Commerce, Bureau of the Census.

ing this inflationary period. (For example, many cities must purchase salt, gasoline, and other items if snow is to be removed and police patrol cars kept running.) In addition, cities are under tremendous pressure from their employees to grant cost-of-living raises—increases that will help them meet inflationary costs and are not based on merit. If inflation is 10 to 15 percent per year (as it frequently was between 1970 and 1975), then cities must increase employee payrolls by a similar amount in order to permit employees to not *lose* purchasing power. The problems created by wage inflation have been the most serious for the nation's large cities. Because property taxes are not directly tied to inflation, cities have found themselves in the position of having to meet inflationary demands without a matching increase in locally obtained revenue. The inevitable result has, in some cities, been delayed by general revenue sharing, but without increased funding, the crisis calls will continue to be sounded.

5. Although the evidence is fragmentary and inconclusive, general revenue sharing may, in the long run, result in increased participation in local politics. Groups that have tended to look to the national government for assistance may now be convinced that important resources are available at the local level and that political power should be brought to bear on the federal government to obtain those resources.[17] This point will be discussed more fully in Chapters 9 and 10.

Whatever the facts might be about the impact of general revenue sharing, it appears that general revenue sharing has continued to receive broad general support. Certainly local officials support it. Testifying before the Senate Finance Committee's Subcommittee on General Revenue Sharing in April 1975, Walter Washington, Mayor of Washington, D.C., stated: ". . . we like the flexibility of the program and would prefer to see it passed one year in advance so that we can take it into account when we do our budgeting."[18] In addition, there is substantial evidence to indicate that more than 95 percent of the nation's mayors and city managers strongly support the program.[19]

The debate over general revenue sharing has been confined largely to decision-makers, but the general public has had extensive involvement and impact in the next policy-choice area—education. The choices affecting educational policy will be certain, as the next section indicates, to generate public discussion and debate.

Education

Background

During the past decade, the nation's urban educational systems have undergone considerable change and have frequently been the center of controversy. Partly because of the widely held belief that education can help solve some of the major problems that exist in American society, programs for policy change have consistently included criticism of the existing educational structures and specific recommendations for changes in them. Probably most interesting is the question of whether the educational system has been asked to perform functions that other institutions, such as the church or family, might better perform. As Edward C. Banfield has argued, "The most widely recommended 'solution' to the problems of the city is more and better schooling. There is almost nothing that someone does not hope to achieve by this means. . . ."[20] Banfield takes the position that ". . . the possibilities for improving the city by reforming its schools are sharply limited."[21] Nevertheless, he goes on to explain how and why school and education policies should be changed. Thus even the conservatives place considerable emphasis on the effect of education on the quality of urban life. A variety of reasons have been given for this increased emphasis on educational policy.

First, education has long been emphasized in America. Even in colonial times, the importance of the basic communication skills of reading and writing was acknowledged. The development of the free public schools meant that poverty could frequently be compensated for by access to public education, which provided the training necessary to succeed in a very competitive economic system.

Second, urban schools, for a variety of complicated reasons, have been affected by decisions reached in other areas, and problems in the schools have sometimes resulted from inaction in these areas. An excellent example is de facto school segregation. De facto (in fact) segregation is not dictated by official policy or law, but is the result of circumstances existing in the community. For example, residential housing segregation often leads to segregated schools unless considerable efforts are made to prevent this situation. Although most Americans are reluctant to admit it, many American cities are in fact racially segregated. Karl and Alma Taeuber conclude that their investigation indicates ". . . strong and consistent support for the conclusion that Negroes are by far the most residentially segregated large minority group in recent American history."[22]

Figure 7-1 depicts a hypothetical city whose class and racial differences are representative of those in most American cities in 1975. The housing and school-related problems that are created by the segregation in this city are clear. Note the tendency for neighborhoods to be fairly well defined and homogeneous. If educational decision-makers had to determine where schools were to be located, what strategies would be available to them? Figure 7-2 indicates two possible strategies. The first would be to place the schools in the center of the homogenous neighborhoods. The second would be to place the schools on the neighborhood boundaries so that each school would be attended by students from neighborhoods that were economically and racially different. An argument has been and continues to be made that schools are best left out of the problem of racial segregation and that ending residential segregation rather than school desegregation is the more realistic answer.

The essential point, however, is that the schools are directly influenced by factors not directly related to the educational system. They are being blamed for the problems created by the absence of effective societal integration. Certainly this concern is an indication of the increased interest in educational decision-making in many cities.

Another important reason for the increased emphasis on educational policy is that parents are more concerned about the quality of the education their children receive. When a group of citizens feels that the schools attended by their children are inferior, requests for action can be anticipated. In many cities lower-class parents have voiced concern over the crowded conditions in deteriorating schools that are staffed, they frequently argue, by teachers unsympathetic to the needs and attitudes of the students. This theme was common in the late 1960s, and it led to a concerted effort by the residents of many cities to gain community or neighborhood control of the schools. As will be indicated in Chapter 8, community or neighborhood control has meant and continues to mean different things to different people, but it has become a catchword, much like "power to the people," used to indicate dissatisfaction with the present situation and a desire for meaningful policy change.

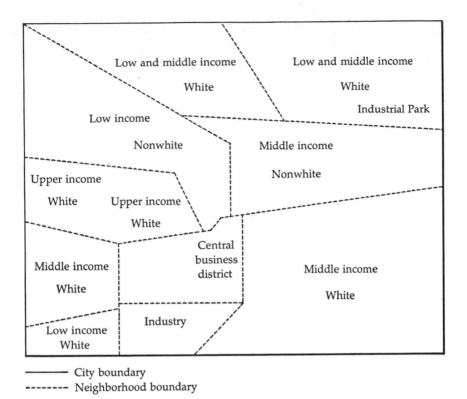

Low and middle income

White

Low and middle income

White

Industrial Park

Low income

Nonwhite

Middle income

Nonwhite

Upper income

White   Upper income

White

Central
business
district

Middle income

White

Middle income

White

Industry

Low income
White

——————— City boundary
- - - - - - - Neighborhood boundary

Figure 7-1   Neighborhoods in a "Typical" American City, 1975

Finally, education has become politicized because of the growing awareness on the part of the educational professionals that they are more open to
public scrutiny and criticism. Thus teachers' organizations have become
more insistent on job security, lower pupil-to-teacher ratios, and such
economic considerations as salaries, fringe benefits, and leave policies. In
most American cities, educational expenditures account for 40 to 60 percent
of the total local government expenditures; this percentage has not increased substantially in recent years. When such a large proportion of the
total budget is spent on the educational program, a fluctuation in the
educational budget becomes a major concern for all taxpayers, and the
question of increased expenditures becomes the subject of intensive debate.[23] Policy and budgetary matters are critical to the professional
educator, and in many cities teacher and administrative organizations have
attempted to have more of a say in such matters as contractual negotia-
tions and school decentralization decisions by increasing their participation
in local politics.

One of the more interesting results of this increased activity has been the
often intense rivalry between the long-established National Education As-

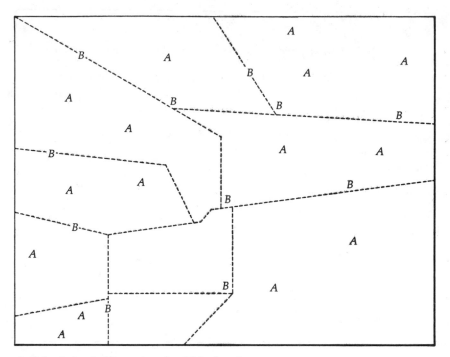

A: Schools located in center of neighborhoods
B: Schools located on neighborhood boundaries

The Bs would establish schools with clientele from different racial and economic neighborhoods. The A pattern would be to continue the isolation of the neighborhood. Obviously, the two patterns are "ideal" types, but certainly the A pattern is dominant in many American cities.

Figure 7-2   Alternative School Placement Practices in a Residentially Segregated City

sociation (NEA) and such organized labor groups as the American Federation of Teachers (AFT). The AFT has forced the NEA, which has long stressed its professional approach to educational problems, to become more aggressive in dealing with public officials when dissatisfied with conditions. As a result teachers' strikes have become more common in the past few years.

This active interest in educational policy-making, combined with the decisions of the courts concerning the schools, has helped to fuel the political controversy that currently exists in many cities facing school desegregation problems.

School desegregation

For the past twenty-five years America's cities have been faced with a continuing and increasing pressure to integrate their schools along racial lines. The question of how best to achieve school integration is central to urban politics, whether in Boston, Indianapolis, Richmond, or San Francisco. Although slavery ended more than a hundred years ago, the United States has not totally committed itself to racial equality. Black Americans still earn less than whites with similar educational and occupational experience and are still subjected to subtle forms of discrimination.

In 1954, the United States Supreme Court struck down the doctrine of "separate but equal" that had prevailed in many areas of the nation for more than fifty years.[24] "Separate but equal" meant that public authorities could provide separate public facilities, such as schools or school buses, for blacks and whites so long as such facilities were in fact equal. In an 1896 decision, *Plessy* vs. *Ferguson*, the Supreme Court had ruled that racial segregation was not unconstitutional if equal facilities were made available.[25] The 1954 decision in the *Brown* case maintained that racial discrimination does deprive the members of a minority group of equal educational opportunity, even if separate and equal facilities are provided, and therefore is a violation of Constitutional rights.

This decision was important because it included schools as public services and prepared the way for consideration by the courts of cases dealing with both de jure (by or according to the law) and de facto school segregation. In the ensuing 21 years, the progress (or lack of progress) made in integrating America's schools has been the subject of debate. Although the Court has consistently reached decisions that have excluded laws requiring de jure racial segregation, it has not always been vigorous in imposing deadlines and specifying requirements for meeting desegregation orders. Promoters of school desegregation have been aided by two provisions of the 1964 Civil Rights Act.

The 1964 Civil Rights Act stipulates that federal funds will be denied any school district that refuses to desegregate. Since the federal government has increased the amount of resources given to local educational districts, this is often an effective incentive to desegregate. In addition, the 1964 Civil Rights Act permits the Justice Department, through the Attorney General, to institute legal suit to end discrimination if, in his opinion, individuals affected by such policies are unable, for economic or other reasons, to institute appropriate lawsuits.

The result of the public controversy over these judicial and legislative actions has been increased concern over school segregation in urban schools.[26] Legal redress has been sought by parents who felt that the schools were de facto segregated—that is, that segregation resulted even though there was no law or policy stating that race was to determine which students were assigned to which schools. (As pointed out earlier, racially homogeneous neighborhoods are responsible for a considerable amount of the racial isolation that exists in neighborhood schools.) Despite the absence of such a law establishing segregation, the federal courts have continued to rule that segregation of public school facilities, no matter how or why, is unconstitutional, and that all due deliberate speed must be taken to de-segregate the schools.

The controversy has at times had ominous overtones. In Boston, during the 1974–1975 school year, racial tensions increased until the city had to use armed police to protect black children being bused from the predomi-nantly black area of the city, under a federal court-imposed integration order, to attend classes in the white ethnic stronghold of South Boston. The "Southies" angrily claimed that they objected to the loss of neighborhood autonomy and not to the busing of pupils to achieve racial balance. For months South Boston was the scene of violent confrontations.

The controversy over the issue of busing has not been confined to Bos-ton, but has been common to most cities having substantial nonwhite populations. The usual rule of thumb is that all schools in a particular school district have to have the same proportion of their students drawn from the racial minority as the proportion of minority students in the district as a whole. Thus, if 15 percent of a school district's elementary school students are nonwhite, the enrollment of each elementary school in that district must be approximately 15 percent nonwhite. To achieve racial balance, most cities must change existing school boundaries and some must institute busing and other means of transferring pupils. Figure 7-3 depicts the geographical problems that are created and gives a variety of possible strategies to meet federal desegregation requirements. As the figure indi-cates, the immediate problem is the racial balancing of the school popula-tion. Option 1 requires the busing of nonwhite students to predominantly white schools. Option 2 requires busing of white students to predominantly nonwhite schools. Option 3 combines both types of busing to achieve racial integration.

It should be obvious that each of the options, plus a fourth one, doing nothing, has real economic and political costs. Certainly Mayor Kevin White of Boston has experienced his share of political problems as a city leader who cannot, due to the power of the federal courts and his lack of direct control over school board policies, do much to influence policy in this area. Either of the first three approaches requires the expenditure of additional funds by the school system, and many contend that this money would be better spent on curriculum improvements and other benefits rather than transportation.

Despite public outcries and dissension, school busing to achieve racial balance in the schools is a fact of life for many American communities. The benefits of increased contact between members of different racial balance in

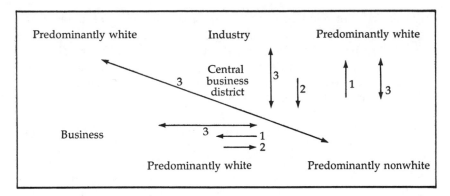

Predominantly white or nonwhite = 95% of area having same racial composition

Total number of school students who are nonwhite = 20% of total school population

Total number of elementary school students who are nonwhite = 25% of total elementary school population

Total junior/senior high school students who are nonwhite = 15% of total junior/senior high school population

Figure 7-3   Possible Desegregation Strategies for a City

the schools is a fact of life for many American communities. The benefits of increased contact between members of different racial groups and the (assumed) equalization of all educational facilities within a school district are thought to outweigh the transportation costs and the loss of neighborhood autonomy associated with busing.[27] Interestingly enough, in some communities, opposition to busing has come from both conservative and radical groups. The conservative sees busing as federal intervention in an area where federal action is not justified and, specifically, as one more step toward the undermining of individual freedeom. The radical sees busing as a liberal attempt to use nonwhites to salve the conscience of bigoted, but guilt-ridden, Americans. Nonwhite children learn more readily in predominantly nonwhite schools that emphasize their common heritage. In addition, forcing nonwhite students to be part of a predominantly white environment during school hours will only increase individual tension and will not result in meaningful improvements or increased opportunities for the students who have been transported.

Outcome

In the mid-1970s, there is little reason to be optimistic about the long-range impact of school desegregation efforts. Residential segregation continues and in many areas has increased, because it has become increas-

ingly difficult for nonwhites to meet the financial burden of home ownership during the inflationary and recessionary tendencies of the past few
years. The effectiveness of integration in terms of improving reading rates
and increasing overall achievement has not been clearly documented, but a
strong case can be made for the conclusion that the results will be marginal
at best and will probably vary considerably from specific example to specific
example. Meanwhile, the political controversy continues.

In 1974, Congress passed an extension of most of the programs included
in the Elementary and Secondary Education Act of 1965.[28] The version of
the bill passed by the House contained an amendment that would have
prohibited ". . . students from being bused beyond the school next closest
to their homes" and would have permitted prior court-imposed busing
orders to be reopened for consideration if they failed to comply with the
"next closest to their homes" ruling.[29] The Senate, in a series of one-vote
decisions, actually expanded the basis for busing, and the conference committee almost failed to resolve the differences. The Senate version finally
prevailed following agreement that the legislation would call for reconsid-
eration of court-ordered busing systems if ". . . the time or distance
traveled impinged on the educational process or endangered the student's
health."[30]

Obviously, Congress has received considerable communication from the
public on this question. Some citizens have argued for constitutional
amendments barring busing, and some groups have utilized the tactic of
passive resistance. The concern may well be that the emphasis on racial
integration may divert valuable attention and resources from efforts to
improve the overall quality of urban school systems. By creating a politically charged atmosphere, busing may render meaningful learning impossible. On the other hand, can there be quality education for all if racial
separation exists? This is obviously a critical question requiring careful
thought.[31]

Closely related to this question is the question of tactics and strategies.
James S. Coleman, whose 1966 report, *Equality of Educational Opportunity*, has been widely cited as a justification of school integration, attracted
considerable public attention when he modified his position in 1975 and
asserted that the political and social costs of school busing to achieve racial
integration might exceed the benefits to be gained, and that busing might
actually aggravate the condition it was attempting to alleviate by increasing
the probability that whites would leave cities where school integration
attempts were likely to be made.[32] This is an interesting and important
example of a policy decision that had major unanticipated consequences,
and it indicates the difficulty of accurately predicting the outcomes of various policies.

One last point should be emphasized. To date, the courts have been
reluctant about ordering busing across school district lines. If the courts'

position on this matter should change, the implications for and the potential impact on urban America would be profound. Most important, integration may force suburban school systems whose curriculums have traditionally been academically oriented to accept less well-prepared students, whereas students from usually inferior inner-city schools may have access to much-improved facilities and curriculums. Although the possibility of this happening is somewhat remote, in the next twenty-five years areawide efforts may be necessary to deal with racial separation in the schools. If such efforts prove unsuccessful, the courts may have to modify their denial of the separate but equal doctrine. In any event, school integration will continue to be a major political issue in America's cities.

Land use planning

Background

In recent years environmentalists and business interests have clashed over the purposes for which urban land should be utilized. As is true of most aspects of urban life, the debate over land use planning has been quite intense. At one extreme are those who advocate that planning, if necessary, is strictly a local matter; at the other extreme are those who maintain that there should be coordinated and integrated land use planning on a state or even a regional basis.

Certainly a major reason for the controversy is the way most land use decisions are reached. Tables 7-3 and 7-4 summarize land use activities, expenditures, and employment for local governments in 1967 and 1968. Table 7-3 shows that costs are highest and that the maximum number of employees are employed within SMSAs. Table 7-4 indicates the existence of a wide range of land use activities. Note (Table 7-4) that a municipality or a county is much more likely to perform some type of land use regulation activity if it is within an SMSA. Note also that a municipality is much more likely to perform a land use activity than a county.

The data support the contention that land use activities are decentralized. This local autonomy often results in unique decisions regarding rules and operating procedures to handle difficulties as they arise. A distinction can be made between two different types of land use policy.

The first is the passive or reactive approach. The policy-making institution enacts a minimum number of restrictions and requirements and readily responds to requests to alter them. Land use personnel perceive themselves as facilitators of growth and development. In contrast, the conservationist approach emphasizes containment of growth—that is, permitting it to occur only if it does not have an adverse effect on other public facilities or on the environment. Perhaps two different approaches to the planning of suburban subdivisions best exemplify the two types of land use policy.

Many suburban areas of the United States have experienced rapid and

Table 7-3   Land Use Expenditures and Employment, 1967

TYPE OF GOVERNMENT	PER CAPITA EXPENDITURE, 1967	NO. OF FULL-TIME EMPLOYEES PER 100,000 INHABITANTS
Metropolitan area governments		
Within SMSAs	$2.16	23.8
Outside SMSAs	.70	7.7
County governments		
Within SMSAs	.54	5.5
Outside SMSAs	.28	2.5
Municipalities		
Within SMSAs, 1960 population of		
50,000 or more	2.31	26.2
5,000–49,999	1.95	22.2
Less than 5,000	.50	14.5
Outside SMSAs, 1960 population of		
5,000 or more	1.34	15.8
1,000–4,999	.48	4.2

SOURCE: National Commission on Urban Problems, *Building the American City* (Washington, D.C.: Government Printing Office, 1968), p. 211.

Table 7-4   Land Use Regulation Activities of Local Governments, 1968

TYPE OF GOVERNMENT	% OF GOVERNMENTS HAVING				
	PLANNING BOARD	ZONING ORD.	SUBDIV. REG.	BLDG. CODE	HOUSING CODE
Metropolitan area governments					
Within SMSAs	46	54	56	54	57
Outside SMSAs	54	46	44	46	43
County governments	15	7	11	5	4
Municipalities with more than 1,000 inhabitants in 1960	58	72	65	78	81

SOURCE: National Commission on Urban Problems, *Building the American City* (Washington, D.C.: Government Printing Office, 1968), p. 208.

virtually unplanned growth. Commercial developers were often able to purchase land at modest rates and to develop it without following any carefully planned development goals because policies requiring planning were sometimes nonexistent. Rapid suburban development frequently meant an increase in the public demand for such services as sewerage, water, education, and public safety. One result was that many suburbs adopted legislation requiring developers to provide certain services such as roads, water, and sewerage without cost to ne city. Naturally, the builder tended to pass these increased costs along to the prospective homeowner, thereby raising the total cost of the home and decreasing the number of people who could afford to move. The end result was a decline in the population growth rate of that area.

An alternative approach has been the carefully planned "ideal" community, in which land use authorities plan the provision and location of such public facilities as hospitals, schools, and parks, as well as the amount, price, and location of housing. This has resulted in a generally improved environment. Land use authorities often also exercise the right to regulate the external appearance of homes, lawn additions, what can and cannot be parked in front of the home, and the size of business signs in residential areas.

Naturally, these two approaches, like the two approaches to overall land use, are attractive to different people for different reasons. Some individuals are willing to give up their rights for what they perceive to be an improved public good. Others feel that they will lose some of their rights and decrease the quality of their lives by allowing land use authorities increased control over their actions. These persons will choose to live in areas where they are not subject to such restrictions.

For whatever reasons, there is little doubt that physical growth patterns in the United States, especially in the urban areas, have not been subject to considerable planning. The magnitude of the problems that are concomitant with urban development is made clear in this passage from the report of the National Commission on Urban Problems, entitled *Building the American City*:

> About 18 million acres of land will come into urban use for the first time in the course of the next 30 years, and the process of rebuilding and rehabilitation will replace large parts of present urban areas. Just as land-use decisions made years ago affect the quality of today's urban environment, so decisions made today and tomorrow will shape the quality of urban life for future generations. Reluctance to provide affirmative guidance for land development will not prevent development from occurring. Rather, inaction now will allow undirected and haphazard development; inaction, therefore, represents a decision about the future urban environment, just as careful positive action does.[33]

A consideration of the politics of the present land use debate is now in order.

Present policy

Several essential questions are being discussed in the present debate over land use policies, and they can be summarized as follows:

1. What level of government should establish land use policies?
2. What criteria should be used in establishing those policies?

3. How "open" should the decision-making processes establishing these policies be?

As the concern for environmental quality increased in the late 1960s, so did the request for federal action to deal with it. The environmental legislation of the late 1960s and early 1970s attempted to deal with the results of growth and development after they had taken place. In the early 1970s there began to be some public interest in enacting land use policies that would increase the power of state and regional authorities to control urban development. At present, a major problem with most local land use decisions is the absence of any coordinating efforts with adjacent or nearby jurisdictions.

In a typical SMSA, there may be 50 to 75 local governments making some type of land use decision. Even if each of them operated in a logical manner, the development of the entire SMSA might be quite haphazard. It has been argued that the state needs to take a more active role in land use planning and control if coordinated planning and development are to be achieved. The National Commission on Urban Problems has maintained that it is necessary to establish ". . . state or regional machinery to reconcile conflicts among local governments and between local governments and special-purpose agencies, and to plan and act on matters demanding a broader-than-local perspective. . . ."[34]

Although the federal government has tried to promote this coordination by requiring evidence of various types of planning before issuing funds and the creation of review boards, such as councils of government, that have limited authority, state or regional land use authorities with sufficient strength have not been established. There have been instances in which public pressure strongly influenced growth decisions (such as the voters of Colorado defeating a referendum issue calling for state funds to help finance the 1976 Winter Olympics), but these have been exceptional.

In early 1975, Representative Morris K. Udall, Democrat from Arizona, tried to have a national land use bill adopted.[35] Udall was an announced Presidential candidate at the time and had consistently sided with environmentalists on the key environmental issues facing Congress. Udall's proposal, HR3510, provided funds for states that developed a statewide land use policy. The proposed legislation utilized the carrot approach in that it offered financial incentives for states that participated but did not require those states that did not wish to participate to do so.

The debate on the bill turned on the question of states' rights versus economic considerations. There is general agreement that the legislation, although it was often publicly opposed because of its tendency to limit the powers of state and local governments, may have been opposed mostly because of the feeling that increased control over development would increase the cost to the private sector and decrease business interests' ability to realize high profits from such development.[36] As Senator Floyd Haskell

(Dem., Colorado) remarked, "I can see why the homebuilders were against it. They want to build any place they can buy land."[37] Others have argued that union opposition to the measure was based on the fear of loss of jobs and the economic loss that would result from planned growth and development.

Similar legislation introduced by Senator Henry Jackson (Dem., Washington) had passed the Senate in 1974, but the House of Representatives voted 204 to 211 against considering a measure similar to the Udall measure, and for all practical purposes discussion of the legislation was finished for that session of Congress. The Udall proposal failed to receive committee approval and was not considered by the full House despite the coalition of freshman representatives and liberals who were elected in November 1974. Only time will resolve the question of whether there ever will be any federal land use legislation.

Outcomes

Obviously, future decisions regarding land use will be critical to urban development. Uncertain as future developments in this area may be, it is safe to conclude that local involvement may result in more and stricter controls in some areas and fewer controls in others. For instance, Oregon residents have persuaded the state government to follow a basic no-growth policy by not attempting to attract new industry or to recruit new residents. Similar happenings may be expected in other areas of the nation as the threat to environmental quality becomes more direct and better understood by more citizens.

At the same time, one can raise the legitimate question of whether increased planning and control will in fact improve the quality of the environment. Planners often largely disagree over what procedures should be followed to ensure successful planning as well as what direction planning should take. The costs of planning efforts are often assumed to be outweighed by the results obtained, but is this always a realistic assessment?

This question cannot be resolved here, but it does indicate the general complexity of the entire planning process. One final point should be made. Planning, as was pointed out in the discussion of urban renewal, can and often does have a variety of unanticipated and often negative side effects. Planners must take them into consideration.

Conclusion

The consideration of the three policy areas in this chapter permits the following conclusions:

1.   Urban policy-making is usually an incremental process.

2. Specific interest groups often interact vigorously during the policy development and implementation stages.
3. Assessment of the impact of specific policies and programs, although frequently difficult, must be carefully done.
4. There has been a general tendency, since the 1930s, for the national government to become increasingly involved in providing resources and other incentives to state and local governments to help them meet their problems.

The difficulty of assessing the impact of a program should not be underestimated. There is now a growing group of professionals who are attempting to make such an evaluation of various programs.[38] They are attempting to answer such questions as: Is a program's impact measured by the number of people it affects? Is it measured by the general conditions it creates? Or is it measured by a combination of these? The problem is that it is often virtually impossible to isolate the interactions that may be taking place at any specific time.

It is important to realize that the three programs discussed in this chapter are actually influencing the quality of life in America's urban centers at the present time. General revenue sharing has been used as a model for other programs involving intergovernmental revenue transfers. Both school busing and comprehensive land use legislation remain divisive and controversial issues. These and other programs attempt to deal with the symptoms and not the basic causes of many of the problems facing urban America. The basic structural reforms that have been designed to bring about major change in urban organization and governance are considered in Chapter 8. Their contrast to the policy choices discussed in both this chapter and Chapter 6 should be carefully noted.

Notes to Chapter 7

1. For two interesting views of this debate over decision-making, see Charles E. Lindblom, "The Science of 'Muddling Through,' " *Public Administration Review* 29 (Spring 1959): 79–88; and Herbert A. Simon, *Models of Man* (New York: Wiley, 1958), pp. 241–260.
2. For an interesting discussion of this aspect of policy-making, see Robert F. Kennedy, *Thirteen Days* (New York: Norton, 1969), pp. 124–128.
3. There are several excellent books about the legislative struggle that preceded enactment of general revenue sharing. See Richard E. Thompson, *Revenue Sharing: A New Era in Federalism* (Washington, D.C.: Revenue Sharing Advisory Service, 1974); and Paul A. Dommel, *The Politics of Revenue Sharing* (Bloomington: Indiana University Press, 1974). See also Samuel H. Beer, "The Adoption of General Revenue-Sharing: A Case Study in Public Sector Politics," paper presented September 4, 1975, at the meeting of the American Political Science Association, San Francisco, September 2–5, 1975.

4. See David A. Caputo and Richard L. Cole, *Revenue Sharing: The First Actual Use Reports* (Washington, D.C.: The Office of Revenue Sharing, 1974), pp. 44–45.
5. Presidential remarks made when signing the general revenue sharing legislation, *Weekly Compilation of Presidential Documents*, October 23, 1972 (Washington, D.C.: Government Printing Office, 1972), pp. 1534–1536.
6. *The Politics of Revenue Sharing*, pp. 68–177.
7. See David A. Caputo and Richard L. Cole, *Urban Politics and Decentralization: The Case of General Revenue Sharing* (Lexington, Mass.: D.C. Heath, 1974), pp. 51–52.
8. Walter W. Heller, *New Dimensions of Political Economy* (Cambridge, Mass.: Harvard University Press, 1966). For a discussion of the history of the concept of revenue sharing, see Maureen McBreen, "Federal Tax Sharing: Historical Development and Arguments for and Against Recent Proposals," in *Revenue Sharing and Its Alternatives* (Washington, D.C.: Government Printing Office, 1967).
9. Michael D. Reagan, *The New Federalism* (New York: Oxford University Press, 1972), pp. 54–88.
10. *Urban Politics and Decentralization: The Case of General Revenue Sharing, op.cit.*
11. Richard P. Nathan, Allen D. Manvel, and Susannah E. Calkins, *Monitoring Revenue Sharing* (Washington, D.C.: The Brookings Institution, 1974). The League of Women Voters has also initiated a major project aimed at assessing the impact of general revenue sharing.
12. *Urban Politics and Decentralization: The Case of General Revenue Sharing*, pp. 70–73.
13. *Monitoring Revenue Sharing*, p. 193; *Urban Politics and Decentralization*, p. 98.
14. *Revenue Sharing: The First Actual Use Reports*, pp. 4–5, 10–11.
15. See the statements made by Clarence Mitchell of the National Association for the Advancement of Colored People and William M. Taylor of the Center for National Policy Review before the General Revenue Sharing Subcommittee of the Senate Finance Committee, April 17, 1975.
16. For a discussion of New York's fiscal problems, see "Mayors Urge Revenue Sharing Extension," *New York Times*, June 27, 1975, p. 1.
17. *Urban Politics and Decentralization*, pp. 103–108.
18. Walter Washington's comments before the Senate Finance Committee's Subcommittee on General Revenue Sharing, as quoted in *Nation's Cities* (May 1975), p.8.
19. *Urban Politics and Decentralization*, pp. 108–116.
20. Edward C. Banfield, *The Unheavenly City Revisited* (Boston: Little, Brown, 1974), p. 148.
21. *Ibid.*, p. 149.
22. Karl E. Taeuber and Alma F. Taeuber, *Negroes in Cities* (Chicago: Aldine, 1965), p. 68.
23. See David T. Stanley, *Managing Local Government under Union Pressure* (Washington, D.C.: The Brookings Institution, 1972), pp. 112–135. See also Harry H. Wellington and Ralph K. Winter, Jr., *The Unions and the Cities* (Washington, D.C.: The Brookings Institution, 1971).

24. *Brown* v. *Board of Education* 347 U.S. 483 (1954).
25. *Plessy* v. *Ferguson* 163 U.S. 537 (1896).
26. For some interesting case studies on this subject, see Robert L. Crain, *The Politics of School Desegregation* (Chicago: Aldine, 1968).
27. For a discussion of the relation between race/economic class and educational opportunities/achievement, see Christopher Jencks *et al.*, *Inequality: A Reassessment of the Effect of Family and Schooling in America* (New York: Basic Books, 1973); James S. Coleman *et al.*, *Equality of Educational Opportunity* (Washington, D.C.: Government Printing Office, 1966); Charles E. Silberman, *Crisis in Black and White* (New York: Random House, 1964), pp. 249–307.
28. *Congressional Quarterly Weekly Report* 32, No. 52 (December 28, 1974): 3423.
29. *Ibid.*
30. *Ibid.*
31. For a discussion of this dilemma, see *Equality of Educational Opportunity*, pp. 3–34, 217–333, and 460–489.
32. See Coleman, *op. cit.*, and for a summarization of the recent adaptation Coleman has offered to his original position see the *New York Times*, June 7, 1975, p. 25, and June 8, 1975, Section IV, p. 7.
33. National Commission on Urban Problems, *Building the American City* (Washington, D.C.: Government Printing Office, 1968), p. 234. See also M.G. Scott, *American City Planning Since 1890* (Berkeley: University of California Press, 1969).
34. *Building the American City*, p. 234.
35. For a discussion of this legislation, see "Land Use Legislation: A Precarious Future," *Congressional Quarterly Weekly Report* 33, No. 9 (March 1, 1975): 428–432.
36. *Ibid.*, p. 431.
37. *Ibid.*
38. The interest of professional political scientists in public policy analysis has increased considerably in recent years. At present there are three journals (*Policy Sciences, Evaluation,* and the *Policy Studies Journal*) devoted exclusively to that subject.

Chapter 8

Possibilities for Institutional Change

Introduction

The preceding two chapters dealt with the specifics of several major programs and policies, but they did not consider the possibilities for institutional change in urban America—that is, changes in the governmental structures whose purpose is to provide public services. Table 8-1 summarizes the levels of government responsible for providing most of the public services in the urban United States. Note that municipalities and townships bear the prime responsibility for police and fire protection, sewage disposal, refuse collection, parks and recreation, water supply, and libraries. In many areas school districts are separate from local governments. The state is frequently responsible for highway maintenance and welfare assistance. When the previously discussed role of the federal government in both categorical grant and revenue-sharing programs is added to this mix, it results in a very complex set of intergovernmental relationships. This complexity clearly affects the decision-making process.

Unfortunately, the study of intergovernmental relations has been largely ignored by political scientists, and the amount of published research on this subject is quite limited.[1] Intergovernmental relationships are both horizon-

Table 8-1 Type of Government and the Provision of Public Services for the Fifty States in 1967

FUNCTION	TYPE OF DOMINANT SERVICE PROVIDER*				
	STATE	COUNTY	MUNICIPALITY/ TOWNSHIP	SCHOOL DISTRICT	SPECIAL DISTRICT
Education	1	3	4	40	0
Highways	46	0	0	0	0
Public welfare	35	11	3	0	0
Hospitals	28	10	2	0	4
Health	29	2	4	0	0
Police	1	0	47	0	0
Fire	0	0	50	0	0
Sewage	0	0	41	0	3
Refuse collection	0	0	49	0	0
Parks and recreation	0	2	44	0	2
Water supply	0	0	45	0	2
Libraries	1	14	30	0	3

SOURCE: Advisory Commission on Intergovernmental Relations, *Governmental Functions and Processes: Local and Areawide* (Washington, D.C.: Government Printing Office, 1974), Table 1-1, p. 3.

*A dominant service provider is one that accounts for more than 55 percent of the direct general expenditure in a particular function.

tal and vertical, as shown in Table 8-2. Vertical relationships, among the local, state, and national levels of government, are the most commonly studied. They are the attempts made by officials in urban centers to influence decisions made by other levels of government. One example is the frequent requests by mayors of large cities for congressional legislation that would increase the amount of financial aid given to their city. Another example is the attempts by citizens of an urban area to obtain state or federal intervention to solve a specific problem or alleviate a certain condition. In Chicago in 1974, a patrolman's group obtained a court-ordered interruption of general revenue-sharing payments made by the Treasury Department to the City of Chicago that was to remain in effect until the city adopted less discriminatory hiring and promotion practices.

Documented evidence is also lacking concerning the nature and extent of meaningful horizontal intergovernmental relationships, but it is reasonable to assume that the increase in horizontal relations between urban municipalities signifies greater cooperation and mutual interest in arriving

Table 8-2 Intergovernmental Relations and Urban Politics

TYPE OF RELATION	EXAMPLES	
Horizontal	Municipality–municipality County–county	State–state Federal–federal
Vertical	Municipality–county Municipality–state Municipality–federal	County–state County–federal State–federal

at joint solutions to common problems. For instance, two suburbs might combine their resources to provide better police and fire protection to adjacent areas of each locality.

Intergovernmental relations are important determinants of policy choices available to decision-makers. Consider for a moment the important area of environmental quality. If a city (B) is downwind of a major city (A), which is a polluter, the residents of B can request that city A do something to alleviate the condition, or they can appeal to a higher level of government (for instance, the state or federal environmental protection agency).

The interaction between central cities and their suburban areas is especially important. If a metropolitan area has only a few relatively large and well-defined cities, the likelihood that there will be meaningful intergovernmental cooperation within that area is usually greater than if the area were composed of many small and heterogeneous communities. Similarly, it may be difficult to obtain much cooperation if the city and surrounding suburbs have different physical characteristics, or if the views of their residents sharply differ. Mutual distrust and a desire for autonomy contribute to the lack of horizontal intergovernmental relations in most metropolitan areas.

The nature of future intergovernmental relations in the United States is briefly considered in this chapter. The first section reviews several attempts to achieve vertical centralization. The second section considers some attempts to strengthen horizontal relationships. The concluding section analyzes the institutional arrangements and their significance for urban public policy. First, however, one last point should be mentioned.

Political theorists and others have long debated the meaning of the Constitution with regard to urban political institutions and policy-making and the nature of federalism in America.[2] The position taken in this chapter is a pragmatic one because no ideological or theoretical position alone suffices to explain present urban governmental institutions. The powers of urban governments have in the past been restricted, but this does not mean that they will not be expanded in the future. Earlier practices, although they obviously will influence future actions, need not solely determine them.

In 1872, Judge John F. Dillon set forth his judgment about the proper role of municipal governments:

> It is a general and undisputed proposition of law that a municipal corporation possesses and can exercise the following powers and no others: First, those granted in express words; second, those necessarily or fairly implied incident to the power expressly granted; third, those essential to the accomplishment of the declared objects and purposes of the corporation, not simply convenient, but indispensable. Any fair, reasonable, substantial doubt concerning the existence of power is resolved by the courts against the corporation, and the power is denied.[3]

Although "Dillon's rule" has customarily been followed in interpreting the legal power of cities, there is every reason to believe that future developments, both in the courts and the legislatures, will render it obsolete. If the urban centers of today are to meet the challenges of tomorrow, they need the ability to develop new intergovernmental relationships.

Changes in vertical relations

This section considers changes in two types of vertical inter-governmental relations that have occurred in recent years. Both have been hailed as major innovations and are useful for gaining an understanding of the dynamics of American federalism.

Crime control

Any discussion of crime in America almost inevitably results in controversy. For whatever reasons, most Americans are concerned about crime. But there are substantial differences of opinion as to exactly what constitutes a crime and whether in fact crimes are reported accurately. The *Uniform Crime Reports for the United States*, compiled by the Federal Bureau of Investigation (FBI), include a variety of statistics on the type and frequency of crime in the United States.[4]

The conclusions that "official police statistics consistently indicate that in general urban areas have higher crime rates than rural areas . . . [and that] the rate of serious crimes per 100,000 population appears to increase with the size of the community . . . "[5] are applicable to most metropolitan areas in the United States. The FBI has developed an index of seven crimes, four of which are crimes against people (murder and non-negligent manslaughter, forcible rape, robbery, and aggravated assault) and three of which are crimes against property (burglary, larceny and theft over $50, and auto theft). These classifications are used to compile a crime index for a particular jurisdiction. Table 8-3 summarizes the violent crimes committed against people and property in the United States in 1965–1973. Note the substantial rise in both crime rates, except in 1972, when property crimes decreased. Note also that crimes against people more than doubled during the period, while property crimes increased drastically, but at a slower rate. The data in Table 8-3 clearly indicate that criminal activity in the United States has increased, and this obviously explains the increased public concern about crime in recent years.

Table 8-4 reports the crime rate in the United States by area in 1973. Note that suburban areas have much lower crime rates than cities with more than 250,000 inhabitants, but substantially higher crime rates than rural areas. But, more interesting, note that the crime rate in suburban areas is higher than that in rural areas for all types of crime except murder. Tables 8-3 and 8-4 indicate that criminal activity in the United States increases as size of area and population density increase.

Table 8-3   Crime in the United States: 1965–1973

| YEAR | CRIME RATES PER 100,000 PEOPLE | |
	VIOLENT	PROPERTY
1965	198.3	2243.1
1966	218.2	2427.7
1967	250.8	2705.4
1968	295.5	3036.2
1969	325.4	3311.3
1970	361.0	3588.1
1971	393.0	3732.8
1972	398.0	3527.1
1973	414.3	3702.1

SOURCE: U.S. Department of Justice, Federal Bureau of Investigation, *Uniform Crime Reports for the United States* (Washington, D.C.: Government Printing Office, 1973), Table 2, p. 59.

Table 8-4   Crime Rate in the United States by Area, 1973, per 100,000 People

| | AREA | | | |
TYPE OF CRIME	TOTAL U.S.	CITIES WITH MORE THAN 250,000 INHABITANTS	SUBURBAN	RURAL
Violent				
Murder	9.3	20.7	5.1	7.5
Forcible rape	24.3	51.4	17.8	12.0
Robbery	182.4	571.5	76.1	17.7
Aggravated assault	198.4	359.9	149.5	110.2
Total violent	414.3	1,003.5	248.5	147.4
Property				
Burglary	1,210.8	1,949.3	1,054.4	564.0
Larceny-theft	2,051.2	2,651.8	1,952.4	677.6
Auto theft	440.1	978.4	307.4	82.8
Total property	3,702.1	5,579.5	3,314.2	1,324.4
Total	4,116.4	6,582.9	3,562.7	1,471.8

SOURCE: U.S. Department of Justice, Federal Bureau of Investigation, *Uniform Crime Reports for the United States* (Washington, D.C.: Government Printing Office, 1973), p. 2.

Various reasons are given for the increase in the crime rate, but caution must be exercised in interpreting the FBI's *Uniform Crime Reports for the United States* for the following reasons:[6]

1.   Reporting problems are common. The definition of a particular crime varies among jurisdictions. What may be robbery in one jurisdiction may be aggravated assault in another. In addition, if a person commits a series of crimes, only the most serious is counted. Thus armed robbery that is followed by murder and auto theft is recorded only as murder. Finally, many serious crimes, such as arson, kidnapping, and assault and battery, may result in substantial physical injury, but are not included in the statis-

tics of the *Uniform Crime Reports for the United States* because they do not fit an appropriate category.

2. A great deal of crime in the United States apparently goes unreported. Crimes against people may not be reported because the victim and the offender are relatives. For a variety of reasons, victims of property crimes may prefer that those crimes not be reported.[7] In addition, there are numerous examples of victimless crimes, such as illegal gambling and prostitution, which are seldom if ever reported. Estimates as to the amount of unreported crime vary, but experts usually agree that inclusion of unreported crime would boost the crime rate between 100 and 400 percent.[8] If this is in fact true, then urban America is even less safe than many have thought.

3. Crime statistics are indeed important resources for urban politicians and law enforcement officials. The mayoral candidate who can attack the incumbent's prior record and the incumbent who can cite crime statistics that indicate a decline in the crime rate are both at an advantage. In addition, police officials often use crime statistics to influence important policy decisions. The police chief who is asking for more funds may have a difficult time obtaining them if the crime rate is low or decreasing. Thus, in some situations, an increasing crime rate is to the advantage of the police and public officials; in other situations, a decreasing crime rate is advantageous.

It is clear that the analysis of crime in urban America is a difficult process. Despite these reservations about the accuracy and use of crime statistics, the following general conclusions about crime in America's cities are possible:

1. Crime is increasing in urban America.
2. Property crime rates have increased significantly in the past 10 years.
3. Crime rates are higher in urban areas of the United States than in urban centers in other countries.
4. The public's concern about crime is high.

An intense campaign has been waged by many local law officials and by the general public to increase federal involvement in the fight against crime. They were assisted in their efforts by the 1968 Presidential campaign of Richard M. Nixon, which, according to Richard Scammon and Ben Wattenberg, was successful partly because it focused on the issues of crime, drugs, racial pressure, and political disruption. By taking a "tough" position on crime, Nixon tapped the fears of the American public. Nixon maintained that the rights given to criminals by the Supreme Court when Earl Warren was the Chief Justice were excessive and emphasized the cost to society when criminals were not vigorously prosecuted.[9]

Even before the 1968 campaign, there was considerable interest in obtaining increased federal action to deal with the rising crime rate. In 1965,

President Lyndon B. Johnson established the Commission on Law Enforcement and Administration of Justice, which became known as the Katzenbach Commission.[10] In its report, *The Challenge of Crime in a Free Society*, the Commission reviewed the problem of crime in the United States and made a series of specific suggestions on how to cope with it. Following is a summary of the Commission's recommendations for a meaningful federal program to combat crime in America. According to the Commission, the program should meet the following needs:[11]

1. state and local planning;
2. education and training of criminal justice personnel;
3. survey and advisory services for criminal justice organizations;
4. national information system coordination;
5. demonstration programs;
6. technological research and development;
7. institutes for research and training;
8. funding for innovations.

Note the emphasis on the planning, training, and research aspects of crime prevention and control. Note also that the implied federal role is to provide the financial resources necessary to effect the changes recommended by the Commission.[12] In other words, the Commission recommended increased federal grants to the states, which would channel part of them to the cities. In terms of the vertical intergovernmental relations discussed earlier in this chapter, the recommended program does not represent a new role for the federal government, but rather an increase in its present role.

It is important to note that, despite the public's increased concern about crime and the favorable political climate for major change, there has been no major effort to change the nature of intergovernmental relations in the United States to deal with crime. No political leader has argued for the creation of a powerful national police force to control crime at the local level. Rather, the common plea has been for a sizable increase in the financial resources made available to the state and local police forces to deal with crime. Even when increased funds were granted to state and local governments, they were not always earmarked for the purpose of reducing crime or changing the conditions responsible for the increase in crime. The conclusion seems inescapable that even though major change in vertical intergovernmental relations may be desirable, useful, or necessary, such change, if and when it does occur, will be an evolutionary process.

The Housing and Community Development Act of 1974

As indicated in earlier discussions, the federal government has been involved in both categorical grant programs and general revenue-sharing programs. One of the major accomplishments of the Nixon and Ford administrations has been the consolidation of a number of categorical grant programs into more unified programs based on the block grant concept. These "special revenue-sharing" programs grant substantial discretion to local decision-makers and reduce administrative costs and requirements while allowing greater federal control than allowed by the general revenue-sharing program. Manpower training and community development are the best examples of such programs and for our purposes the Housing and Community Development Act of 1974 is most important.

Title I of the Housing and Community Development Act of 1974 created the Community Development Block Grant Program.[13] This program replaces the categorical grant programs dealing with urban renewal, Model Cities, water and sewer facilities, open spaces, neighborhood facilities, and rehabilitation and public facilities loans. Under this program, federal funds go directly to the general-purpose local government unit having the broadest legal authority to deal with community development. Cities with populations of more than 50,000 and most counties with a population of more than 200,000 receive funds according to a formula that takes into account the size of the unit's population, their poverty level, and their housing conditions. Other cities may compete for the remaining funds, and those cities with populations of less than 50,000 that are already receiving funds for urban renewal or Model Cities programs will continue to receive funds until those programs are completed.

The funds received by the city or county can be used in any part of the city or county as long as the needs of low- and moderate-income groups and urgent community development requirements are met. The Department of Housing and Urban Development (HUD) administers the block grant program and is responsible for its overall quality. The emphasis is on careful planning, implementation, and evaluation of development efforts rather than the piecemeal approach that characterized the categorical aid programs. Cities receive funds only after they develop a satisfactory comprehensive plan for general community development.

The legislation is unique because it

1. combines several major programs;
2. decreases the administrative costs of grant application procedures;
3. emphasizes coordinated planning with balanced development as its main objective;
4. requires citizen input at various stages of the community development process; and
5. represents a compromise between the general revenue sharing and categorical aid approaches.

Although it is too early to assess the ultimate impact of the program, it is important to estimate what some of the program's effects will be. For instance, how will different urban groups benefit from the block grant funds and will the funds be allocated where most needed? To what extent will political participation by different community groups affect the decision-making process and hence the future of the program?

In many respects, the Housing and Community Development Act represents a compromise on the question of federal control over federal funds and thus is an important change in the attitude toward vertical intergovernmental relations, which in the past have been defined in absolute terms. The establishment and outcome of future programs will depend on the success or failure of this one, and obviously, future vertical intergovernmental relations will be directly affected by what transpires as a result of this legislation.

Changes in horizontal relations

Centralizing urban governments

As was previously mentioned, the entire question of horizontal intergovernmental relationships has received little attention from policy analysts. Local governments in particular have been ignored. However, their importance should not be underestimated because they are frequently in contact with neighboring units of government, and actions taken or not taken in one locality often directly affect the residents of other localities. For example, in a metropolitan area having 25 separate governmental jurisdictions, the law enforcement practices concerning illegal gambling, drug traffic, and prostitution affect the entire area.[14] If enforcement practices differ among jurisdictions, one can expect a difference in citizen behavior.[15] Similarly, if one city has a major industrial plant that emits toxic substances, the entire region will probably be polluted. Finally, the lack of housing in one area may lead to increased crowding or the deterioration of already existing housing in other areas.

Reformers and those advocating orderly policy-making have sometimes stressed the need to develop mechanisms to coordinate the policies of these multiple governments and to attempt to make them consistent with one another.[16] This goal can be accomplished by means of a council of governments, an area planning commission, federation, consolidation, or some combination or variation of these. Consolidation and federation are considered here because they are the most widely discussed, and understanding them is important to understanding the dynamics of urban intergovernmental relations.

Figure 8-1 depicts a representative standard metropolitan statistical area in the United States in the mid 1970s; Table 8-5 compares the main county, county *E*, with the surrounding counties. Figure 8-1 shows that policies and circumstances outside the control of a particular jurisdiction may substantially affect the quality of the environment within that jurisdiction. For example, if the residents of county *D* do not have good sewage-treatment

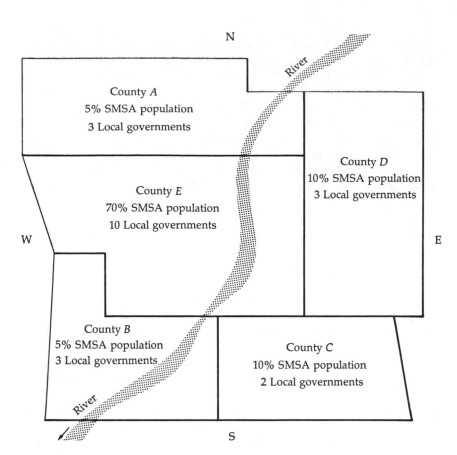

Figure 8-1   Representative Metropolitan Area

facilities, major water problems will be created for the residents of county *E* and county *B*. If the prevailing winds are from the west and northwest, industrial air pollution from counties *A*, *B*, and *E* might cause deterioration of the air quality of counties *C* and *D*.

Regional policies and actions also affect social and economic developments. If decisions are made in any of the counties surrounding county *E* that will attract business and industry away from that county, the leaders of county *E* may be faced with the problem discussed in Chapter 3: an increasing demand for public services that cannot be met because of the decreasing resource base. The movement of industries (and hence employment) to the suburbs, primarily because of the availability of less expensive land, has been well documented by urban economists.[17]

The differences in the population composition of the counties are considerable, as indicated in Table 8-4. County *E*, which includes the central city, is the population center of the regional area; 43 percent of the SMSA's

Table 8-5 Population Characteristics of Component Units of Representative SMSA

COUNTY	% OF SMSA POPULATION	% OF COUNTY POPULATION	% WHITE-COLLAR	MEDIAN FAMILY INCOME	% NONWHITE	% ETHNIC
County A	5					
Unit 1	1	20	90	$15,000	—	3
Unit 2	1	20	85	11,900	—	2
Unit 3	3	60	95	16,100	1	2
County B	5					
Unit 1	1	20	25	7,800	1	3
Unit 2	2	40	30	8,200	1	7
Unit 3	2	40	20	8,000	1	6
County C	10					
Unit 1	9	90	50	9,300	1	15
Unit 2	1	10	40	8,700	1	35
County D	10					
Unit 1	1	10	20	6,600	5	25
Unit 2	7	70	65	8,900	2	60
Unit 3	2	20	30	7,100	6	35
County E	70					
Unit 1	11	18	15	9,200	12	25
Unit 2	43	62	50	9,500	35	35
Unit 3	7	10	20	7,800	15	10
Unit 4	2	3	70	13,500	1	15
Unit 5	1	1	60	12,200	1	20
Unit 6	1	1	60	11,900	2	18
Unit 7	1	1	20	11,000	12	65
Unit 8	1	1	5	4,500	21	40
Unit 9	1	1	35	7,800	2	60
Unit 10	2	2	20	9,300	4	70

population lives in unit 2 in county *E*. In addition, county *E* has all but a small proportion of the region's nonwhite population and the heaviest concentration of ethnic populations. Counties, *A*, *B*, and *C* are more homogeneous than county *D*.

Given these socioeconomic and population characteristics, several possibilities for governmental reform exist. The first is the consolidation of all the governmental units within any one county. City-county consolidation would be a major centralizing step. It would usually result in county-wide elections for all major political offices, countywide tax rates, and countywide provision of services. The Advisory Commission on Intergovernmental Relations (ACIR), created by Congress in 1959 to investigate and recommend ways to improve intergovernmental relations in the United States, summarized the claims of consolidationists as to the benefits of county government as follows:

1. Public services within the metropolitan area will be more adequate and more efficiently provided.
2. The residents of a metropolitan area will have greater access to and control of regional decision-making.
3. Comprehensive and coordinated programs will be developed in accord with an explicit metropolitan plan.
4. Interlocal functional conflict will be abolished.[18]

The main point of the argument is that consolidation will restore order and rationality where they are thought to be lacking. For example, assume that all 26 units of local government listed in Table 8-5 have individual police and highway departments. Figure 8-1 indicates that many of the outlying areas of a particular jurisdiction are closer to the center of the next jurisdiction than to the center of their own jurisdiction. County *B*'s northern and eastern edges are closer to the centers of county *A* and county *C* than to the center of county *B*. If the police and highway departments were consolidated by county, the new police and highway departments would be able to (1) provide services more efficiently and more equitably to the entire county; and (2) enjoy economies of scale (reduced costs because of increased size) in purchasing and obtaining supplies.

Consolidation will also increase the opportunity of citizens to interact with the officials of the political institutions that directly affect them, not merely the political institutions in the jurisdiction where they reside. Theoretically, this increased access should open up the political system and make it more responsible to the problems that affect the entire county. On the other hand, there may be times when policy decisions may be quite beneficial to the residents of a large area of the county, but may create unanticipated and adverse problems for the residents of other, smaller jurisdictions. Then the interests of the larger group would prevail because of the principle of the greatest good for the greatest number.

Opponents of consolidation often maintain that such centralization of power disregards basic rights of individuals to form governments to govern themselves. A related argument is that as the size of governmental units increases, governments lose contact with their constituents and become less responsive to their needs and demands. The published research on the attitudes of opponents of consolidation is not extensive, but several conclusions can be drawn from it.

First, reaction to consolidation is often closely related to self-interest. If a resident assumes that consolidation will result in increased taxes or a decrease in public services, opposition can be expected. On the other hand, if a resident feels that consolidation will result in increased public benefits or lower taxes, support will be forthcoming. In addition, if consolidation causes the elected political leaders of the various jurisdictions to lose their positions (there may only be one mayor instead of 10), it would be logical for them to oppose it.[19]

Second, opposition to consolidation is often dictated by a person's philosophical and, at times, ideological beliefs. David Booth, in his study of the attempt to consolidate the governments in Nashville and in Davidson County, Tennessee, concluded that community leaders who opposed consolidation did so because of their concern that this was part of the ". . . Communist plot to take over the world."[20]

Third, although it is not always discussed in the debates over consolidation, racial concern is often apparent. Interestingly enough, the concern is not just expressed by suburban whites. That this is possible is illustrated by Table 8-5. In the hypothetical SMSA, the nonwhite population is 18.4 percent of the total population. A very small percentage of the populations of all the counties except *D* and *E* are nonwhite. Less than 3 percent of the population of county *D* is nonwhite. However, more than 23 percent of the population of county *E* is nonwhite, and more than one-third of the population of unit 2 within that county is nonwhite. The white residents in most of the jurisdictions view consolidation, especially consolidation of more than one county, as a way of increasing the political power of the nonwhite population because it broadens the resource base for the provision of services, thus giving them an incentive to participate and possibly increasing their influence on areawide decisions.

But nonwhites may interpret consolidation as an attempt to decrease their power. For example, since the nonwhites residing in unit 2 of county *E* are 35 percent of that city's population, their political strength should be increasing. If unit 2 is experiencing the usual pattern of population movement common to such cities (whites leaving in large numbers and being replaced by nonwhites), nonwhites obviously can expect their political power to increase. Thus they probably will interpret any attempt to enlarge the boundaries of government as a direct attempt to dilute their political power. On the other hand, the argument can be advanced that the resources necessary to meet the pressing problems of unit 2 may be obtained only by combining surrounding governmental units and thereby increasing the resource base. This argument will be discussed in more detail in later chapters.

In summary, then, it is important to note the conclusion reached by a team of researchers that studied officials who publicly opposed consolidation in Indianapolis, Indiana: "Elite opposition, even in a single geographic area, may encompass a wide variety of complex views and . . . it may be a mistake to assume, as have most observers, that a single broad generalization is applicable to such opposition."[21] Similarly, Amos Hawley and Basil Zimmer concluded from the research they conducted in the 1960s that "the opposition of suburban residents to governmental consolidation is, in fact, one of our most unequivocal findings . . . central city residents were far from agreement that consolidation is desirable."[22] Motives are difficult to assess, but it is clear that residents of particular governmental jurisdictions, although they may be dissatisfied with city services, are quite likely to be reluctant to give up the autonomy and control that the local jurisdiction provides them.

Consolidation can also be analyzed from a political point of view. For instance, what are the political forces that help to bring consolidation about? The few consolidated areas that do exist in the United States are consolidations of one county and not of an entire metropolitan area. The most widely cited examples of city-county consolidations are Baton Rouge, Louisiana; Nashville–Davidson County, Tennessee; Jacksonville–Duval County, Florida; and Indianapolis–Marion County, Indiana. Extensive documentation exists concerning these four areas[23] as well as attempts at consolidation that failed. Most of these consolidations occurred when a majority of the central city residents and a majority of the county residents voted in favor of a specific consolidation plan.

Table 8-6 illustrates four possible outcomes of voting in consolidation referendums. If a majority of both central city and county residents were to vote in favor of consolidation, as just described, the consolidation effort would be defeated in three of the four examples listed in Table 8-6. Note that in example *D*, even though a majority of those voting voted Yes, the consolidation effort failed. This is a common result when a majority is required in each jurisdiction, rather than in the entire area, to adopt consolidation.

A public referendum is the usual way of obtaining approval of consolidation proposals, but the consolidation of Indianapolis–Marion County, Indiana, the largest consolidated area in the nation, was effected in an unusual way.[24] Because of the strength of the Republican party in the state legislature and the strong leadership of Republican Mayor Richard G. Lugar, consolidation of Indianapolis and Marion County was accomplished by legislative action. The state legislature did not require a public referen-

Table 8-6 Four Possible Outcomes of Voting in Consolidation Referendums

JURISDICTION	% OF TOTAL COUNTY POPULATION	EXAMPLE A % VOTING FOR	EXAMPLE A OUTCOME	EXAMPLE B % VOTING FOR	EXAMPLE B OUTCOME	EXAMPLE C % VOTING FOR	EXAMPLE C OUTCOME	EXAMPLE D % VOTING FOR	EXAMPLE D OUTCOME
Central city	51	50	Does not pass	51	Passes	40	Does not pass	80	Does not pass
County									
Suburbs	34	51		70		90		48	
Rural areas	15	10		35		90		45	

NOTE: Assumption is that same percentage of voters vote in each of the jurisdictions for all 4 examples.

dum, but simply adopted consolidation as the new form of government for the area. Although the specifics of this consolidation are too complex to discuss here, it does seem to have been brought about by social, economic, and political factors that were unique to this situation, and therefore no useful conclusions can be drawn from it. Direct state legislative action, however, may be a new strategy for those who favor consolidation and wish to eliminate the need for extensive public debate and perhaps even a referendum.

Some conclusions are possible about the impact of consolidation on the quality of life in the areas that have adopted it. According to the ACIR Report, consolidation has

1. considerably expanded public services;
2. increased political accountability and responsiveness;
3. eliminated duplication of services;
4. increased financial resources;
5. created some economies of scale;
6. not eliminated minority dissatisfaction with governmental services; and
7. encountered difficulty in providing uniform and differentiated services.[25]

Consolidation is apparently difficult to achieve, and even when such reorganization is accomplished, the results are not always as planned.

Probably most important is the fact that consolidation does not always reduce the conflict between the areas within the newly created governmental jurisdiction. An underlying assumption of consolidation is that the residents of the areas are indeed willing to concede that areawide problems and decisions must at times take priority over purely local wants and needs. As the situations previously discussed in the consolidation section indicate, such concessions are seldom made.

Federation is similar to consolidation, but the two concepts differ in several important respects. A federation is an areawide unit of government that usually has limited responsibilities. Written agreements define the powers of the federation and the relationships between this areawide unit and the local units of government. The prerequisites of federation are the realization that there are commonly desired areawide goals, and the willingness of the local units to relinquish much of their autonomy. The entire five-county area in Figure 8-1 would constitute a federation; an areawide government would be responsible for some services, but the local jurisdictions would still be responsible for others. At present, two metropolitan areas in the United States (Miami–Dade County, Florida, and Minneapolis–St. Paul, Minnesota) and one Canadian city (Toronto) have a federated form of government.

In Miami–Dade County, there are two tiers of local government: the local units and the areawide unit. Both tiers have equal legal power. In this federation, such services as transportation and welfare are provided by the areawide tier of government.[26] A service becomes part of this areawide institution's responsibility when it becomes too costly for the local units alone to finance, or when it does not require extensive transfers of corporate wealth. Despite the general acceptance of this two-tiered system, a series of lawsuits have challenged the legality of the assignment of responsibility for providing some of the public services.

Minneapolis–St. Paul is a unique federated system. It has no direct service responsibilities and thus is not considered a general-purpose unit of government. The ACIR Report states that "The Twin Cities Metropolitan Council, created in 1967, has resolved intra-metropolitan policies and programs, coordinated and controlled the activities of hitherto independent metropolitan bodies, and acted as the policy board for practically all of the federally encouraged areawide programs in the state."[27] Given the Council's limited formal power, its apparent success must be attributed to a variety of factors. Probably the single most important one is the awareness in the Twin Cities metropolitan area of the importance of collective decisions and their impact throughout the entire area. The Metropolitan Council has controlled suburban development by establishing policies to regulate sewage disposal and the maintenance of highways and airport facilities.

In both of these examples, federation has apparently alleviated some of the pressing problems facing the metropolitan areas, but it has not resolved those problems. The desires of the local units of government have not always been reflected in the formulated area plans. In general, if an areawide unit of government begins to grow too powerful, it may be subjected to the same criticisms as are frequently made of consolidation. On the other hand, an areawide unit of government may have difficulty mediating disputes between local governmental units unless it has some powerful enforcement mechanism.

In sum, although federation may prove quite useful, it frequently fails to accomplish many of the goals desired by the local governmental units. In fact, it may actually reduce accountability by limiting direct public access to the policy-maker.

Decentralizing urban governments

In this section two types of community reorganization efforts are considered that have been aimed at increasing citizen control over governmental services: neighborhood autonomy and neighborhood federation. The assumption of both is that even a city with a population in excess of, say, 100,000 people may in fact be too large and that its political institutions must therefore be restructured so that they will be more responsible and representative. In other words, it must be decentralized from the metropolitan area. The city depicted in Figure 8-2 is one that can be easily divided into seven discrete neighborhoods, identified by the letters. Table 8-7 summarizes the basic socioeconomic composition of each neighborhood. The table shows that neighborhoods *D* and *F* are the two most dissimilar, whereas neighborhoods *A* and *B* and *E* and *G* are quite similar. Despite these apparent similarities, the aggregate data in Table 8-7 indicate the differences that exist.

Neighborhood autonomy Perhaps the strongest recent argument for decentralization to the neighborhood level has been advanced by Milton Kotler.[28] Kotler, who was active in neighborhood organizing in Columbus, Ohio, has maintained that "to understand this new political movement, we must understand the nature of the neighborhood, so long ignored or misunderstood, and with that understanding we must examine the nature of the modern revolution of local control."[29] Kotler's main point is that modern cities have been imperialistic in forcing neighborhoods having strong identities and recognizable needs for different types of city services to become part of the larger city. The result has been the continued growth of the central city without an increasing qualitative or quantitative improvement in the provision of city services to the neighborhoods.

To Kotler, the neighborhood is the key for several reasons. First, it is composed of people with similar socioeconomic backgrounds and shared interests and needs. Second, the neighborhood, not the larger city, is a common reference point for the people who live there—it represents their life. Third, the neighborhood has distinct physical characteristics that make its needs for public services unique. Because of the age, condition, and purpose of its buildings and streets, for example, each neighborhood requires different public services, and thus one citywide agency cannot possibly effectively serve all of the city's neighborhoods. Advocates of decentralization thus reach the inescapable conclusion that the neighborhood must assert its independence and assume the responsibility of providing services to its citizens.

Equally important, ". . . the neighborhood achieves an economy of its own to yield enough wealth to preserve its local political liberty."[30] This cannot be done by simply increasing the neighborhood's control over the provision and delivery of services or by waging strong, aggressive action against the larger city. It can be accomplished only by establishing a type of neighborhood corporation that will make decisions that cover ". . . the same areas as those of any government—namely, finance, imports and exports, war and peace, territorial defense and laws."[31] Everyone in the neighborhood must have a vested economic and political interest in that neighborhood. In addition, internal decision-making must be sound, equitable, and efficient; otherwise, the corporation will lose its power and potential and will be of little value to the neighborhood.[32]

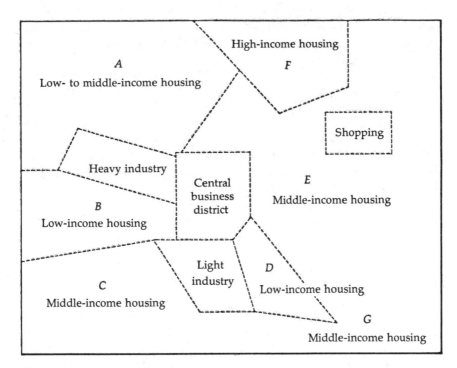

Figure 8-2   The "City" and Its Neighborhoods

Table 8-7   Characteristics of Neighborhoods in Figure 8-2

NEIGHBORHOOD	% OF CITY POPULATION	% NONWHITE	MEDIAN INCOME	% WHITE COLLAR
A	10	50	$ 7,200	10
B	15	60	7,400	15
C	20	10	9,200	30
D	10	90	5,400	15
E	20	5	10,200	45
F	10	1	17,500	90
G	15	10	11,000	60

Instead of the one city government that is assumed to exist in the hypothetical city (Figure 8-2 and Table 8-7), neighborhood decentralization, if the citizens of the individual neighborhoods demanded it, would result in seven separate autonomous units of government. As Table 8-7 indicates, not all the neighborhoods would have the same economic resource base. Neighborhoods D, A, and B (in that order) have the lowest median income; neighborhoods F, G, and E (in that order) have the highest. However, advocates of neighborhood autonomy would maintain that the citizens of neighborhoods A, B, and D also have access to business wealth because they are adjacent to industrial and commercial developments. Such financial resources could be utilized to provide the services required by the neighborhood.

In his classic statement justifying neighborhood autonomy and explaining how it can be brought about, Kotler discusses the transfer of authority.[33] He is aware that present city administrators are unlikely to yield control without a struggle, but he argues that a clear and concise demand for neighborhood autonomy may succeed if the neighborhood can demonstrate its own independence and lack of political allegiance to the larger unit. To Kotler, negotiation for the transfer of power from the city officials to the neighborhood leaders is the key, because the police and military authorities possess armed power and will readily use it if provoked.[34] In sum, neighborhood decentralization will succeed only if the neighborhood is cohesive, organized, and dedicated to changing the normal structure of community decision-making.

Unfortunately, it is impossible to assess the success or failure of the neighborhood plan as envisioned by Kotler because examples of its occurrence are few. Obviously, the threat of decentralization has been and continues to be a powerful rhetorical statement of groups or neighborhoods who contend that neighborhood control, for whatever reasons, is desirable. Certainly one could argue that, carried to its extreme, neighborhood control could complicate urban life if each neighborhood were to become a self-contained municipality. In addition, is it really reasonable to assume that a neighborhood is capable of supplying the financial resources necessary to provide the wide range of public services required by American communities today? Finally, how will neighborhood control affect attempts to achieve racial integration? If neighborhood autonomy and control are to be of prime importance, is it not logical to assume that community interests are bound to be subordinated? The key question, of course, is the relative importance of the various theoretical and political questions to the individuals in the community. Their feelings on these issues will determine their decision as to which form of government is more desirable.

Neighborhood federation   Neighborhood federation began to be advocated in the early 1970s, partly as a response to the justification of and drive for neighborhood control. In this system a two-tiered government is responsible for different services but its center is located at the city level rather than at the metropolitan level. Services that are more efficiently provided at the city level, such as police and fire protection and sanitation, are provided by the city. The neighborhoods, the second tier of local government, have increased control over the delivery of these services and also have increased, and sometimes even, total control of education, social welfare programs, and neighborhood development.

Perhaps the most interesting endorsement of the federated approach was made by Joseph Zimmerman in his book, *The Federated City*.[35] Zimmerman contended that "most citizens in large cities appear to be interested only in the delivery of quality public services. As long as quality services are delivered on the neighborhood level in adequate amounts, the average citizen will be little interested in community control of governmental institutions and functions, administrative reform, or electoral reform. . . . Only the atypical citizen will devote much time to civic activities when the local government is functioning efficiently, delivering the desired services, and providing the desired facilities."[36] Zimmerman thus concludes that "a positive approach to the reform of large city government in the United States would involve the conversion of the existing unitary system into a federation, improvement of city hall–neighborhood communications, [and] decentralized delivery of services by the upper-tier government where possible. . . ."[37]

One of the problems of neighborhood federation, which is typical of any federal system of government, is the assignment of powers to the respective levels. Here, the problem is extremely difficult because any concession of power to the neighborhood is a reduction in the already-existing powers of the central government and therefore is not likely to be easily accomplished. In addition, communication between the participant groups is frequently unsatisfactory because of the mutual distrust that often exists between the city's leaders and neighborhood residents.

The costs of federated government and the difficulty of obtaining common agreement have also obstructed efforts to achieve neighborhood federation. It has been a common practice for mayors to obtain direct citizen input on important community problems and issues by creating advisory boards and other organizations that are responsible for making policy recommendations. However, many citizens feel that membership in these organizations implies agreement with the policies advocated by the mayor. They may also feel that the organizations are not truly representative. Although many would agree with Zimmerman's statement that ". . . structural change and tinkering alone cannot solve the multitudinous problems . . . in central cities, . . ."[38] many would disagree with his recommended solution.

Conclusion

In this chapter, a variety of structural reforms have been considered that could have a major impact on governmental organization at all levels. It should be clear that diversity is and will probably continue to be the dominant characteristic of governmental organization in the United States. As was explained earlier, few metropolitan areas have exactly the same form of government, and even where similar forms exist, the local political climate effects public decision-making and possible outcomes. The intriguing question is whether this diversity is beneficial or harmful to the quality of decision-making. Although this question cannot be adequately answered here, it is possible to argue for certain changes, based on past experiences and an estimate of future needs, that might improve the quality of public decision-making:

1. A recognition that real political differences exist within any neighborhood, city, and metropolitan area.
2. A mechanism to enable the government to tap these differences and use them in a constructive way.
3. A realization that since governments are composed of human beings, no governmental structure will be perfect.
4. A realization that the relationship between process and substance needs to be fully considered and developed.

Each of these suggestions deserves consideration. Several of them are returned to in Chapter 10.

First, anyone who maintains that economic, political, and social differences do not exist within urban populations is simply ignoring reality. Governments must attempt to reconcile these differences without discouraging the political debate that is an essential part of the democratic system. Any governmental institution that is predicated upon the absence of conflict, and therefore does not provide for its resolution, violates democratic principles.

This suggestion is closely related to the second. Differences between citizens need to be thoroughly understood and valued for their uniqueness. Governmental organizations should reflect these differences.

Third, that governments are "human" is often overlooked because it is so obvious and because of the emphasis on technology in the modern world. Critics of public institutions fail to take this fact into consideration. This is not to say that imperfection, whether in the form of dishonesty, graft, or incompetency, should be advocated or tolerated, but that imperfection should be expected by both citizens and decision-makers.

Finally, is it really desirable to have the decisions wanted by the majority if they are reached in a manner that violates the procedural norms that are essential to the maintenance of a democratic society? If the suggested reform resolves the problem in question but does so undemocratically, then the cure is worse than the illness. In other words, action that violates accepted and legitimate norms may be necessary to achieve a substantive change; when this is true, the substantive change probably will not be forthcoming.

The assumption that structural change will automatically solve the pressing problems of America's urban centers is overly simplistic and potentially dangerous because it ignores the political differences that may be responsible for the problems found in a particular urban area. The avenues available to individuals and groups that wish to influence the urban policy-making process are discussed in the next chapter.

Notes to Chapter 8

1. For an interesting perspective on the importance of intergovernmental relations, see Carl W. Stenberg and David B. Walker, "Federalism and the Academic Community: A Brief Survey," *Political Science* 2 (Spring 1969): 155–167. For a discussion of the regional aspects of intergovernmental relations, see Martha Derthick, *Between State and Nation* (Washington, D.C.: The Brookings Institution, 1974).

2. See James Bryce, *The American Commonwealth* (New York: Macmillan, 1916); Daniel J. Elazar, *The American Partnership* (Chicago: University of Chicago Press, 1962); James Sundquist and David Davis, *Making Federalism Work* (Washington, D.C.: The Brookings Institution, 1969); and Michael D. Reagan, *The New Federalism* (New York: Oxford University Press, 1972).

3. John F. Dillon, *Commentaries on the Law of Municipal Corporations* (Boston: Little, Brown, 1911), Vol. I, Section 237.

4. The *Uniform Crime Reports for the United States* are published regularly by the FBI; the yearly reports are generally considered to be the definitive estimate of the criminal activity occurring during a particular year.

5. Marvin E. Wolfgang, "Urban Crime," in James Q. Wilson, ed., *The Metropolitan Enigma* (New York: Doubleday, 1970), p. 270.

6. *Ibid.*, pp. 279–283.

7. Commission on Law Enforcement and Administration, *The Challenge of Crime in a Free Society* (Washington, D.C.: Government Printing Office, 1967), pp. 20–22.

8. *Ibid.*

9. Richard M. Scammon and Ben J. Wattenberg, *The Real Majority* (New York: Coward, McCann and Geoghegan, 1970), pp. 200–211.

10. See *The Challenge of Crime in a Free Society*, pp. 1–15, for the specifics of the Commission's mission.

11. *Ibid.*, pp. 279–291. List is taken from p. 285.

12. *Ibid.*, pp. 283–285.

13. For a summary of the legislation, see Karen Kerns, "Community Development Block Grants: The First Year," *Nation's Cities* 13 (July 1975): 21–36.

14. For discussion of police behavior in eight communities, see James Q. Wilson, *Varieties of Police Behavior* (Cambridge, Mass.: Harvard University Press, 1968).

15. *Ibid.*, pp. 278–299.

16. For a general discussion of this point, see Advisory Commission on Intergovernmental Relations, *Governmental Functions and Processes: Local and Areawide* (Washington, D.C.: Government Printing Office, 1974).

17. John F. Kain, "The Distribution and Movement of Jobs and Industry," in James Q. Wilson, *The Metropolitan Enigma* (New York: Doubleday, 1970), pp. 1–43.

18. *Governmental Functions and Processes*, p. 113.
19. Richard L. Cole and David A. Caputo, "Leadership Opposition to Consolidation," *Urban Affairs Quarterly* 8 (December 1972): 256.
20. David Booth, *Metropolitics: The Nashville Consolidation* (East Lansing: Michigan State University Press, 1963), p. 27.
21. Cole and Caputo, p. 256.
22. Amos H. Hawley and Basil G. Zimmer, *The Metropolitan Community* (Beverly Hills, Calif.: Sage, 1970), p. 138.
23. For a discussion of these consolidations, see Advisory Commission on Intergovernmental Relations, *Regional Governance: Promise and Performance* (Washington, D.C.: Government Printing Office, 1973), pp. 17–36 and 47–74.
24. For a detailed discussion of the consolidation of this area, see *Regional Governance: Promise and Performance*, pp. 47–74.
25. *Governmental Functions and Processes*, p. 113.
26. *Ibid.*, p. 111.
27. *Ibid.*, p. 112.
28. Milton Kotler, *Neighborhood Government* (Indianapolis: Bobbs-Merrill, 1969). See also Alan A. Altshuler, *Community Control* (Indianapolis: Pegasus, 1970); and Howard Hallman, *Neighborhood Control of Public Programs* (New York: Praeger, 1970).
29. *Neighborhood Government*, p. xii.
30. *Ibid.*, p. 37.
31. *Ibid.*, p. 52.
32. *Ibid.*, p. 61.
33. *Ibid.*, pp. 75–79.
34. *Ibid.*
35. Joseph Zimmerman, *The Federated City* (New York: St. Martin's Press, 1972).
36. *Ibid.*, p. 97.
37. *Ibid.*, p. 82.
38. *Ibid.*, p. 97.

Chapter 9

Citizen Participation Options

Introduction

This chapter deals specifically with the various options and strategies that are available to the urban citizen who is interested in influencing the formulation and/or implementation of public policy. The distinction between these two objectives is important and should not be ignored. The strategies that should be used by anyone who wishes to influence decisions while they are being made differ from those that should be used when the policy is actually being implemented.

In any discussion of the options available to the citizens of urban America, several important questions must be considered. What motivates individuals to take political action? Do they get "involved in politics" because they feel that political participation is a civic obligation? Do they do it because of some personal want or need? Or because they are "fed up" with what political decision-makers are (or are not) doing for them? There are no easy answers to these questions, partly because most of the available public opinion data focus on the attitudes and preferences of citizens with regard to national, rather than urban, politics.[1]

Nevertheless, it is possible to define some of the problems faced by those who wish to study political participation. First, and probably most important, is the problem of determining when and why individuals take political action. Most will do so when they are convinced it will serve their own self-interest. However, different people define self-interest in different ways. Thus, some will take political action only if they are positive that they can influence policy. Others will participate so long as they think there is any likelihood that their voices will be heard.

Perhaps a good example is urban renewal. It is logical to assume that citizens residing within the renewal area will want to become involved, but quite often those who are not affected by the program in any way become involved because they are concerned about its implications. If residences are razed without the owner's receiving just compensation, the issue may attract the attention of others than those who are directly affected by it. In sum, it is often difficult to explain and assess individual motives. Perhaps the best that can be done is simply to describe who participates under what set of conditions and then to speculate why. That is one of the aims of this chapter.

A second problem is the definition of "participation." To most Americans, participation means a specific act, such as registering to vote or voting, working for a political candidate or a political cause, or contributing money to a political organization. These are all considered traditional aspects of participation, but what about participation in civil disturbances or committing armed robbery? Is it conceivable that such actions are classified as political participation by some urban residents? In this chapter, a distinction is made between traditional and nontraditional forms of political participation.

Finally, the significance of political participation is frequently difficult to determine. For instance, voter turnout in many communist nations often approaches and even exceeds 90 percent, but this does not mean that the political system is open and democratic. Similarly, voter turnout at municipal primaries is often less than 10 percent of those eligible to vote. Does this mean that everyone is satisfied with the present situation? Or does it mean that they are so frustrated with the system that they refuse to waste their time and resources by attempting to change it? Both perspectives will be returned to latter in this chapter.

These three problems indicate that we may never know all we wish to know about participation, but they do not make such consideration impossible.

Traditional participation

Electoral politics

Any discussion of traditional participation must consider the level and form of that participation. Urban citizens, for the reasons given in the following paragraphs, have played important roles at both the local and national levels of government, but have not had the political power they might be expected to have at the state level.

Participation of urban residents in local politics has not been widespread. Robert Dahl found that the voter turnout in New Haven, Connecticut, was lower in mayoralty elections than in Presidential elections.[2] Dahl also found that, for most citizens in that city, political participation was rare. Only 16 percent of the citizens included in his survey sample had any contact with political or governmental officials, and only 47 percent ever discussed local politics with friends.[3] Dahl concluded that ". . . one of the central facts of political life is that politics—local, state, national, international—lies for most people at the outer periphery of attention, interest, concern, and activity."[4] Dahl then traced the development of the myth that participation is widespread and is necessary for democratic government.[5] The essential point, however, is that urban citizens are in fact not overly involved in local politics. What are the reasons?[6]

First, it is entirely possible that most people are satisfied with the results of local decisions and therefore do not actively participate in nominating or supporting candidates for public office.

Second, some citizens may decide that participation is a waste of time and effort. They may think that regardless of which candidate they choose to represent them, the results of that representation will be the same. Sometimes support for a particular candidate does not result in the expected changes and citizens become alienated from the political system to such a degree that they refuse to participate in subsequent elections.

Third, it is possible that the costs of political participation may be too high. A person who has to take time from his job or use his own financial resources in order to vote may decide that such sacrifices are not worthwhile. In addition, discussion of politics may complicate one's business or social relationships if the political leaders in the community become offended or feel that such discussion poses a potential threat to them.

The Alford and Lee study of local voting indicated that voter turnout is often less than one-third of the adults eligible to vote.[7] Table 9-1 describes the voter participation in a "typical" primary in a large city, and gives some indication of the extent to which political machines can effectively dominate local politics. The table shows that voter turnout in primaries is often quite low. Many potential voters are disqualified because they fail to register—sometimes because they consider the primary a low-priority item. These are exactly the circumstances that allow a political machine to dominate.

It is clear from Table 9-1 that party *B* can expect to win the general election unless the voters who align with it fail to vote or unless large numbers of them vote for the candidate supported by party *A*. The members of party *B* believe that despite these contingencies, their candidate will have a nearly insurmountable advantage in the general election. Thus the

Table 9-1   Voter Participation in a "Typical" Urban Primary Election

VOTER PARTICIPATION	%	N
Total electorate registered party A	35	35,000
Total electorate registered party B	65	65,000
Voters registered party A voting	20	7,000
Voters registered party B voting	35	22,750
Total registered voters voting	30	29,750

party primary is the key election in this community, for it is here that potential challenges to the party's dominance could have their greatest impact. If the organization's candidate is defeated in the primary, the person who defeated him is virtually assured of election in the general election. It is in the primary that the importance of numbers and the machine's dominance becomes clear.

As Table 9-1 indicates, 22,750 voters of party B voted in the primary. Assume that this was a two-candidate contest for mayor, and that the required number of votes for victory in the primary is 22,750/2 + 1 = 11,375 + 1 = 11,376. That means if the leadership of party B can "deliver" slightly more than 11 percent (100,000 registered voters) of the total city electorate and only a little more than 16 percent (65,000 registered voters) of the party's faithful, they can expect to win not only the primary, but also the general election. Thus the critical number for the machine is not the number needed to win the general election, but the number required to control the primary.

Table 9-1 could be used to describe the partisan electoral politics of many American cities, but the one that most immediately comes to mind is Chicago, where powerful control is exercised by the Democratic party machine. The party machine has been very successful in controlling local nominations, and when it was challenged in 1975, when the liberals contested Mayor Daley's nomination, a massive organizational effort was exerted that left the reformers badly beaten in the primary, and Mayor Daley went on to win an overwhelming victory in the general election.[8]

In sum, machine domination does not always lead to widespread public acceptance of a particular party, but a little organization does go a long way toward securing victory in urban politics. Because of the machine's restricted size, it can more easily dominate local elections if voter turnout is low. Thus a machine is often quite selective in encouraging participation, especially in the primary. As was indicated in Chapter 4, participation is encouraged, but only if that participation results in support of the party in control of the machine.

If participation in local elections is low, participation in state legislative contests within urban areas is also likely to be low. Lack of knowledge about specific candidates and their positions on policy matters, as well as lack of information concerning the role and importance of the state legislature, frequently contributes to low voter interest and to reliance on party identi-fication. Again, both conditions contribute to the success of the candidates of well-organized political parties.

As mentioned earlier, state legislators have traditionally been hostile to the needs of the cities—partly because, before 1964, when the Supreme Court ruled that the "one man, one vote" concept was also applicable to state legislative districts,[9] geography rather than population was the basis for representation in many of the state legislatures. The 1964 decision required state legislatures to redraw their district lines according to popula-tion distribution and thus increased the power of the urban population. Unfortunately, there is little evidence as to what effect the reapportionment decisions have had on politics at the state level. However, there is evidence to indicate that the suburban areas surrounding many SMSAs were under-represented in state legislatures before 1964[10] and received more seats as a result of the one man, one vote decision.

There is little evidence to indicate that voting for United States represen-tatives or senators is done at a higher rate in cities than in other areas. However, there is evidence to indicate that Presidential elections account for the fluctuation of voting rates in many urban areas. In addition, Presi-dential elections increase turnout rates in all areas, and in many states, the voter turnout in the large metropolitan areas is critical to the outcome of the election. Obviously, Democratic presidential candidates attempt to in-crease turnout rates of low-income, inner-city residents, whereas Republi-cans want the suburbanites to vote. These efforts to encourage citizens to register and vote are considerable and often play an important role in determining who wins.

Urban residents realize their numerical advantage and their political im-portance, and bloc voting has been important in many Presidential elec-tions. Analysts of the 1960 Presidential election, especially Theodore White, have stressed the importance of the urban black vote in electing John F. Kennedy over Richard M. Nixon.[11] Scammon and Wattenberg conclude from their analysis of the 1968 Presidential election that the combined low- to middle-income white ethnic vote helped to turn that election in favor of Richard Nixon.[12] The point is that the potential for considerable influence exists, but urban residents have not, in most areas, been sufficiently organized and politicized. As the needs of the urban areas for governmental assistance increase, the political organization and leader-ship needed to tap that potential may develop.

The chances for success of any proposed electoral reform will depend on the impact it is anticipated to have on election results. Thus a switch to a direct popular election method of selecting the President is likely to be regarded as an attempt to weaken the voting strengths of large, concen-trated groups—especially the nonwhites—because under the electoral col-lege system these groups have significant power in the states where they are located. Thus any proposed change is bound to be hotly debated if a particular group thinks that its power is threatened.

Policy implementation

Certainly attempts by citizens, whether individuals or groups, to influence the implementation of public policy are part of the American historical tradition. Attempts to influence the implementation of public policy have been frequent and have been aimed at bringing pressure to bear upon the administrators responsible for a particular program.

The lone individual has at times been quite successful in changing the policies of urban governments. Dahl details an interesting example of a woman in New Haven, Connecticut, whose organizational efforts were instrumental in changing the implementation of policy in that city.[13] In such cases, success is greatly dependent upon the ability of the individual to bring the specific grievance to the attention of both the decision-maker and the general public. Thus some willingness to carry the fight to an extreme is often needed, such as outspoken criticism at public hearings on construction or relocation.

The group strategy that has been most successful is to coalesce either in support of or in opposition to a specific issue and to exert persistent and well-organized efforts at every step of the policy-making process. The following example illustrates the vigilance that is necessary if a group wishes to influence the formulation and implementation of public policy decisions.

Assume for a moment that the residents of a particular neighborhood have requested more adequate park facilities in their area of the city. Initially, attempts might be made to bring this need to the attention of the director of the parks department or the elected council member representing that district. If the council is elected on an at-large basis, then the requests might be directed to a council member sympathetic to the group. If the director of parks agrees that the request is reasonable and necessary, chances are that the next planning and budgeting request will include a request for funds for the increased services. The residents will then have to ensure that the request remains in the projected budget throughout the budgetary process. If this is a "lean" year for the city, their task will be much more difficult than it would be if the city were not experiencing fiscal difficulty. In the latter situation, they would only have to be sure that their request was part of the new expenditures; in the former, another item would have to be reduced or eliminated before they could be sure that their request was supported. This could make the process both more "political" and less likely to succeed.

If the group is successful in having the funds included in the budget and finally appropriated, they will still have to monitor the decision-making process to ensure that the park is planned and administered in accordance with their desires. For instance, if the neighborhood residents are elderly, they might favor adequate all-weather indoor facilities rather than outdoor facilities. In addition, the hours of operation of the park and the amount and quality of maintenance devoted to its upkeep will be important in determining the park's utility and attractiveness.

The point is that group action must be sustained over a long period, must consider the many different aspects of policy-making and administration, and must be very well organized if it is to have the maximum and desired impact on the policy-making and administrative processes. The question then arises as to the costs and resources needed for effective group action. These are summarized in Table 9-2. As indicated in the table, the success of a group depends not merely upon its own characteristics, but also upon the nature of the policy-making and implementation processes that it attempts to affect. The larger the group, the greater its potential to have significant influence; the more resources it may have at its disposal, the more likely are its efforts to be effective. However, if decisions are not actually reached when the group assumes they are reached, then group pressure at that point is unlikely to bring about change. During an interview conducted in 1968–1969 as part of the author's research into local budgetary decision-making, a respondent stated the following:

Q. How does the council reach its decision?
A. Well, we caucus. There are 6 Democrats and 5 Republicans and we Democrats caucus before the public meeting. We decide on what the agenda items will be and our vote on them. That way we can recess and recaucus or postpone action if something comes up that we hadn't expected or which might embarrass us.
Q. What about the public's attempts to influence policy?
A. We either know the positions ahead of time or agree to no changes regardless of what the public says or does. If we say no changes, the group could make the most convincing case imaginable and we would have to say no to their request. Of course we are careful to do this on grounds other than opposition to what they want. Just about anything can be turned down by citing the lack of funds or the feeling that this is special legislation and not really beneficial to the entire city.[14]

Thus the group would be given a hearing and the opportunity to make its request, but the response to that request would have been predetermined— hardly an open decision-making process.

Also important is the last determinant of the nature of the policy formulation and implementation process (Table 9-2)—whether the administrative officials are willing to consider the requests of citizens in a realistic and

Table 9-2 Determinants of Group Success in Influencing Formulation and Implementation of Public Policy

DETERMINANT	OPTIMUM NECESSARY FOR INFLUENCE
The group	
Size	The larger the better
Internal organization	Cohesive, visible
Resources available	Volunteers, money, time
Ability to communicate	Effective goals set; positions clearly stated
The policy formulation and implementation process	
Nature of decision-making	Open, decisions clearly stated
Budgetary situation	Room for expansion; resources available
Commitment of decision-makers to equity in services for all citizens	Positive
Willingness to consider citizen views	Open, realistic

open manner. If a department head feels that acceptance of a request will weaken his position or that of his department, then it is unlikely that the request will be accepted. Similarly, if administrative officials think that the matter under consideration is highly technical (say, achievement levels in schools or causes of air pollution), they may assume that the group is uninformed and thus not qualified to judge the situation realistically, and will ignore the group's requests.

In general, it is rare for a group to have significant and sustained impact on the policy-making process. Perhaps it is because of this failure of traditional methods to achieve results that new methods and procedures have been developed and have been increasingly resorted to by groups attempting to influence the formulation and implementation of public policy in urban America.

Nontraditional approaches

Electoral politics

Despite claims to the contrary, few attempts at innovation in electoral politics have been made at the urban level. Certainly there have been instances in which "reform" candidates have obtained public support of their attempts to defeat the machine and to bring "good" government to a particular city,[15] but these individuals have used existing techniques and have attempted to develop counterorganizational strengths in order to deal effectively with already existing political organizations.

Perhaps the best recent example is the Democratic reform movement in Chicago. Led by several local council members, the reform Democrats have attempted to establish effective political organization outside the traditional Democratic party organization controlled by Mayor Daley. They have attempted to strengthen their organization throughout the city and have been effective in increasing public opposition to "boss" rule and in embarrassing Daley and the regular Democrats by gaining recognition at the 1972 Democratic Convention. However, reformers must abide by the election results and, for whatever reasons, the voters of Chicago repudiated them in the citywide elections in 1975 and re-elected Mayor Daley. This strengthened the power of the regular Democrats and their contention that they are the group most representative of Chicagoans.

Probably because the task facing those who want reform achieved through the electoral process is difficult and often impossible, and because many policy-making systems are not in reality structured as depicted in Table 9-2, the most dramatic and successful attempts to influence public policy are now the nontraditional approaches. Thus the failure of traditional methods of access is likely to continue; such methods may in fact reduce the effectiveness of a particular group in attempting to achieve its stated policy aim.

The preceding has considered the difficulties of utilizing electoral politics; the next section considers the various strategies that have been followed in attempting to influence the implementation of urban policy.

Policy implementation

Three types of behavior are characteristic of those attempting to influence policy implementation: collective organizational efforts, group economic and political action, and violence. The implications of these actions are frequently ignored. However, these behavioral patterns have occurred and will continue to occur in urban society. They must be considered in any meaningful analysis of possible citizen influence on future urban policy-making and implementation.

The first type of behavior, collective organization, has been quite common in some cities. This technique is used when individuals and/or groups feel they need to bring continuous pressure to bear upon a group of decision-makers—usually when they perceive the electoral process as being closed.[16]

The method of Saul Alinsky for organizing community groups is an excellent example of this approach.[17] Alinsky maintained that group strength is critical for success and thus as many different groups as possible should be combined into a coalition.[18] The members of the individual groups must accept in advance the aims of the larger coalition and agree to follow the strategies that will be decided upon. The assumption is that diverse groups having many different goals can reach agreement on several basic issues and goals common to all. The first task of the community organizer, then, is to obtain the agreement of the groups to these goals— often a long and complicated process. The next task is to establish very specific goals. Thus it is not enough to desire "more open" government or "better job opportunities." The goals must be well defined so that the group can bargain more effectively. The unit under pressure will thus be forced to respond to specifics; and it will be aware of what the group is willing to accept and where compromise will be necessary.

Another reason for this emphasis on group identification and the establishment of objectives is that they increase group solidarity and thus the strength of the coalition. Once the coalition has obtained approval of its objectives, it can reduce the level of its activities so long as it monitors the implementation process to be sure the goals agreed upon are in fact implemented.

The Alinsky approach has been most successful in Rochester, New York, and in the Chicago area. It is most likely to result in success if strong groups with the potential to form a coalition are already in existence and if the desired objectives of the group can in fact be met by the institutions under pressure. One difficulty with the Alinsky approach is that many governmental agencies and institutions often lack the legal power to meet group objectives. For instance, assume that jobs are desired and that private industry is unwilling or unable to provide them. The ability of the government to provide jobs can be quite limited, and thus specific requests made to governmental institutions cannot be granted.

Closely related to the Alinsky approach is the argument that direct political organization is the key to influencing the policy-making process. Stokely Carmichael, a prominent black activist leader of the 1960s, and Charles Hamilton, a black political scientist, develop this point of view in their book *Black Power*.[19] Carmichael and Hamilton maintain that blacks (and, by implication, other groups that feel left out of the policy-making process) need to "take care of business."[20] The "TCBing" is done by developing effective and ongoing political organizations at the local level whose goal is to influence both electoral outcomes and administrative decisions at that level. The emphasis is on overt political action: registration of voters, selective support of candidates, and development of a "black consciousness"—an awareness within the black community of its problems and needs. After the local area has been organized and its power sufficiently developed, coalitions with other similar organizations are possible and eventually city control is achieved.

Both the Alinsky and the Carmichael-Hamilton approaches assume that it is possible for groups without power to organize and that government institutions are indeed willing and able to respond to the demands made by these groups. In this respect, they are really quite optimistic.

Neither approach applies exclusively to either racial or class politics; both can be used by other groups to achieve their desired policy ends (for example, ethnic groups that feel they have been ignored, as some have been during the busing controversy). This approach could result in an increased politicalization of groups in urban areas and make the political process more responsive to a wider array of needs and demands. In fact, the realization that such political organization is desirable and necessary may be a very healthy sign because it may indicate that despite the cynicism that resulted from frustration of their earlier efforts, individuals and groups are still willing to contribute their time and scarce resources to efforts to influence the policy-making process because they feel that there are positive benefits to be gained from such participation and that policy-makers, despite their past failures, may still be responsive to public pressure and particularly to their demands and needs.

This optimism is seldom associated with the second type of behavior—group economic and political action. Here the assumption is that the larger society and its political institutions are likely to be unresponsive to the group's needs and that the most fruitful opportunity for group betterment lies in attempts to develop effective economic and political organizations independent of the larger society. These independent political and economic organizations are seen as specific alternatives to already existing institutions.

One of the most interesting examples of this approach is the neighborhood corporation, which is an attempt to increase neighborhood loyalty and pride by actually selling "shares" in the neighborhood to each resident.[21] Assume that a group wants to develop neighborhood business without the assistance of outside financing. Shares can be sold to neighborhood residents for nominal sums and the capital thus raised can be used to obtain revenue from banks, industry, and government. In this way, individual residents share the credit for the success of any program and also have a direct reason for participating because they benefit from patronizing the neighborhood-controlled businesses. This strategy clearly assumes that the neighborhood is indeed self-contained, that it has the ability to develop its own financial base, and that support can easily be rallied for political and economic programs.[22] In other words, neighborhood residents are assumed to share common feelings and to be willing to invest in the corporation. As the residents become more aware of their collective strength, it is only a matter of time until the corporation becomes more viable, expands its operations, and ultimately becomes the dominant economic force in the neighborhood. Eventually, the success of the corporation provides an incentive for the neighborhood's residents to be more forceful and innovative in developing autonomous political institutions to deal with their problems and needs; thus they become less dependent upon the services and institutions of the central city government.

An alternative is to take a separatist stance from the beginning. The Black Muslims are an excellent example.[23] Stressing the unique aspects of black heritage and the black experience in the United States, the Muslims offer an alternative for black persons who are dissatisfied with the treatment they have received from the members of white society or from black individuals who prefer to associate themselves with that society. The Black Muslims emphasize physical separation and the superiority of Muslim ways to those of the larger white society. The very essence of the Muslim appeal is that black individuals have been denied the opportunity to grow and develop by the members of the inferior white race that oppresses them. Thus, if Black Muslims are given a chance to renounce the individuals who oppress them, they will benefit from a rewarding set of experiences that will bring strength not only to them but to all others who hold Muslim beliefs.

Both of these strategies have proven effective at different times and for different numbers of people. The important point is that both strategies reflect a general distrust of the larger society, which is seen as manipulating groups and individuals and attempting to assign them to an inferior status. However, such organization is not attempted only by nonwhites and low-income persons. Certainly the local groups that have been organized in some urban areas to protest busing to achieve school integration fit these models.[24] The individuals who are active in such groups think that the decisions made by the judges and other decision-makers have violated their basic rights and ignored their needs and wants. Thus efforts must be made to organize to regain control of institutions or situations.

In summary, such collective efforts to organize may be quite detrimental to the stability of the political system. They may represent the last desperate attempts by frustrated and ignored individuals and groups to influence policy and decisions without resorting to violence.

It is often difficult to differentiate between types of violence. For example, active protest is the selective and limited use of violence in order to draw the public's attention to a particular set of conditions.[25] Individual acts of violence can also be differentiated from group activity.

Violence is often avoided in discussions of viable political strategies, either because it is considered unacceptable behavior or because it is thought to be counterproductive. The fact of the matter is that violence, whether organized crime or simply random acts of violence against individuals, is a very real part of urban life in America, and thus deserves careful consideration.

The 1960s were turbulent years in many American cities; prolonged civil disturbances were common. These disturbances often followed the pattern described in Table 9-3; many of them resulted in considerable property damage and personal injury. It is difficult to imagine the extensive property damage that resulted from the disturbances in Newark, Harlem, Detroit, and the Watts area of Los Angeles. The disturbances, although each tended to be unique, did follow similar stages of development and occurrence. The five stages occurred over a period of several weeks and sometimes months and often resulted in divisiveness and bitterness.

Table 9-3 Description of "Typical" Civil Disturbance of the 1960s

STAGE	RESULT
Triggering incident	
Arbitrary arrest	Crowd gathers; tensions increase
Disputed arrest	Grievances begin to mount
Alleged brutality	Sporadic violence begins
Disruptive stage	
Sporadic looting	Participants lack specific targets
Extensive property damage	Chaos prevails; arson common
Harassment of authorities	Police and firemen interfered with when responding to calls
Active stage	
Widespread looting	Confused efforts made by local law and order officials to quell the disturbance
Extensive arson and property damage	Authorities unable to handle the situation
Territory is controlled by participants	Martial law declared
	National guardsmen and/or federal troops brought in
Control stage	
Order restored	Extensive show and use of force by authorities
Extensive arrests made	Area effectively sealed off and control maintained
Investigation begun	"Blue-ribbon" panel appointed
Post-disturbance stage	
Business activity decreases	Official investigating commission investigates
Authorities reduce control	Surveillance by police and other armed officials decreased
Specific grievances are investigated	Attempts made to redress grievances
Life returns to "normal"	Attempts made to re-establish normal conditions

Divisiveness and bitterness also characterize the debate over what should be done to bring the situation under control. Bear in mind that mayors were often reluctant to request state or federal assistance because they felt such requests would indicate that they could not handle the situation. In addition, events often developed so rapidly that local officials were unaware of the magnitude of the problems they faced until it was too late for them to deal effectively with those problems. Local officials frequently had to decide whether their approach should be restrained or whether it should utilize all available force as a sign of their serious intent to bring the disturbance under control.

The Report of the Kerner Commission, the "blue ribbon" panel appointed by President Johnson in 1967, indicates that strategies to achieve control varied widely and that confusion often characterized the efforts of local police and firemen.[26] The following conclusions can be drawn from the Report of the Kerner Commission:

1. Most of the participants in the disturbances were black males.[27]
2. Looting and arson were widespread.[28]
3. Injury and death occurred more frequently among the participants and innocent bystanders than among the members of law enforcement agencies.[29]
4. The violence was apparently an expression of long-smoldering dissatisfaction with urban conditions.[30]
5. The underlying causes of the disturbances were basic and indicated the necessity for American society to adopt innovative policies if these events were not to be repeated.[31]

When all was over and done with, two important questions remained to be answered: why had the violence occurred and what were its results?

The conclusions reached by the Kerner Commission as to the basic causes of the disturbances was not widely shared. Conservatives often maintained that the violence was part of an organized conspiracy to weaken the United States or that it was a reaction to the federal government's failure to fulfill its promises.[32] The failure of the War on Poverty and especially that program's community action provision was usually cited as the worst example of the latter.[33]

The conservatives were quick to point out that the failure of liberal programs caused the disturbances; liberals were equally quick to point out that the disturbances were nothing more than a normal response to quite undesirable conditions and to the unresponsiveness of public officials to the needs of the protesters.[34] In short, the disturbances were justified and were evidence of the alienation of the black population from the rest of American society.

Considerable efforts were made to establish the real reason for the disturbances, and anyone who could offer a novel or interesting explanation, whether valid or not, was assured extensive media coverage. Political scientist Peter Lupsha was extremely successful in placing the disturbance in a theoretical and historical perspective.[35] Lupsha contended that urban violence can be classified according to both the specificity of the target and the leadership of the group(s) causing the violence. Lupsha classified the various types of violence according to the following categories: specific target and well-organized leadership, specific target and diffuse leadership, diffuse target and well-organized leadership, and diffuse target and diffuse leadership. Lupsha maintained that the civil disturbances fell in the last category because they lacked specific targets and were not well organized, nor did they have well-defined leadership.[36]

Lupsha then went on to refute the other theories offered to explain the violence and contended that the ". . . anger of our black citizens is not the irrational rage of frustration, it is an anger arising from a rational evaluation of the system."[37] Lupsha concluded that ". . . the gap between the theory and the practice of government in the United States . . . is one of the root causes of urban violence."[38]

This is the significance of Lupsha's and similar conclusions:[39] the assertion that the political system itself is responsible for the violence and that until the system becomes more responsive and open, periodic violence can be expected. Implicit in this position is the recognition that violence may very well be a rational, pragmatic, and necessary response by individuals who are unable to gain governmental attention (and perhaps concessions) in any other way.

It is this last point that has been so systematically ignored in considerations of the impact of violence on public policy. Certainly a critical question is whether such violence results in any positive benefits for the groups causing it. My own attempt to assess the impact of the civil disturbance that occurred in Washington, D.C., in April 1968 on subsequent policy decisions in that city indicates that the most tangible outcome was a city directive to district police officers not to use the term "boy" when arresting or otherwise dealing with black males.[40] This directive may have symbolic value, but it is obviously not a major policy change and it is unlikely to lessen tensions or improve the quality of life in Washington.

Thus violence may not be as productive as many have contended. In general, the disadvantages of such action outweighed the advantages. For instance, the housing and commercial sections of black neighborhoods were badly damaged during the civil disturbances, and the results were an increase in substandard housing and the likelihood that the quality of the living conditions of many black residents would deteriorate further.[41] In addition, local police authorities received special funds for training and equipment to enable them to deal more effectively with future disturbances. However, the funds were limited and the programs often skirted important issues. Given the available information, it is logical to conclude that the violence that characterized these urban disturbances was not effective in redressing grievances or in gaining concessions from those in power.

Lest the impression be given that violence is resorted to only by urban blacks, two other examples of its use should be mentioned. First, white residents have used violence to prevent school busing to achieve racial integration. School buses have been dynamited and school property has been destroyed in these attempts to block busing, even though the courts have clearly established the precedent and approved the busing program. Whites have also formed coalitions that have, at times, advocated the use of violence when necessary to block court-ordered busing for integration purposes.

Second, some groups have used guerrilla tactics aimed at disrupting society to such an extent that the authorities will simply refuse to meet the costs of controlling the violence and will accede to the demands of the groups responsible for the violence.[42] This strategy appeals to many radical groups because they know that urban society, because of its complexity, is dependent upon a variety of vulnerable services such as water and communications, and disruption of any of these services would have serious ramifications. Urban commando groups are often the subject of intense media speculation, but the assumption that authorities would actually surrender to them is rather naive and difficult to accept.

Thus violence appears to have very limited utility as a tactic to bring about change. Resort to violence may be symptomatic of the deep and pervasive problems affecting society and society's inability to deal with them, but as a practical strategy violence seems to be a desperate rather than a rational attempt to maximize a group's impact on public policy.

Conclusion

This chapter has indicated that the options available to individuals and groups are quite limited and may not always have the desired effect on policy development and implementation. This could very well be the most serious flaw in a system of government in which power is decentralized and effecting changes in policy is a complex process. Because policy formulation is usually accomplished in a series of decision-making steps, individuals who lack sufficient time and money may be unable to participate. Add to these restrictions the need for technical information and it becomes apparent that many individuals and groups are completely removed from or have limited access to the policy-making and policy implementation processes.

Perhaps what is needed is a greater realization of the need for local control and an increase in the willingness of public officials to let individuals and groups have a larger say in decisions that specifically affect them. As was indicated in Chapter 8, this probably will mean a reversal of the movement toward centralization that has been urged by reform advocates. The problem, however, is twofold. First, what decisions can in fact be decentralized? Second, what are the appropriate mechanisms to shift some of the responsibility back to the local level? Certainly decisions in either of these areas will result in conflict, and thus the influence of individuals and groups on public policy is unlikely to increase significantly in the future unless some of the structural changes reviewed in Chapter 8 are effected, and the chances that this will happen are slim.

In the remaining chapter the information presented thus far is used as a basis for the discussion of the policy options available to decision-makers attempting to solve pressing urban problems.

Notes to Chapter 9

1. See Chapter 3, pp. 57–67, in which the results of the ten-city study conducted by the Department of Housing and Urban Development and administered by the National League of Cities and the United States Conference of Mayors Secretariat are discussed.
2. Robert A. Dahl, *Who Governs?* (New Haven, Conn.: Yale University Press, 1961), p. 277.
3. *Ibid.*, p. 279.
4. *Ibid.*
5. *Ibid.*, pp. 279–281.
6. The reader is encouraged to review the exchange between Dahl and Walker regarding the causes of low participation. See Jack L. Walker, "A Critique of the Elitist Theory of Democracy," *American Political Science Review* 60 (June 1966): 285–295; and Robert A. Dahl, "Further Reflections on 'The Elitist Theory of Democracy,' " *American Political Science Review* 60 (June 1966): 296–305.
7. Robert R. Alford and Eugene C. Lee, "Voting Turnout in American Cities," *American Political Science Review* 62 (September 1968), p. 803.
8. This victory occurred despite Mayor Daley's stroke a year before the election and indictments of many highly placed local Democratic leaders on criminal charges. For a discussion of the role of the machine today, see Raymond E. Wolfinger, "Why Political Machines Have Not Withered Away and Other Revisionist Thoughts," *Journal of Politics* 34 (May 1972): 365–398.
9. See Robert A. Goldwin, ed., *Representation and Misrepresentation* (Chicago: Rand McNally, 1968).
10. See Paul T. David and Ralph Eisenberg, *Devaluation of the Urban and Suburban Vote* (Charlottesville: Bureau of Public Administration of the University of Virginia, 1961), pp. 11, 16.
11. Theodore H. White, *The Making of the President: 1960* (New York: Atheneum, 1960), pp. 424–425.
12. Richard M. Scammon and Ben J. Wattenberg, *The Real Majority* (New York: Coward, McCann, and Geohegan, 1970), pp. 45–71.
13. *Who Governs?*, pp. 192–199. See also William K. Muir, Jr., " 'The Hill' Against Metal Houses," Interuniversity Case Program case series, No. 26 (University: University of Alabama Press, 1955).
14. Author's personal interview transcripts.
15. Pittsburgh in the early 1970s is a good case in point; Gary, Indiana, under Mayor Richard Hatcher's leadership, and Newark, New Jersey, under Mayor Kenneth Gibson, are also excellent examples. For a discussion of these efforts as they apply to the War on Poverty, see J. David Greenstone and Paul E. Peterson, "Reformers, Machines, and the War on Poverty," in James Q. Wilson, ed., *City Politics and Public Policy* (New York: Wiley, 1968), pp. 267–292.
16. See Saul D. Alinsky, *Rules for Radicals* (New York: Vintage, 1972); and Saul D. Alinsky, *Reveille for Radicals* (Chicago: University of Chicago Press, 1946).

17. *Ibid.*
18. *Rules for Radicals*, pp. 125–164.
19. Stokely Carmichael and Charles V. Hamilton, *Black Power* (New York: Vintage, 1967).
20. *Ibid.*, pp. 178–185.
21. Milton Kotler, *Neighborhood Government* (Indianapolis: Bobbs-Merrill, 1969), pp. 39–50.
22. *Ibid.*
23. C. Eric Lincoln, *The Black Muslims in America* (Boston: Beacon Press, 1961), pp. 33–229.
24. School busing procedures have been the center of controversy in Boston.
25. For a discussion of a variation of this definition of active protest, see Michael Lipsky, "Protest as a Political Resource," in *American Political Science Review* 62 (December 1968): 1144–1158.
26. *Report of the National Advisory Commission on Civil Disorders* (New York: Bantam, 1968).
27. *Ibid.*, pp. 128–129.
28. *Ibid.*, pp. 114–115.
29. *Ibid.*, p. 116.
30. *Ibid.*, p. 117.
31. *Ibid.*, pp. 410–483.
32. See Edward C. Banfield, *The Unheavenly City Revisited* (Boston: Little, Brown, 1974), pp. 211–233.
33. See Aaron Wildavsky, "The Empty-Head Blues: Black Rebellion and White Reaction," *The Public Interest* 11 (Spring 1969): 3–17.
34. See the *Report of the National Advisory Commission on Civil Disorders*, pp. 203–282.
35. Peter A. Lupsha, "On Theories of Urban Violence," *Urban Affairs Quarterly* 4 (March 1969): 273–296.
36. *Ibid.*, p. 275.
37. *Ibid.*, p. 294.
38. *Ibid.*
39. For the statement of a similar position, see Robert M. Fogelson, *Violence as Protest* (New York: Doubleday, 1971). For a more general discussion of discontent, see William A. Gamson, *Power and Discontent* (Homewood, Ill. Dorsey Press, 1968).
40. Author's unpublished manuscript, "Results of Urban Violence: An Impact Analysis," p. 11.
41. *Report of the National Advisory Commission on Civil Disorders*, pp. 358–361. See also National Advisory Commission on Civil Disorders, *One Year Later* (New York: Praeger, 1969).
42. For a discussion of this type of violence, see Martin Oppenheimer, *The Urban Guerrilla* (Chicago: Quadrangle Books, 1969).

Chapter 10

Current Policy Choices

Introduction

It is impossible in a concluding chapter to summarize all that has preceded, just as it is impossible to cover everything that has not been mentioned thus far. In this chapter the various policy options available to decision-makers are discussed and an attempt is made to place them in a broad theoretical perspective. Difficult decisions will be necessary concerning which choices are most desirable, but the final choices are the responsibility of the political participants. Before analyzing the options in detail, the four assumptions on which this discussion is based should be mentioned.

The first assumption is that no matter how much progress is made, decision-makers and citizens will continue to want an improvement in the quality of life in urban centers; their goal will be absolute, rather than relative. If good conditions or solutions are experienced, an attempt will be made to make the good better and ultimately the better the best. Thus a distinction must be made between good, better, and best.[1] An example will be helpful here.

Assume that 20 percent of a country's population is considered to be living at the poverty level and that a massive and innovative governmental program is begun to end that poverty. At the completion of the program, empirical evidence indicates that it has reduced the number of poor to 10 percent of the population. This would be a significant accomplishment and would mean that major social, economic, and political changes had taken place in that society. Yet a logical reaction would be to ask why the other 10 percent of the population remains in poverty and what other programs might more effectively solve their problems. This reaction is simply a reflection of the human desire for perfection; however, this continuing dissatisfaction with the way things are is an important ingredient contributing to the dynamic nature of American policy-making—that is, the continual modification of public policy decisions. It helps to explain earlier decisions and is useful in predicting the likelihood of increased action in particular areas in the future.

The second assumption is that decision-makers must take into account the many similarities *and* differences among the nation's urban centers. (The influence of socioeconomic and political variables on policy formulation and implementation has been discussed in previous chapters.) The policy decisions made in a wide variety of cities have common elements, partly because the nation's cities face similar problems and the citizens in many cities have similar characteristics and share similar political opinions and attitudes. However, the point is that those responsible for policy formulation and implementation should not ignore the very real likelihood that major differences exist both within cities and within SMSAs. Major differences are also likely to exist between cities, and these differences also must be taken into account if the policy process is to be responsive to the needs of the residents of America's urban centers.

Two further conclusions can be drawn from the discussion of the Urban Observatory Program and the citizens' evaluations of city services and the overall quality of life in Chapter 3. The first is that when a variety of attitudinal variables are combined (see Table 10-1), the attitudes of the respondents in the 10 cities toward city government and its services are more likely to be mixed and negative than positive.[2] Note the variation in outlook scores: Boston has the highest proportion of negative outlook scores (59.2 percent) and San Diego has the lowest (13.5 percent). Baltimore is the only city other than Boston where more than half of the respondents (55.8 percent) show negative outlook scores. Albuquerque (19.9 percent) and Denver (20.8 percent) are the only cities other than San Diego where less than 25 percent of the respondents show negative outlook scores.

Even more interesting is the fact that San Diego has the highest proportion of positive outlook scores, yet these positive responses were given by only 21 percent of the San Diego respondents. This indicates the general dissatisfaction found in many American cities. In three of the cities, less than 10 percent of the respondents show positive outlook scores, whereas

Table 10-1   Citizen Outlook Scores: 1970

	OUTLOOK SCORES					
CITY	POSITIVE		MIXED		NEGATIVE	
	%	N	%	N	%	N
Albuquerque	17.7	75	62.4	264	19.9	84
Atlanta	11.8	47	57.9	230	30.3	120
Baltimore	6.6	29	37.6	164	55.8	244
Boston	9.5	41	31.3	135	59.2	256
Denver	15.6	47	63.6	192	20.8	63
Kansas City, Kans.	16.1	27	51.2	86	32.7	55
Kansas City, Mo.	6.2	21	48.7	164	45.1	152
Milwaukee	16.8	65	58.1	225	25.1	97
Nashville	12.6	46	50.4	184	37.0	135
San Diego	21.0	99	65.5	309	13.5	64
All respondents	13.4	497	52.5	1953	34.1	1270

SOURCE: The Urban Observatory Program data tape, funded by the Department of Housing and Urban Development and administered by the National League of Cities and the United States Conference of Mayors Secretariat. See footnote 2 at the end of this chapter for a description of the questions asked and procedures used in computing the scores.

only 13.4 percent of all the respondents show positive scores. The conclusion is inescapable: most urban citizens do not have a positive outlook toward their government and a much higher proportion of all respondents have mixed or negative views (52.5 and 34.1 percent, respectively).

It is interesting to speculate whether any of the individuals in these three categories are likely to change their opinions. For instance, if a significant number of those in the "mixed" outlook category should change their views to negative, more than one-half of the total respondents would then hold negative views. Such a change could have vast implications for future policy decisions in some urban areas.

Table 10-1 clearly indicates that changes are necessary to improve the outlook of urban citizens toward their government. Bear in mind that the cities listed in the table are considered among the most attractive in which to live in the United States.[3] Thus one might expect to find even more negative outlooks in other American cities.

However, Table 10-1 should not be considered a rationale for any and all governmental programs. Merely because the citizens in many cities share negative outlooks does not necessarily mean that they face the same problems or that these problems require the same solutions. This point is supported by Table 10-2, which summarizes the association between negative outlook scores and respondent characteristics. If the problems of this sample of respondents were common to a particular category of citizen (say, the elderly, the poor, or those with low level of education), one would expect to find a high degree of statistical association between these characteristics and negative outlook scores. Table 10-2 indicates that negative citizen outlook

Table 10-2 Negative Outlook Scores and Respondent Characteristics

CITY	RESPONDENT CHARACTERISTICS*				
	SEX	AGE	RACE	EDUCATION	INCOME
Albuquerque	NS	.01	.07	.06	NS
Atlanta	NS	NS	NS	.05	NS
Baltimore	NS	.09	NS	NS	NS
Boston	.05	NS	NS	.03	.10
Denver	NS	.02	NS	NS	.01
Kansas City, Kans.	.10	NS	NS	NS	.03
Kansas City, Mo.	NS	NS	NS	NS	.03
Milwaukee	NS	NS	NS	NS	.10
Nashville	NS	.02	NS	NS	NS
San Diego	NS	NS	.01	.08	NS

SOURCE: The Urban Observatory Program data tape, funded by the Department of Housing and Urban Development and administered by the National League of Cities and the United States Conference of Mayors Secretariat.
*Significance level = or < .10. "NS" means not significant.

scores *are not* associated with any particular variable across the ten cities and that negative citizen outlook scores are probably a product of individual and not group perceptions. In fact, the pattern is so inconsistent that it is logical to assume that the urban policies developed for a particular racial or income group may not be very effective unless individual city adaptation is permitted. Furthermore, programs designed for a particular racial or income group will not succeed unless they increase positive citizen perception of governmental services and activities. This would require more than mere attempts to eliminate poverty or to provide better housing.

It is also important to note from Table 10-2 that dissatisfaction with city governance and services is not confined to the low-income, nonwhite population of the ten cities. Given that mixed and negative outlook scores predominate among all respondents, future public policy decisions affecting these cities and urban areas in general must take into account the needs and wants of all the city residents, not just particular subgroups, if such policies are to be effective and citizen outlook is to be improved. However, it may be impossible for most urban governments, as presently structured, to provide the range of services apparently needed and desired by urban residents because such governments lack resources and find it difficult to decentralize decision-making in order to increase citizen satisfaction.

The third assumption is that there is a need to differentiate between process and substance in questions relating to urban policy. The distinction between these two terms is often not clearly understood and the resulting confusion can lead to a variety of problems. *Substance* refers to the specific policy outcomes that affect the lives of individuals, such as tax rates, patterns of law enforcement, and educational opportunities. *Process* means how those decisions are reached.

For example, assume that a citizen wishes to change the zoning provisions applicable to his neighborhood. In order to have his request heard, he must file a petition, attend a public hearing, and then await the decision of the appropriate public agency. These steps are all procedural steps—they are the process by which a decision is reached. The decision that is reached is the substantive response to his request for action; it represents the results of the decisional process. In short, the person learns whether he can or cannot do what he requested.

In attempting to distinguish between process and substance, there are three sources of complication. First, a relationship does not always exist between procedural rules and subsequent substantive decisions. In other words, a change in process does not always result in a change in substance. Some observers argue that procedural reforms are necessary if basic substantive changes are to be forthcoming. Thus, the early reform advocates maintained that the recall, initiative, and referendum, all procedural aspects of policy-making, would lead to a much different set of substantive decisions.[4]

Second, it is not sufficient to make a substantive change that satisfies most people if that change and the manner in which it is made and implemented fail to meet acceptable procedural norms.

For example, what if an urban center should decide to control its future growth by establishing rigid housing and zoning policies that, in effect, exclude "undesirables." A common criticism of such efforts is that they are exclusionary and even discriminatory. Thus the desired substantive goal, balanced and orderly growth resulting in improved environmental quality, is difficult to object to, but the procedures used to obtain it, exclusionary and restrictive zoning policies, may be unacceptable to many people. The point is that the balance between process and substance is critical if a particular policy is to be both acceptable and capable of being implemented by governmental officials.

A final aspect of this process-substance question is the relationship between policy-makers and the average citizen. Assume that citizens are concerned about police brutality in making arrests. This concern results in a request by citizens for action by the appropriate officials. Those officials must consider not only their substantive response to the request, but also the procedures that will be followed in dealing with the citizens' request and obtaining the police department's response. Then the officials discuss the information they have accumulated and reach a decision.

The "expert" frequently plays an important role in evaluating citizens' requests. If it is decided that the expert is in a better position to evaluate citizens' needs than are the citizens themselves, the procedures that are followed in handling such concerns are vastly different than they would be if the citizens were considered to be knowledgeable about the situation and the various options that are available to policy-makers.

Under the original antipoverty legislation, community action agencies were to consist of and be controlled by the poor, on the assumption that the poor themselves were qualified to make policy decisions.[5] The Model Cities legislation was designed to maximize citizen involvement by allowing extensive citizen representation on the decision-making boards. Naturally, these arrangements cause problems for the expert, who saw his views either ignored or modified by citizens who lacked his training and expertise but who knew instinctively what the appropriate policy decision should be and how it should be implemented. (It will be interesting to follow the role of the average citizen in the planning and implementation stages of the block grant program, which is part of the 1974 Community Development Act.)

The planner, who is also an expert, similarly affects the lives of others, and thus it is again logical to ask whether those affected by his plans have the right to be consulted. For instance, assume that a major highway is being planned and that the least expensive of the possible plans would also force the most people to relocate. Should the planner reject this plan because of its social costs, or should his decision be influenced solely by economic considerations? If the citizens affected by the highway are adamantly opposed to the plan, is the planner obligated to revise it?

The key distinction here is the distinction between a negotiating and a consulting relationship.[6] In a negotiating relationship, the participants (expert and citizens) attempt to reach a compromise acceptable to both sides. If such compromise cannot be reached, then subsequent policy decisions cannot be made because of the stalemate. In a consulting relationship, the expert requests information from and considers the views of the members of the affected group, but is not bound to abide by their requests or recommendations.

Politics in urban America has long been dominated by the expert— whether reformer, urban renewal planner, or economist—and it is only in recent years that even the consulting relationship has been initiated in some cities. Some experts have suggested that they have a moral obligation to side with the groups affected by their decisions, in order to counterbalance the prestige and influence of other experts responsible for initiating and implementing policies.[7]

The essential point is that policy proposals that fail to consider the distinction between process and substance are quite likely to be unsatisfactory and unacceptable to many urban groups and may even cause greater strife and dissatisfaction than the policy they are replacing.

The fourth and final assumption, which is often ignored by those who advocate reform and policy change, is that the resources available for implementing any policy alternative are scarce, and that the costs and benefits of any policy decision must be weighed not only in terms of the desired end but also in terms of the implementation process required to reach that end. Each part of this assumption should be more fully explained.

First, it is obvious that the supply of resources available for implementing urban policy changes is not infinite. Consequently, there is little room for "wasting" resources by adopting ill-conceived plans or implementing them in an inefficient manner. This is one of the main points of Banfield's argument against extensive government intervention in matters affecting urban policy,[8] but Banfield's position is not identical with the one taken here.

Second, citizens and policy-makers should realize that some things cannot be obtained by governmental action and others that may be obtainable exact such high costs as to make them undesirable. Thus an important part of urban policy-making is to weigh benefits in relation to costs. Cost-benefit analysis is a method of evaluating and comparing the costs and benefits of various policy options so that a choice can be made among them that is based on maximizing benefits and minimizing costs. Although this type of analysis is certainly useful, it does have drawbacks.

For example, some of the costs of a particular policy option may be difficult to measure. It is possible to estimate the cost of relocating X number of families if Y number of housing units are destroyed, but the psychological costs to the individuals who are forced to relocate are difficult to state in dollar terms. The benefits gained by the community whose housing units were destroyed are also difficult to assess.

Moreover, the implementation of certain policies may be imperative regardless of the costs. A current example of such a policy is busing to achieve racial integration in the schools. In the mid-1960s many urged that integrated school environments were necessary if racial separation were to end and the achievement levels of nonwhite pupils were to be raised,[9] although few predicted that busing would have resulted in such controversy. However, according to James Coleman, it now appears that busing has had an unintended result: it may have increased the exodus of whites from the central cities to the suburbs.[10] Thus the unanticipated costs may outweigh the benefits and the results may even be counter to the proposed intention of the policy. When the policy was decided upon, the overall benefit of increasing educational opportunity for nonwhites was perceived as being worth the costs involved. However, urban residents, both white and nonwhite, may not be willing to meet those costs. If that occurs, a change in the busing policy is likely to be required.

Cost-benefit analysis also tends to be subjective. The costs and benefits, as well as the policy decided upon, are viewed differently by different people, and thus conclusions differ.

Finally, resource considerations are not likely to be the only determinants of public policy. Political questions will also be at the core of the policy discussion.

These four assumptions are the basis of the policy options that are discussed in the remainder of this chapter. Each option will be considered from a variety of perspectives and the likelihood of its implementation will be considered.

The centralizing option

The first option is to increase the involvement of the federal government in urban policy matters. It is not necessary that the powers and responsibilities of the states or urban centers be reduced, but only that the role and power of the federal government be increased. The arguments in favor of this option are as follows.

1. Many of the problems facing America's cities are indeed national problems, and thus a national strategy is necessary to deal with them. For instance, programs aimed at increasing job opportunities are more likely to succeed if the federal government is responsible for initiating and administering such legislation. In addition, the migration from one major city to another that has resulted from the difference in services provided by those cities could be reduced if the federal government were to assume more responsibility for some of those services.

2. Only the federal government has the necessary financial resources (obtained primarily from the federal income tax) to deal effectively with urban problems. Solutions to the pressing urban problems require massive amounts of funds and it is unrealistic to expect either the states or urban centers to provide them.

3. States and urban centers, for a variety of reasons ranging from political indifference to inability to establish and administer the appropriate programs, have not and will not undertake serious and comprehensive efforts to ameliorate urban problems. In most state legislatures conservatives from rural areas can defeat or at least block legislation that does not benefit them directly and most urban centers lack the economic resources necessary to handle pressing problems.

4. Urban residents are not able to muster the support they need at the local and state levels and therefore must appeal to the federal government. The expectation is that the decisions reached there will be more favorable to urban residents because they are more likely to gain recognition at that level and because the resources needed for solutions are more likely to be available at that level. This is a variation of E.E. Schattschneider's argument concerning the arena of political conflict.[11] Schattschneider claimed that those without power at one political level may gain power by taking the fight to the next level.[12]

What substantive and procedural changes would result if the centralizing option were chosen? Substantively, the federal government would provide more funds to the cities. Federal involvement in transportation, housing, sanitation, environmental protection, and antipoverty programs would increase. The federal government would play a more important role in the planning process—various policy options would be reviewed and decisions would be based on local community and national needs.

If the federal role were to continue to increase, many of the services now performed by urban governments would become the obligation of the federal government. Thus the numerous local police and fire agencies might be replaced by one national agency with standardized training and equipment. Federal involvement in urban mass transit might result in the creation of a national corporation (perhaps similar to Amtrak, which was funded to provide national rail service) that would plan, build, and operate mass transit systems in the nation's urban centers.

The procedural changes resulting from the selection of the centralizing option could have far greater impact than the substantive changes. Assume that the categorical grant or grant-in-aid approaches discussed in Chapter 6, according to which a unit of local government receives funds if it meets certain federal requirements, continue to be the predominant federal fund-allocation programs. A procedural change might be that federal officials would not release funds until urban centers adopted an areawide approach to certain problems. Several questions might be raised by this change. Can the states veto the urban centers' requests for funds or the purposes for which they plan to use the funds? Can the federal government require the local units to meet specific and difficult performance standards before releasing the funds?

Imagine that a city requests federal funds to improve the training of its police personnel. Does the federal government have the right to know the nature of the training and which police personnel are to receive it? If the federal government feels that other practices in that police department (say, minority recruitment and advancement) or other policies of the recipient government are unsatisfactory, does it have the power to refuse to grant such fund requests until these practices and policies are changed to its satisfaction?

Assume that a growing city requests federal funds to plan its growth and to improve sanitation in areas where most of the growth is occurring. Can and should the federal government influence that growth by requiring that a certain racial or economic mix of potential residents have a say in the planning process before federal funds are forthcoming? Should the federal government require that all jurisdictions coordinate their plans with the plans developed in their immediate vicinity or region?

Both of the preceding examples illustrate the interesting procedural questions that a substantive change to increased centralization might raise. Obviously, these four arguments are not the only ones that can be made in support of the proposal, but they are the arguments most frequently heard.

The decentralizing option

This option has two variations. Each is unique, even though both share common characteristics.

Local autonomy

The following arguments are usually advanced in support of this variation of the decentralization option.

1.   The costs of federal involvement far outweigh the benefits. The programs seldom meet their stated objectives and often exacerbate an existing situation.[13] Governmental programs that are not planned, financed, and controlled by the local community are bound to be failures; the more money invested in such a program, the greater the failure.

2.   Federal programs cannot be adjusted to meet local needs. Such programs are based on a strict definition of the "problem," and any locality whose problems do not fit this definition is in difficulty.[14]

3.   The gains in substantive resources from increased federal action are likely to be outweighed by the losses in procedural rights and powers caused by such action. The administration of the program by the local unit is subject to periodic and often arbitrary review and audit by the federal bureaucracy. To meet these requirements, cities are sometimes forced to hire additional auditors and other professionals, thus decreasing the amount of resources that can be used to "solve" the problem.

Supporters of local autonomy maintain that the cities themselves are responsible for raising revenues and solving their problems. If the leaders of the cities are not willing to assume such responsibility, then the state and federal governments are under no obligation to assist them, just as state and federal authorities do not have the right (assuming that policies are being made and implemented in a legal manner) to intervene and argue about whether a policy is equitable or in the best interests of the city.

The theme of the local autonomy position is that that government governs best which governs least. The assumption is that the federal government has very limited ability to affect many of the problems facing the city and thus a much wiser course of action would be to decrease governmental involvement in as many areas as possible. This position contrasts with another variation of the decentralizing option.

Local autonomy with federal support

The following arguments are made in support of local autonomy with federal support:

1.   The federal government, although it may mean well, cannot effectively administer categorical aid programs because their requirements are too specific and cannot be adapted to meet the unique problems of most cities. Thus requirements that might be applicable to New York City are likely to be inapplicable to Denver or Los Angeles.

2.   The administrative costs of hiring and training personnel and filing reports, all of which are required of a city that participates in the categorical grant program, are far too high and divert funds from the programs to be

implemented. Even if administrative costs were kept at a reasonable level (10 to 25 percent of the total program), they would still detract significantly from the program's overall effectiveness.

3. Although federal bureaucrats may have good intentions, it is impossible for them to be aware of and understand all the unique problems of particular cities. Thus their decisions are based on their own perceptions and not on a particular city's needs as defined by responsible city officials, and many city problems may be ignored.

A solution proposed by those making this argument is that federal funds should be made available to the cities, but a minimum number of strings should be attached (or, preferably, none). Thus the local units would be able to use those funds to meet locally designated needs and not the needs specified by a federal bureaucrat or by Congress.

It is possible to argue that these funds should go directly to neighborhood organizations or to regionally organized agencies that deal with specific problems, rather than to city agencies. Obviously, this position is held by those who feel that local governmental institutions are largely unresponsive to their needs because of a lack of resources.

These two variations of the decentralizing option indicate that the available policy alternatives are few. Suggestions that the states be abolished or that the nation be divided into 10 or 15 states are simply not going to be accepted for very pragmatic political reasons. Instead, variations of the available alternatives are possible. Table 10-3 summarizes the policy options that have been discussed in this chapter. The various political forces that could help to determine which of the policy options are followed are discussed in the remainder of this chapter.

Table 10-3 Policy Options Available for Urban America

OPTION	CHARACTERISTICS
Centralizing	Increased federal aid
	Increased federal bureaucracy
Decentralizing	
Local autonomy	End of federal programs
	Reliance on local resources and leadership
Local autonomy with	
federal support	Increase in federal funds
	Decrease in federal requirements for using funds
	Increase in local initiative in using funds

Limitations on policy selection

The political forces that affect policy choices have been described in detail in the preceding chapters, but the likelihood that certain changes will occur has not been discussed. Political observers, whether they are on the right or on the left, frequently forget that many of the problems that affect urban politics also affect national politics (for example, inadequate resources, absence of concrete goals, institutional paralysis). For the following reasons, policy changes are unlikely to be easily and rapidly accomplished.

1.   The political institutions that are responsible for making policy decisions affecting urban America are quite diverse, and it is unlikely that they will be changed overnight. The state legislatures are one example. Since all the states but Nebraska have a bicameral (two-house) legislature, it is unlikely that a major change in one will result in a major change in another. Another example is the United States House of Representatives. Many assumed that the gains made by the Democratic party in the 1974 Congressional elections would result in a disciplined and liberal House, but they have not.

It is quite obvious that in American politics, the more things change, the more they remain the same. Thus those who expect decision-making institutions to accomplish major and rapid change are bound to be disappointed. Delay is almost assured by the system of checks and balances, the monolithic bureaucracy, and the debate that is part of the democratic system.

2.   The opportunities of the individual citizen to influence the nomination and election of most policy-makers, as well as their positions on important issues, are limited. The number of people involved in the decision-making process is so large that an individual can seldom have any influence. In addition, the "average" man has limited resources (especially financial) and is too busy responding to day-to-day needs to participate effectively in national politics.

At the local level, both the number of citizens with the potential for participation in the decision-making process and the possibility that such citizens will be able to participate increase, but the policy-making power of governmental institutions at that level may be limited, and thus such participation frequently is not meaningful.

3.   Another limitation on the impact of governmental action is that there are some urban problems that governmental action, no matter how carefully reasoned and administered, may not be able to influence. One example is the racial hatred that exists in many urban centers. Certainly government can try to restrain the behavior that results from the hatred, but it cannot completely eliminate such feelings. If the condition that calls for governmental action is simply unresponsive to that action, it is not fair to blame the government if its efforts fail.

Closely related to this point is the question of the relevancy of governmental action in a particular area. There may be instances in which nongovernmental institutions, such as economic or religious groups, can have a greater impact on urban problems than the governmental institutions themselves. For instance, poverty might be substantially reduced if large business firms were to recruit and train the poor and provide incentives for them to seek employment and training. This is not to advocate the cessation of government activities; it is merely a suggestion that nongovernmental institutions should become more responsive to the needs of urban America.

4. There is a lack of class cohesiveness in the United States (class *cohesiveness*, not class consciousness). Members of various socioeconomic groups need to utilize their resources, whether wealth or numbers, to influence the policy decisions that affect them. Economic and class differences in the United States have been obscured by ethnic and racial differences, thus making cooperative efforts by members of the same economic class who belong to different racial or ethnic groups difficult if not impossible to achieve.

As was discussed in Chapter 6, the War on Poverty quickly became viewed as an attempt to help the black poor, rather than the poor in general. Thus opposition to it came not only from whites earning adequate incomes who opposed governmental action in this area, but also from poor whites, who felt they were being excluded from the program. One of the most effective obstacles to policy changes aimed at assisting the poor has been the racial and ethnic divisiveness that exists among the poor.

5. Policy choices must be considered in the light of technological changes that may occur. Certainly the automobile has had a tremendous impact on urban life, but one wonders if subsequent technological developments will be as important, or more important. For example, what will happen if technological developments permit the recycling of natural resources to such an extent that concern about their depletion is no longer necessary? Similarly, what will happen if technology becomes so advanced that "work" as it is known today becomes outmoded and humans are replaced by computer-directed machines?

In addition to facilitating increased control over the physical environment, technological change may increase control over society; individual freedoms are likely to be affected by improved police surveillance techniques, stronger mind-controlling drugs, and more advanced surgical techniques. There is obviously a danger that technological advances may have unintended and harmful results, and thus governments will be faced with the problem of harnessing them.

Clearly, policy change will evolve slowly; nevertheless, significant change is possible and even likely, but considerable energy and time will be required to bring it about. Such change will probably result from the efforts of patient, well-organized citizen groups, such as consumer advocates and environmental protection groups.

The success of these groups is often reflected in the electoral victory of a public official supportive of their efforts. For example, one reason for the Democratic victory in the elections for governor and United States senator in Colorado in 1974 was that the Democratic canidates spoke out in favor of balanced growth and conservation, two issues that were uppermost in the minds of the state's voters at the time. Another example is Governor Daniel Walker's victory in Illinois in 1972. Walker defeated not only the Republicans, but also the wing of the state Democratic party controlled by Mayor Daley.

In addition to these limitations on policy choice, several other developments could influence the policy-making process at the various levels of government. Some of the coalitions that might form in future years are depicted in Table 10-4. Coalitions may be formed on the basis of class, race, and/or geographical location. The three coalitions that might be formed on the basis of class are perhaps the least openly discussed in the United States because some people are not aware of their existence, some prefer not to admit the possibility of their existence, and others admit that they exist but prefer to ignore them. The prime motivation for such concerted activity would be the shared economic interests of the individuals in the various classes. More specifically, (1) the upper and middle classes would benefit from maintaining the poor in their inferior position and not permitting them to develop significant political strength. Thus this coalition could result in political oppression and restrictive legislation that would make it difficult for the poor to escape poverty.

If coalition (2), in which the have-nots combine forces with those who have a little against those who have the most, were to be formed, the upper classes might be forced to make major economic and political concessions, but if Floyd Hunter[15] and C. Wright Mills are correct,[16] such concessions will not be made because the upper classes will be able to manipulate enough people and influence enough political actors that major policy changes affecting them will not be forthcoming.

Many would contend that coalition (3) dominates American politics today (certainly George Wallace would): the lower and upper classes have effectively combined forces to dominate policy-making at the expense of the middle class. The middle class is required to carry the major share of the

Table 10-4   Possible Political Coalitions That Will Affect Future Urban Policy Choices

BASIS OF COALITION	COMPOSITION OF COALITION
Class	
1	Upper class and middle class versus lower class
2	Middle class and lower class versus upper class
3	Middle class versus upper class and lower class
Race	
4	White versus all nonwhite
5	White versus black versus other nonwhite
Location	
6	Suburbs and rural areas versus central city
7	Central city and rural areas versus suburbs

tax burden of liberal programs designed to aid the poor (such as busing and job-training programs), while the upper class enjoys the benefit of tax loopholes and shelters.

Coalition (3) might result in the recognition by the middle class of their present situation and a resolve to organize and bring about policy changes that would benefit them. The wealthy liberals and the poor would then have to double their efforts in order to stave off the political power aligned against them. The motivation for the link between the lower and upper classes is mutual exploitation. The lower class realizes that only the rich can intervene and direct substantial resources their way, so they align themselves with that class; the wealthy think that such intervention will increase the animosity of the middle class toward the lower class, thus enduring the continued dominance of the upper class.

Racial coalition (4), whites against nonwhites, would result in formal and informal practices that would deny opportunities to nonwhites. Policy decisions would be made on the basis of which racial group would benefit and what the costs to the other racial groups would be.

Coalition (5) is a variation of coalition (4). The splintering of the nonwhite racial groups indicates a lack of cohesiveness among them and thus the possibility that they would be less likely to cooperate on policy matters in the future. The whites might also attempt to divide and conquer minority groups by creating disagreement among them that would obscure their mutual interests and make it difficult for them to work toward common goals.

It is easy to argue that present divisions within American society are not as discernible as these five coalitions might suggest and that the existence of crosscutting pressures might make behavior difficult to predict and even more difficult to explain. Coalitions (6) and (7), however, are new and different interpretations of current political phenomena and their formation is much more likely to occur. Coalition (6) may already be the dominant pattern in many parts of the United States: suburbs and rural areas, because of their dominance in the state legislatures and in Congress, have combined forces to block policy decisions favorable to the central cities. Mass transit facilities, which receive limited support from both the federal and state governments, are an excellent example. The Bay Area Rapid Transit System (BART) presently serving the San Francisco area was hailed as an attempt to link the outlying areas and downtown San Francisco. It received support because it was seen as a regional approach and not merely mass transit for the city of San Francisco. Similarly, Chicago was successful in obtaining increased state funding for mass transit only when it agreed to allow a regional transportation authority to operate transportation facilities in the northeastern part of Illinois.[17]

Coalition (7) offers the most promise for urban America. It assumes that as the central city becomes less wealthy and as the rural areas lose wealth to the suburbs, a coalition will naturally form that is mutually beneficial to the central cities and the rural areas. By combining their political strengths, they may be able to overcome the dominance of the suburban interests and influence policy decisions that would result in an improvement in the quality of life of not only residents of the central cities and rural areas but also residents of the suburbs, because the policy changes could very well mean a decrease in the divisions and hostilities between the areas. The coalition would be able to forge important cooperative efforts at the state and federal levels and could be quite important in any presidential election.

This brief description of the coalitions that may be formed and the results of their interaction should be indicative of the possible changes that could affect urban America. Change is quite likely to occur, but it will not be rapid. Policy-makers will no doubt remain reactive to, rather than anticipative of, future change, and policies may not always be comprehensive or clearly stated. The key to America's future, and especially the future of its urban areas, is the determination on the part of its political leaders to agree on the rudiments of certain broad policy changes. If such agreement is reached, then the United States can look forward to a promising future.

Notes to Chapter 10

1. For an interesting discussion of this point, see Edward C. Banfield, *The Unheavenly City Revisited* (Boston: Little, Brown, 1974), pp. 279–286.
2. In tabulating an individual citizen outlook score, the following questions and responses were used:
   1. Over the past five or ten years, do you think that local government here in (*city*) has gotten *better*, has stayed about the *same*, or do you think it is *not as good* as it used to be?
      1. Better
      2. Same
      3. Not as good
      9. NA
   2. And overall, how would you rate the way (*city*) is run?
      1. Excellent
      2. Very good
      3. Good enough
      4. Not so good
      5. Not good at all
      9. NA
   3. Considering what people in (*city*) pay in local taxes, do you think the people generally get their money's worth in services, or not?
      1. Yes
      2. No
      3. NA
   4. In some cities officials are said to take bribes and make money in other ways that are illegal. In other cities, such things almost never happen. How much of that sort of thing goes on in (*city*)?

1. Great deal
2. Some
3. A little
4. Almost none
5. Don't know
9. NA

For all four questions, 9's were recoded to 0's. For question 2, response 2 was recoded to 1, response 3 was recoded to 2, and responses 4 and 5 were recoded to 3's. For question 3, response 2 was recoded to 3, and for question 4, responses 1 and 2 were recoded to 3, responses 3 and 4 were recoded to 1, and response 5 was recoded to 0. The citizen outlook score was then computed for each respondent who had answered all four questions (12.8 percent or 546 had answered none of the questions); the scores ranged from 4 (most positive) to 12 (most negative). Those respondents with citizen outlook scores of less than 5 were labeled "positive," those with scores of 5 to 8 were labeled "mixed," and those with scores of more than 8 were labeled "negative." These are the categories used throughout Tables 10-1 and 10-2.

3. For a recent and popularized attempt to measure the attractiveness of American cities, see Arthur M. Louis, "The Worst American Cities," *Harpers* (January 1975), pp. 67–71.

4. Lincoln Steffens, *The Shame of the Cities* (New York: Hill and Wang, 1957), pp. 1–19. (Originally published in 1904).

5. For a discussion of the ability of the poor to make their own decisions, see Richard L. Cole, *Citizen Participation and the Urban Policy Process* (Lexington, Mass.: D. C. Heath, 1974), pp. 11–15.

6. For a discussion of these relationships, see Harry Eckstein, *Pressure Group Politics* (Stanford, Calif.: Stanford University Press, 1960), pp. 15–39.

7. Alan A. Altshuler, *The City Planning Process: A Political Analysis* (Ithaca, N.Y.: Cornell University Press, 1965).

8. *The Unheavenly City Revisited*, pp. 260–278.

9. *Equality of Educational Opportunity* (Washington, D. C.: Government Printing Office, 1966), pp. 1–34, more commonly known as the Coleman Report.

10. For a discussion of James Coleman's current position on school integration, see *The New York Times*, June 7, 1975, p. 25; and *The New York Times*, June 8, 1975, IV, p. 7.

11. E. E. Schattschneider, *The Semi-Sovereign People* (New York: Holt, Rinehart and Winston, 1960).

12. *Ibid.*, pp. 6–9.

13. *The Unheavenly City Revisited*, pp. 260–278.

14. See the various editorials in *Nation's Cities* in 1972 and 1975 on the subject of the mayors' objections to the categorical grant approach to urban problem-solving.

15. Floyd Hunter, *Community Power Structure* (Chapel Hill: University of North Carolina Press, 1953).

16. C. Wright Mills, *The Power Elite* (New York: Oxford University Press, 1966).

17. See "Recent Aid by Regional Transit Authority to Chicago Area Transit Systems Analyzed," *Chicago Tribune*, March 23, 1975, Sec. 2, p. 4.

Index